D1250615

Playing Hockey
the Professional Way

OTHER BOOKS BY THE AUTHORS

Play the Man
by Brad Park with Stan Fischler

Goal! My Life on Ice
by Rod Gilbert with Stan Fischler and Hal Bock

Playing Hockey the Professional Way

by Rod Gilbert and Brad Park

with a Preface by Emile Francis

HARPER & ROW, PUBLISHERS
New York   Evanston   San Francisco   London

PLAYING HOCKEY THE PROFESSIONAL WAY. Copyright © 1972 by Rodrigue Gilbert, Douglas Bradford Park, and Allan Eisinger. All rights reserved. Printed in the United States of America. No part of this book may be used or reproduced in any manner whatsoever without written permission except in the case of brief quotations embodied in critical articles and reviews. For information address Harper & Row, Publishers, Inc., 10 East 53rd Street, New York, N.Y. 10022. Published simultaneously in Canada by Fitzhenry & Whiteside Limited, Toronto.

STANDARD BOOK NUMBER: 06–011521–1

LIBRARY OF CONGRESS CATALOG CARD NUMBER: 72–79667

Contents

Preface

I HAVE known Rod Gilbert for better than sixteen years. He played for me when I was coach of the Rangers' Guelph Biltmores in the Ontario Hockey Association. Later, we both came to New York—Rod as player and I as a general manager and coach. Rod has developed into one of the finest hockey players in the National Hockey League—a fact that was attested this past 1972 season when he was named to the first All-Star team.

Brad Park, on the other hand, has played for me since 1968. I selected him in the 1966 amateur draft, and he proved to be a tremendous choice. Brad has made the first All-Star team twice and the second team once in the four years he has played professional hockey.

Rod and Brad are truly exceptional players. And I, like all coaches in the NHL, am on a constant lookout for players of their caliber. Of course, players of their ability don't come along every day.

But how do we rate a hockey player's abilities? When a scout for our team reports to me on a prospective player, he rates the young player as being either "excellent," "good," "fair," or "poor" in each of the six following categories:

1. Skating ability
2. Stickhandling ability
3. Scoring accuracy
4. Positional play
5. Playmaking effectiveness
6. Ruggedness

From our scout's report card, I determine whether or not to pursue the young man further. Among the final deciding factors in making any of my selections, however, are the player's leadership qualities and his ability to get along with his teammates. Incidentally, both Rod and Brad are assistant captains on the New York Rangers.

Rod and Brad also have the ability to teach hockey and work with young players. The proof of this fact is the success they have had with their Skateland Summer Hockey School. In this book they have further demonstrated this ability. I would recommend their book to all young hockey players and fans. Rod and Brad really know what the game is about.

—EMILE FRANCIS
General Manager and Coach,
New York Rangers

Playing Hockey the Professional Way

1

The Game of Ice Hockey

HOCKEY is the fastest team sport in the world. Each 60-minute game consistently combines the players' skating speed of 18 to 24 miles per hour with a rubber object propelled 90 to 110 miles per hour at a heavily padded man in front of a goal 6 feet wide and 4 feet high. The phrase "never a dull moment" may well have been coined at a hockey game by a spectator who needed words to describe the furious action of the speed-burning sport. Hockey is competitive excitement maintained at a continuous breakneck pace—assured by explosive body contact at sizzling speeds, when defenders throw the same type of blocks as linemen in football.

While hockey is a wonderful spectator sport, it's still a greater game to play. Both of us have been playing hockey since we were very young. We've had our happy moments and our sad ones, but it's our profession and, to be a little corny, our way of life. But, as we look back over the years, one fact is most prevalent: If a man didn't enjoy playing hockey it would be the toughest job in the world.

Hockey is a precision sport, depending to an enormous degree on finesse, timing, and teamwork. The professional hockey player must also be proficient in such skills as skating, stickhandling, passing, shooting, checking, and so on. There's still another important factor in learning to play hockey: You must know how to take a few cuts and bruises. They are just part of the game. So, if you can't take the cuts and bruises in either life or hockey, forget about playing our game. But, you still can be a loyal fan.

Writing about something you've been doing since you were five years old can be difficult. We both have written books on our hockey careers (*Goal! My Life on Ice* by Rod Gilbert, published by Hawthorn Books,

1

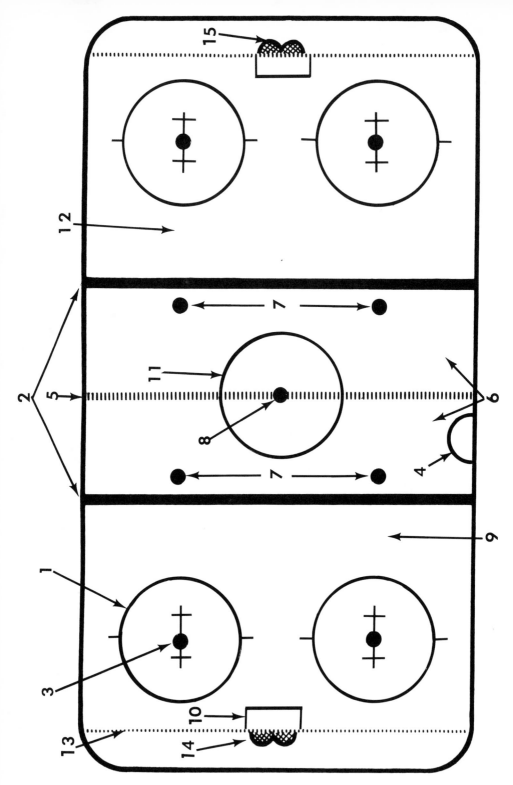

Most NHL rinks measure 85 × 200 feet. The various locations and markings on the rink are as follows: (1) face-off restraining circle; (2) blue lines; (3) face-off spot; (4) referee's crease; (5) center line; (6) neutral zone; (7) face-off spots; (8) center face-off spot; (9) defending zone; (10) defending goal crease; (11) center ice circle; (12) attacking zone; (13) goal line; (14) defending goal net; (15) attacking goal net.

Inc.; *Play the Man* by Brad Park, published by Dodd, Mead & Company). However, writing a book on how to play hockey was something else. So much that we do out on the ice is automatic to us. Sure, we've been teaching young people from the ages of six to eighteen how to play hockey at our Skateland Summer Hockey School in New Hyde Park, New York. In fact, it was the writing of instruction sheets for our students that led us to write this book. But to tell the complete story of how to play hockey was a great challenge.

Before going into the how-to-play aspects of hockey as we have learned it over the years and now teach it in our school, let's take a quick look at where it is played, its basic principles, and the rules governing the game. Of course, if you're familiar with the basics of hockey, you might skip the next few pages.

THE RINK

Let's start with the rink on which hockey is played. It is a round-cornered rectangular ice surface 200 feet long and 85 feet wide. These dimensions vary a bit from rink to rink but not by very much. For instance, the Pittsburgh Penguins' rink is 205 feet long; at the Chicago Stadium, the home of the Blackhawks, the playing surface is only 188 feet in length. Of course, a strong-skating, good-passing team usually performs best on the larger surface.

The playing area is surrounded by a wooden wall, known as the boards, or dasher boards, which is 3½ to 4 feet high. Shatterproof plate glass or wire screen generally extends above the boards around the rink to protect the spectators from being hit by the puck. Incidentally, in some rinks these boards are resilient, in others they're stiff and give little rebound.

Oftentimes new fans are confused by the markings on the ice. Ten feet from the boards at each end of the rink is a 2-inch red goal line that spreads across the ice. Centered on each goal line is a goal net, or cage. This net is 4 feet high by 6 feet wide, just small enough to make scoring difficult and just big enough to make defending it difficult for one man. It is curved in back from 1 foot deep to 3 feet deep at its center and its sides and back are covered with a white twine. The goal cage is anchored to the ice with pins that extend up through the ice into the pipelike goalposts. In front of each net is a small rectangle called the goalie's crease. That spot is off limits to the opposing players. If you're in the crease, any goal that goes in the net is disallowed. The exception is when you're shoved in the crease and held there by a member of the other team. Many goalies employ not-so-gentle taps on the ankles to keep an enemy from getting next to their crease.

The segment of ice between the goal lines is divided by three 12-inch lines—two of them blue lines 60 feet from the goal lines and the third one a red line which divides the ice in half. The portion of the ice surface in which the goal is situated is called the defending zone of the team defending the goal; the central portion is known as the neutral zone (center ice); and the portion farthest from the defended goal as the attacking zone. In rinks that are not the "official" length, the difference is in the neutral zone; the defending and attacking zones are always the same size.

Play is started by what hockey people call a face-off. That's our version of basketball's jump ball. That is, two players face each other about 3 feet apart, and one of the officials drops the puck between them, inaugurating play. (The puck is a vulcanized rubber disc, frozen before the game, that is 3 inches in diameter and 1 inch thick, and it weighs between 5½ and 6 ounces.) Actually there are five face-off circles, one at center ice and two in each team's defensive zone, one to the left and one to the right of the goaltender. There are also four small face-off spots or drops in neutral ice—that area between the blue lines in the center portion of the rink. Two of these spots are drawn 5 feet from each blue line. Play at the start of each period and after each goal is started by a face-off at center ice. When plays are whistled down, causing face-offs, the infraction rarely occurs precisely at center ice. That's why there are eight other face-off locations—four circles and four spots—on the ice besides the one in the middle of the rink.

Then there's the referee's crease, a red semicircle against the boards near center ice, which is off limits to the players when there's an argument going on. If the referee makes a call you don't like, your team's captain or assistant captain can argue and skate after the official. But once the referee reaches his crease, the argument ends because players can't follow him into that area.

Behind each goal, electric lights are set up for the use of the goal judges. A red light signifies scoring of a goal. Where an automatic light system is employed, a green light signifies the end of a period or a game. A red light can't be turned on when a green light is showing thanks to a special switching device. But before this switching arrangement was mandatory, we lost a game in Los Angeles that we hadn't really lost. Ross Lansberry of the Kings put the puck into the net at the instant the green light went. The goal judge flashed the red light. An argument followed. Some 15 minutes after the game actually ended, the referee decided the red light went on before the green. Although game films later showed clearly the reverse to be true, Lansberry's goal went into the record books as being scored at 19:59 of the third period and we lost the game 5–4. With the new automatic light systems in use in the National Hockey League today, this couldn't happen again.

A buzzer, siren, gong, or other suitable sound device is also used to signal the end of a period or a game. In addition, at a rink there's usually some form of electric clock for the purpose of keeping the spectators, players, and game officials accurately informed of all time elements at all stages of the game, including the time remaining to be played in any period and the time remaining to be served in penalties.

Immediately alongside the ice, in the neutral zone, are the players' benches. There are separate door (gate) openings leading from each bench to the ice. Also alongside the ice in the neutral zone are the penalty boxes, or benches, where penalized players must sit out their sentences in the sin bins. There are, of course, separate penalty boxes for each team. Most fans don't realize the location of benches is one fine point in the strategy of winning hockey games. While no bench or penalty box for one team can be closer to its goal than the other team's, the situation can be worked to the home club's advantage. The home team has the right to assign the players' bench and penalty box to the visiting club, as well as to select the goal it wishes to shoot at for two of the three periods. (Hockey is played in three periods of 20 minutes for a game total of 60 minutes, and the goals are changed after each period.) Since, as you will see later in this book, it's usually more important to try to move players into your defending zone as quickly as possible than to put them in the attacking zone, the home team will always select the players' bench and penalty box nearest to the goal they will be defending for two periods.

Our seating positions on the players' bench are also determined by the goal we're protecting. For instance, if this goal is at the left of the bench, as it is when we're on home ice during the first and third periods, our defensemen who are on the bench sit at the extreme left side of the bench while our spare goalie's seat is on the far right end. The forward line replacements move down the bench toward the left. That is, the forwards just coming off the ice always sit first at the right end of the bench then move toward the left so that when they're ready to go back on the ice, they're at the left end next to the defensemen.

Here the Rangers' forward line prepares to make a change on the fly as they jump over the dasher boards.

The Toronto goalie has just made a poke save against Rod Gilbert. Vic Hadfield (11 front, extreme right) is in position for a rebound.

During the second period, when the net we're defending is to the right of our bench, the defensemen sit on the extreme right end of the bench and our spare goalkeeper is on the left. The forward line replacements move down the bench toward the right.

Home ice has other advantages too. Each rink has its own idiosyncrasies and the home players should be able to capitalize on them much more quickly than the visitors. These idiosyncrasies take the form of lively or dead boards, which give the puck a fast or slow rebound. A team that knows just how the puck will ricochet has an advantage over the team that doesn't. There are also psychological advantages for the home team because of the thousands of fans who are rooting behind them. When the visitors score a goal, the rinks are usually deathly silent. When the home team scores, or gets a rally going, the place is usually wild with enthusiasm.

One thing that seems to puzzle a lot of people about the rink is the ice itself. How does it get its color? How are the line markings made? How thick is it? Well, here's how icemaking is accomplished at our home rink—New York's Madison Square Garden. Like most arenas in the United States, the Garden is used for many events—boxing, rallies, circuses, basketball, roller derbies. The night before a hockey game, while any given event is going on, brine is circulated through pipes embedded in the Garden's concrete subfloor. Then, after the event is over, the top floor boards are removed and the dasher boards are installed. Incidentally, the brine which is used to lower the temperature of the concrete subfloor is at 10 degrees above zero.

When the desired temperature of concrete surface is reached, workmen, using a hose, apply a thin film of water over the floor. When this freezes the process is repeated two more times. Then, the entire ice surface is covered with a water solution containing a whitening agent. After three more water sprayings, the markings are applied by hand painting. Templates and forms are used to assure a uniform paint job. Once the markings are down, the surface receives 14 more water-spray applications. Some eight hours later, the ⅝-inch-thick ice surface we skate on is ready for use. If you're curious, it takes about 6,000 gallons of water to flood Madison Square Garden—we asked one of the workmen.

Between periods, the ice is resurfaced by a machine called a Zamboni—named after its inventor and maker. This machine picks up the fine ice shavings and then applies a thin film of hot water to smooth the surface. When the hockey game is over, workmen, usually the same night, quickly break up the ice and remove it from the concrete subfloor so that another activity can get underway at the Garden.

THE TEAM

A hockey team consists of six players. By positions, they are called the left wing, center, right wing, left defense, right defense, and goalkeeper. But the most important point to keep in mind is that hockey is a team sport and teamwork is vital to success. And as you read further in this book, you'll find that, in spite of the speed of our game, we do have a definite pattern of plays. True, unlike football or basketball, we don't have too many set plays or hard-and-fast systems. But, while it may appear to new fans that play on the ice may be helter-skelter, hockey is *not* a game of individuals, with each man playing the puck on his own, forgetting about the rest of the team. Our game is a team sport.

The wings and center are called forwards and play together on a unit, or line. There is frequent platooning, but, in general, the same three forwards always play together and the same two defensemen play together. The forwards usually stay on the ice from 1 to 2 minutes during a particular time, or shift. Forwards normally rotate in three shifts; that is, a team usually skates three forward lines. The defensemen remain in action for the same periods of time, usually 1 to 2 minutes, but teams carry only two regular defensive units, plus one extra defenseman to take the place of an injured or penalized player of the regular unit. The goalie is the only player who usually goes the entire 60 minutes of a game.

Oddly enough, hockey is the only sport in which players may be substituted at any time without a stoppage of the action. When the puck is in play the substitutes enter the game on the fly by jumping from the bench to the ice as the other players approach the bench gate. Of course, changing on the fly can present some problems; sometimes a team finds itself with an extra skater on the ice because of a foul-up when making a line change. To avoid the 2-minute penalty for playing with too many skaters on the ice, the Rangers and most clubs in the NHL substitute by position. For instance, when changing a forward line, the center skates onto the ice only when the center he is replacing has skated to the bench, while the left wing replaces the other left wing and the right wing replaces the other right wing. Our defensemen change in the same manner. Our coach, Emile Francis, makes the decision when the line and the defensive pair are to change. But such changes are only made when our team is moving into the attacking zone. It's never wise to change players when play is in your defensive zone since this will give your opponents a momentary player advantage which could cause trouble.

When you're a midget player, changing on the fly presents an added problem. At age seven, Brad Park played for the Eglington Aces. "Our home rink in the Scarborough section of Toronto had a professional quality. The sideboards were enormous. In fact, they were so high we'd never climb over the boards and drop to the ice because the five-foot drop would have killed us. Instead, the coaches would take us around the waist and lower us out of the benches, gently, to the ice. While on the bench we stood all the time so we could see the game."

Basically, here's what players at each of the positions do:

Goalie. He is the court of last appeal as it is his responsibility to keep the puck from entering the goal. He can stop the puck in any manner —using his stick, glove, or body. He very seldom leaves the vicinity of the goalkeeper's crease. As we describe later, each goalie has his own style of play. Some skate to cut down a skater's angle, others are scramblers—lunging, kneeling, and flopping on the ice. Eddie Giacomin of our team likes to roam to the side, behind, or out in front of the net to field the pucks and shoot them to his teammates. Jacques Plante, a veteran NHL goalie of several teams, was the first to go behind the net to field the puck and pass it to a teammate, but Giacomin has embellished that style to great advantage. He has also developed a technique of passing the puck and firing it down the ice out of danger when he sees the opportunity that no other goalie has ever utilized to such an extent. Perfecting the use of his stick has given Eddie more mobility than any goalie in the league, and, in a sense, gives us a third defenseman on the ice. Actually, his style has helped other fine goaltenders to improve their style.

Defensemen. It is the duty of the defensemen (like Brad Park) to keep the opposition from getting a close shot at the goal. They are supposed to block shots, clear the puck from in front of the net, and guard opposing forwards. Offensively, defensemen pass the puck to the forwards and follow the play to act as a rear guard. The defensemen must also know how to shoot from just inside the attacking blue line (or from what is called the points). More on the various duties of defensemen is given in subsequent chapters.

Forwards. Forwards (such as Rod Gilbert) are usually considered the

Rod Gilbert (top) is a right-hand shot, while Brad Park (bottom) is a left-hand shot.

real offensive of a team. With the exception of facing off (a special assignment usually given to the center), the three forwards must be able to do the same things. To visualize their areas of play, imagine the ice surface divided lengthwise into three equal lanes. The wings are responsible in their lanes and patrol up and down, moving out only for good reasons. They must be the fastest skaters and the best shots on the team. While the left wings usually are left-handed shooters and the right wings right-handed, there are exceptions. One of Rod's childhood idols and one of the all-time greats of hockey, Maurice "Rocket" Richard, shot left-handed and yet played right wing. This, in effect, meant he took most of his shots from the "wrong" side. Richard tallied 626 lifetime NHL goals, including both regular season and play-off games. It's an oddity of hockey that better than 75 percent of the players shoot from the left, whereas in baseball more than 75 percent of the players bat right-handed. On the 1971–72 Rangers, for instance, only six players—Ab De Marco, Bill Fairbairn, Bruce MacGregor, Bobby Rousseau, Gary Doak, and I—of the seventeen skaters who regularly suit up for games fire from the right side.

National Hockey League rules permit a team to have 17 players, plus two goalkeepers, in uniform for a game. A few players like the Rangers' Rod Seiling, the Black Hawks' Jerry Korab, the Canadiens' Jim Roberts and Serge Savard, and the Bruins' Carol Vadnais can play both positions—defenseman and forward—with ease. In fact, before Brad Park entered the junior status, "I was a forward. But at about the age of fifteen I started to put on a little weight and my body-checking ability began to jell. My coach—who was my father—switched me to defense. Incidentally, playing on a team coached by your father isn't always easy. Once we won a game 6–0 and he came into the dressing room and blasted us. 'You guys got a shutout,' he said, 'but you made mistakes left and right.'

"Next time we won 1–0 and he said we had played a great game. He, like most coaches, was fickle. He once dropped my brother, Ron Park, from the team because he didn't think he was good enough. But, I must give my dad a great deal of credit. He worked hard with me when jobs were hard to find and our family didn't have much money. He'd work during the day and plan his work schedule to mesh with Ron's and my hockey games. I'd play a game at 6:30 P.M. and my older brother would play at 8:30 P.M. It's interesting to note that my coauthor, Rod, played defense until he reached the junior classification. [The various classifications of hockey are explained later.] We both

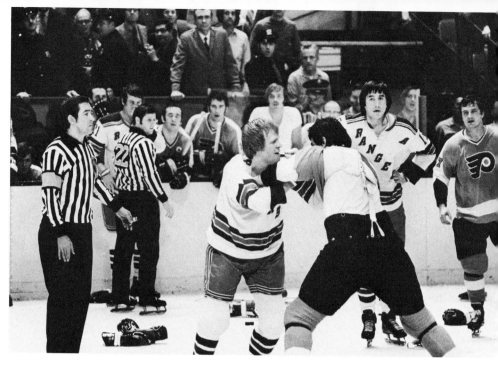

Our "policeman" during the 1971–72 season was Glen Sather. Here he is in action against Rick Foley of the Philadelphia Flyers.

A hockey game is started by a face-off at the center ice circle.

agree that a young player should learn to play at forward and defense. The experience gained will be of great help when you later play an established position."

Often players are given specific jobs on a team above and beyond their regular duties. For instance, there are penalty killers and power-play specialists. The former are players sent out onto the ice to thwart the opposition's attack when a team is short-handed because a teammate is in the penalty box. In such cases, the regular-strength team usually sends out its best shooters in hopes of getting a power-play goal. (Most coaches generally put out only one defenseman in power-play situations.)

In some cases a team will assign a player—usually a forward—the role of shadow. This simply means that a player is given one star player on the opposing team and told to keep him from scoring. For example, in the 1972 Stanley Cup finals, Walt Tkaczuk of our team was given the tough task of shadowing Phil Esposito. Esposito during the regular season had scored 66 goals, an average of almost one a game. The result of Walt's work in the finals: Esposito didn't score a goal. By the way, if you don't know, the Stanley Cup is the championship trophy of the National Hockey League.

Almost every hockey club has a policeman, a rugged player who is responsible for the well-being of his teammates. With everything else, hockey is also a game of intimidation, with no mercy shown for the weaker opponent. Thus it's the role of the club policeman to protect his smaller or less combative teammates from unwarranted physical punishment. This type of hockey player can change a game around by keeping the opposition honest. Two of the best policemen in the league are Orland Kurtenbach of the Vancouver Canucks and Ted Harris of the Minnesota North Stars.

THE PLAY OF HOCKEY

As the game is about to start, both teams line up in position on the ice for the opening face-off. The center is at the center spot in the neutral zone, flanked by his left and right wings. The wings are about midway between the edge of the restraining circle and the boards and a few feet on their own side of the center line. The two defensemen station themselves near their own blue line, about 10 feet apart. The goalkeeper stands between the goalposts just inside his crease line. The referee is at center ice with the puck, facing the game timekeeper,

Rod Gilbert (top) scores his fortieth goal in a season. This record as it appeared on the official Madison Square Garden score board.

while the linesmen stand at the side boards facing each other, but on opposite blue lines.

The game is started by a face-off at the center spot. The two opposing centers stand squarely facing their opponent's end of the rink about one stick length apart, one foot on either side of the center face-off spot and with the full blade of the stick flat on the ice. When the puck, dropped by the referee, strikes the ice, the players facing off play it with their sticks. No other player may enter the restraining circle until this occurs. Sometimes a face-off will be done over because one of the centers was able to hit the puck before it touched the ice.

Once a team has control of the puck, it's on the offensive and it will try to move the puck into the attacking zone and score a goal. The team without the puck is on the defense and it will attempt to prevent the scoring of a goal. The attacking team can bring the puck into the opposing team's zone in only two ways—stick-handle it in, or shoot it in. The defending players try to get the puck away from the attackers by blocking or checking them with either their bodies or their sticks or by intercepting the puck. It's not necessary to shoot the puck into the netting behind the goalie to score. If the *entire* puck crosses the goal line inside the posts, even if it is in the possession of the goalkeeper, it is a goal, *unless* (1) an attacking player kicks the puck, or otherwise deliberately directs the puck into the goal by any means other than the stick, or (2) an attacking player is in the goal crease and is in no way held in by a defender while a teammate scores.

It is within the rules for an attacking player to carry the puck into the goal crease area and still score. It's also within the rules for an attacking side to score a goal by having a shot deflect off a teammate, as long as the teammate doesn't intentionally steer the deflection into the goal with his hand or skate. If the same shot deflects into the goal off a defender, or if a defender inadvertently directs the puck over the goal line, it is a goal. In such a case, the attacking player who last played the puck, in the referee's opinion, is awarded the goal. One of the most famous goals of hockey was scored by Red Kelly, now coach of the Pittsburgh Penguins. While playing for the Toronto Maple Leafs, Kelly shot the puck into his own net accidentally, in a game against the New York Rangers. This not only proved to be the winning goal in the game, but was a key goal in Andy Bathgate's record-breaking ten-game goal-scoring streak. Bathgate, the last Ranger to touch the puck, was given official credit for the goal. Of course, in such a scoring situation, no assists are given.

If the goalie carries the puck across the goal line, as shown here, it is considered a score.

While a goal doesn't count if it is kicked in by an attacker, if that same attacker kicks it in off a defender other than the goalkeeper, it does count. In this case, the kicker is credited with the goal. On the other hand, if a shot is deflected in off a teammate, the teammate gets credit for the goal and the shooter gets an assist. By the way, no more than two assists can be credited on any goal, and those assists go to the two players who handle the puck immediately preceding the goal. In other words, when a goal is scored the official scorer may give two, one, or no assists, depending on how many helped in the scoring of the goal. A point is awarded to a player for each assist or goal he scores.

The team scoring the most goals is adjudged the winner and receives two points in the league standings. If the game ends in a tie, special arrangements are made. This depends on the individual league's rules. Some declare a tie game; others play a 10-minute sudden-death overtime period. If the score is still tied at the end of this time, it is considered a tie game. In either case, both teams receive one point in the standing. In some contests, such as the Stanley Cup playoff, the sudden-death is continued until one team scores. In the 1971 playoff, we both were involved in triple overtime, the longest game in modern Ranger history. Of course, what makes this game vivid in our minds is that we beat Chicago 3–2. Incidentally, the longest Stanley Cup game was six overtime periods in 1936, in which Detroit beat the Montreal Maroons 1–0.

Often friends we've met in New York—sometimes people who have never seen hockey before—go to games. They'll ask us what they should watch for and the answer is most simple: Just follow the puck. When you grow up with hockey as we did, it comes naturally. Skating, playing, watching the sport . . . it was all part of our childhood. But many Americans have to learn our game. It's like Canadian kids getting adjusted to baseball. We can imagine that the speed of our game could make it tough for someone watching it for the first time. Our advice to our friends is this: Don't try to look for the technical things right away. Let your eyes get adjusted to the speed of the game, the changes of direction, the constant action. Keep your eye on the puck. It's that little piece of rubber around which this game revolves. If you can follow it, you'll pretty much be able to follow the flow of the game.

After you've seen a few games, you'll notice the refinements. You'll see guys like Jean Ratelle work the trailer play again and again, and pretty soon you'll look for it when Ratty (our nickname for Jean) is on the ice. The trailer play is executed—just as it sounds—with one man trailing the puck carrier. The man with the puck will skate in, perhaps fake a shot, and then leave the puck for his trailer. The goalie sometimes never sees the trailer and can't get set for the shot. Often the puck carrier on the play will screen the goalie's view. Sometimes his own defensemen will block the goalie's sight of the puck. See what we mean about the whole team being responsible for success or failure?

You often hear complaints from fans who never see the puck go in on scrambles in front of the net. Don't feel too bad. Sometimes goalies don't see those either. But, when you go to a game, try to follow the pattern of play. If it's moving too fast, don't worry. Just sit back and enjoy the speed and agility of the players. And please do us one big favor. Don't throw anything onto the ice during the course of a game. When skating at the speed we do, a penny or some other small object tossed by a thoughtless fan could cause injury to a hockey player. This happened to Rod once and resulted in a very serious back injury that could have cost him his career.

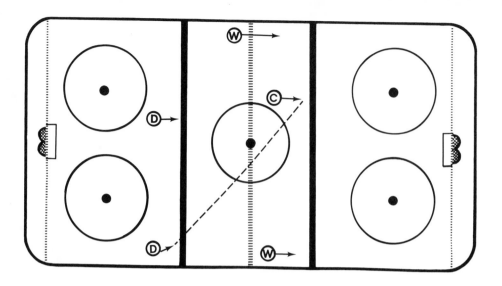

Any time a player passes the puck over two lines to a teammate, the play itself is offside (top). When a player shoots the puck over the red line, the blue line, and then the goal line and a rival player (except the goalkeeper) touches it first, "icing" is called (bottom).

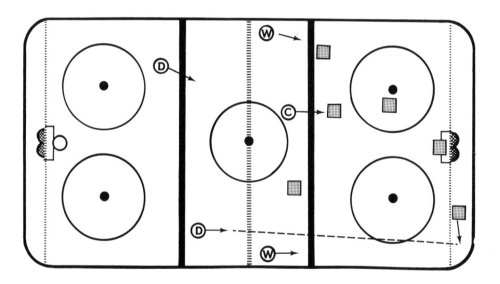

THE RULES

Three main rules cover the majority of infractions in hockey. They are primarily spectator-designed, as they force playmaking and teamwork, discourage stalling, and maintain speed. The three infractions are governed by the blue lines and center red line, and each calls for a face-off.

Offside Passes. While the rules may be spectator-designed—that's a quote from the official NHL rulebook—many new fans are thrown by the offside infraction whistled down by the officials. Just between us, sometimes those offside calls throw the players too. But really understanding what an offside pass is all about isn't that hard. In logical sequence picture an attack beginning from your end, moving up ice. Let's take an imaginary game between, say, the Rangers and Boston. Suppose we have the puck in our end and are getting ready to move out. There are two restrictions on our forward movement. First, we can't pass the puck from our zone farther than the red line. The puck carrier can skate the puck out and take it as far as he cares. It is only on passes that he is restricted. That's why the wings don't take off and skate away, leaving the center with no one to pass to. The wing must stop short of the red line and wait for the center to throw a pass or carry the puck out himself. Once the center is in neutral ice—the area between the blue lines—he can pass up to but not over the Boston blue line. Again, the wings have to wait for him and for the puck. Simply stated, the offside rules say that no pass can travel over two lines. If you remember that, it will be easy to recognize offside pass violations that come from faulty passes.

Offsides. The second infraction occurs when any member of the attacking team crosses the defending team's blue line ahead of the puck. Let's say Rod Gilbert sees an opening, sidesteps a defenseman, and breaks into Boston's end while one of his teammates is still handling the puck at mid-ice. "If he passes the puck to me, or follows me across the blue line, I'll be offside. That's because the puck must always precede all of the attacking players over the defending team's blue line.

"Often you'll see a player pull up as he approaches a line or skate right by the puck. If he crosses that line ahead of the puck or picks up the puck after crossing a line ahead of it, he'll be offside. That rule eliminates players' hanging back in an opponent's zone while play moves out into the neutral zone. It would be nice if I could just hang around the other team's net, waiting for one of my teammates to grab the puck and throw me an ice-length pass. No defenseman to worry about. Only a goalie to beat. Hockey would be too easy if you got away with things like that."

If we're attacking in Boston's end of the ice and lose possession to one of their players, they're going to try to clear it out of their zone. If they succeed, we must clear the zone too—and that means all of our players must get out before we can resume the attack. No attacking player can cross the red center line or opposing team's blue line ahead of the puck. If he does, he's offside. You can have one leg in the zone, but as long as your other skate is straddling the restraining line, you won't be offside. Often you'll see players almost doing splits to keep one skate back of the line so they won't be offside. The position of the player's skates and not that of his stick is the determining factor in all instances in deciding an offside. A player is onside when *either* of his skates is in contact with or on his own side of the blue line at the instant the puck completely crosses the outer edge of that line regardless of the position of his stick. Should the skates of the player propelling the puck cross the line ahead of the puck, it too is considered an offside.

For a long time there was no red line in hockey. Then Frank Boucher, a great Ranger player, coach, and executive, suggested the innovation in 1943. Until Boucher came up with the red center line, teams were not allowed to pass the puck out of their own ends. They had to carry it out with their sticks. "You could see," Boucher told Rod Gilbert, "teams bottled up for minutes at a time in their own side. That's why I suggested a red line in the middle of the ice so teams could pass the puck out of danger without penalty."

Icing the Puck. This occurs when you shoot the puck up the ice from your side of the red center line and across the opposing team's goal line (not into the goal, of course), and the puck is first touched by an opposing player. Play is stopped and the puck is then brought back for a face-off in the circle deep in your defensive zone.

Icing is a strategic maneuver to take the pressure off your team, and sometimes it can be used for other purposes too. Rod Gilbert remembers during the 1968 playoffs against Chicago a battle of wits between Ranger coach Emile Francis and Chicago's Billy Reay. Emile wanted Ron Stewart, one of the better defensive forwards in the NHL, to shadow Bobby Hull. Reay, of course, was trying to avoid that match-up and get Hull's line on the ice against anybody but Stewart. In New

York, Emile as the home coach had the last option on starting lineups and always had Stewart out against Hull to do his shadowing job. But when the series shifted to Chicago, Francis had to name his starting lineup first. He started Phil Goyette's line with Bob Nevin at right wing. Reay countered with Hull's line, which meant Bobby would be up against Nevin instead of Stewart. Emile wasn't prepared to let Reay win that showdown. He used icing as a strategy in this spot. Goyette won the game-opening face-off and got the puck to Arnie Brown, one of our defensemen. Brown iced it—deliberately—causing a stop in play. The Goyette line skated off and Stewart's line came on the ice to face Hull.

A deliberate icing sometimes can backfire as a strategy. Once, a couple of years ago, the Rangers had to settle for a tie against Toronto because of an inopportune icing. We were leading 3–2 in the last minute and we were concerned with just eating up time. Play was in our end and the Leafs were pressing. One of our defensemen got the puck, and instead of skating clear of our zone and holding on to it, he just shot it the length of the ice. Icing was called and the puck was brought back for a face-off. There were only 6 seconds left on the clock, but in hockey that's enough time to win a face-off and get a shot. That's just what Ron Ellis did, and instead of winning 3–2, we were tied, 3–3.

There are four conditions when icing is not called:

1. When a team is shorthanded as a result of a penalty, it can't be called for icing. That is, you can shoot the puck the length of the ice to break up an attack and not have officials bring it back on you.

2. If the puck cuts across part of the goal crease, no icing will be called.

3. When a defending opponent, in the judgment of the linesman, could have played the puck before it crossed his own goal line, there is no icing.

4. When a member of the team which ices the puck touches it before the defending opponent, no icing is called and play continues. This is, of course, when he's not offside.

There's also a stoppage of play when the puck goes outside the playing area at either end or either side of the rink, or strikes any obstacle above the playing surface other than the boards, glass, or wire; it is faced off from where it was shot or deflected. If the puck becomes lodged in the netting on the outside of either goal, making it unplayable, or when it is "frozen" between opposing players intentionally or otherwise, the referee stops play, and the puck is faced off at either of

Brad Park freezes the puck against the net. Once the referee loses sight of the puck, he calls for a face-off.

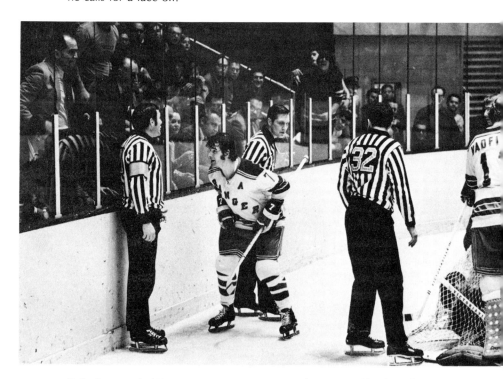

Only the captain (C) or assistant captain (A) can dispute an official's call. Here Rod Gilbert (note the A on his uniform) lets the referee know what he thinks of one of his decisions.

the adjacent face-off spots. If the referee believes that the stoppage was caused by a player of the attacking team, he can conduct the face-off in the neutral zone. Should a scramble take place, or if a player accidentally falls on the puck, and the puck is out of sight of the referee, he immediately blows his whistle and stops the play. The puck then is faced off at the point where the play was stopped.

THE OFFICIALS

There are eight officials in hockey—the referee, two linesmen, two goal judges, a game timekeeper, a penalty timekeeper, the official scorer. The latter five are called minor officials. They receive this title only because the referee and the two linesmen are major officials. There is nothing minor about their duties. While the referee and linesmen are salaried, none of the NHL minor officials are paid. They are appointed by the league as men of high standing in their local communities. In other words, except for the Stanley Cup playoff games, when the minor officials are imported from neutral cities, all are from the cities where they officiate. It's to the credit of these minor officials— and to hockey—that their natural hometown interests don't interfere with their objectivity.

Referee. He has full control of a hockey game. While he receives assistance from the linesmen and goal judges, the final decision on everything, from the time a game will start to whether or not a goal beat the buzzer, rests with the referee. He is the only official with power to administer a penalty that will put a man off the ice. However, he doesn't call infractions of icing, offside, and offside passes.

Although the referee and linesmen are clad in identical uniforms, the referee can be distinguished by a red arm band. The referee can be replaced only if an illness or accident makes it impossible for him to continue. Then he appoints one of the linesmen to take his place.

Linesmen. They call the infractions of icing, offside, and offside passes. They chase the puck after stoppage of play and drop the puck for face-offs in the neutral zone. Generally, they can't call penalties but can report these infractions to the referee. The exceptions to this are when a team has too many players on the ice and when an object is thrown from either bench onto the ice. These are infractions that may be called by the linesmen. Of course, the referee may call upon a linesman to give his version of an incident that may take place during a game. Last year, for instance, Rod Gilbert had a goal taken away by

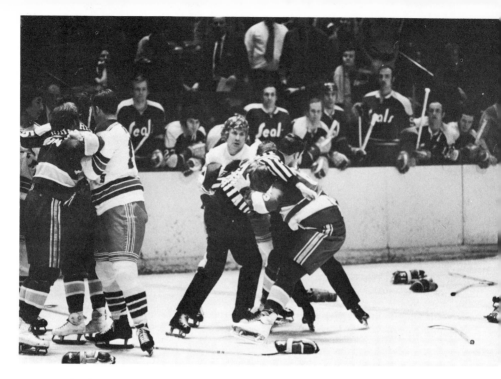

The linesmen have the unenviable job of breaking up fights, such as this one between the Rangers' Hadfield and Seals' Stewart (top); the result was one linesman flat on his back holding his punched nose. Of course, Vic received a game misconduct and a fine; but because the referee deemed that the punch that knocked down the linesman was accidental, he wasn't suspended.

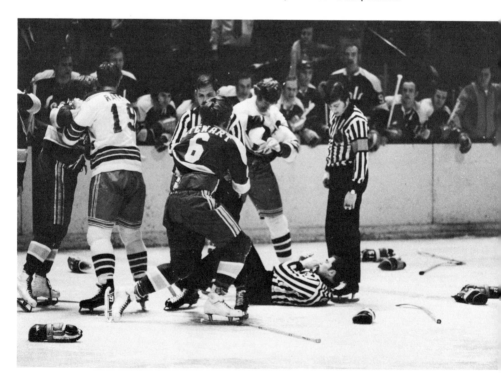

a linesman that cost the Rangers a victory. "While standing in front of the Toronto goal, I had a puck deflect off my thigh into the net. The red light went on and the referee signaled a goal. But, the Toronto players argued that I hit it with my hand, which is of course illegal. After a short discussion, the referee asked the linesman nearest the play for his opinion. He agreed with the Toronto players, and no matter how I tried to prove that both my hands were on my stick, the referee took the word of his linesman and my goal was disallowed. The game ended in a 2–2 tie."

The linesmen have the unenviable job of breaking up fights, while the referee assesses the penalties. This can be quite dangerous, as one linesman discovered last year when he was accidentally "decked" by our captain, Vic Hadfield, in a fight with Bob Stewart of the California Seals.

Goal Judges. They're seated in a screened area, outside the playing surface, behind each goal. It is their job to determine whether or not the puck has crossed the goal line. (The referee, of course, has the final decision on the legality of goals.) If it has, a red light in front of the goal judge's area is turned on to signify a score.

Game Timekeeper. He operates the master clock which tells how much time has elapsed in each period, and he is responsible for the buzzer, gong, siren, or other sound device which signals the end of a period.

Penalty Timekeeper. He checks the time served by penalized players and keeps an accurate account of the time penalties are imposed and when they lapse.

Official Scorer. He keeps the official sheet to record the goals scored, the scorers, the players to whom assists have been credited, the time of goals, the goalkeepers' saves, and the penalized players and the time of penalties. The referee reports to the official scorer the name or number of the goal scorer, but the official scorer credits the assists.

PENALTIES

Penalties, like the officials, are a necessary evil of hockey! Of course, when a team is penalized, the entire strategy of the game changes on both sides. Usually several times during the game each team will be forced to play shorthanded when one or more of its players is sent to the penalty box. At no time, however, is a team made to play more than two men below full strength. Should a third penalty be called, it is

Most common penalties in hockey: tripping;

hooking;

elbowing;

cross-checking;

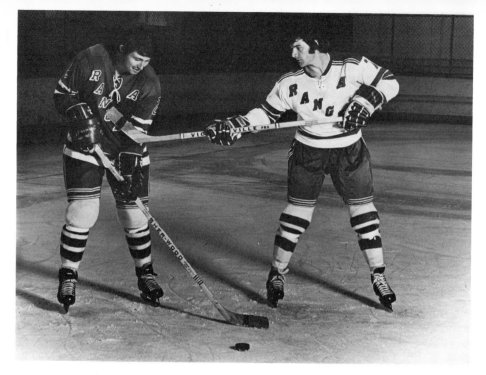

spearing;

holding;

interference;

high sticking.

delayed until the first expires. Nevertheless, the third player penalized must at once proceed to the penalty box but may be replaced by a substitute until such time as the penalty time of the guilty man commences. Incidentally, should the team with the advantage score, the penalized player returns to the ice except where a major or match penalty has been called.

During a hockey game, no greater anger is voiced by the hometown fans than when a penalty is called on their team or an infraction by an opponent is missed by the referee. We must remember that the vast majority of penalties are judgment calls—and we both have questioned some referees on their judgment—and what makes the situation more confusing is that each referee *seems* to have a slightly different interpretation of some of the basic rules. To further complicate the matter, few fans are really familiar with the rules involved in any single infraction.

Rather than describe each infraction with the official interpretation, we believe that the preceding photographs will better explain the major rule violations and the officials' calls.

There also are other penalties for such infractions as delaying the game, handling the puck, playing with too many players on the ice, roughing, fighting, boarding, butt ending, throwing a stick, playing with a broken stick or illegal equipment, falling on the puck (other than the goalkeeper).

There are basically five types of penalties:

Minor Penalties. These call for a player, except the goalie, to be ruled off the ice for 2 minutes, during which time no substitute is permitted.

Major Penalties. These are 5 minutes long, and are imposed when two players resort to fighting instead of hockey, or when a player cuts his opponent, drawing blood, while committing an illegal act. No substitute is permitted for the offending player.

If the second major penalty occurs in the same game to the same player, he is banished to the penalty box for 15 minutes, but a substitute is permitted after 5 minutes have elapsed. The third major penalty to the same player in the same game means his expulsion from the remainder of the contest, but a substitute is permitted to replace the man so suspended after 5 minutes have elapsed. In professional hockey a fine may also accompany a major penalty.

When coincidental major penalties are imposed against an equal number of players of each team, the penalized players must take their seats in the penalty boxes, and they aren't allowed to leave until the first stoppage of play following the expiration of their respective penalties. Immediate substitutions may be made for the players so penalized and neither team is considered shorthanded.

Misconduct Penalties. These are 10-minute penalties, generally called against players who become abusive in language or gesture. The penalized player is put out for 10 minutes but doesn't leave his team shorthanded. In professional hockey, an automatic fine against the offender is also assessed. In amateur hockey, many young players tend to argue with officials. Remember that the official is the "government" controlling the game and his final decision must not be criticized especially in an abusive way.

When a player receives a minor penalty and a misconduct penalty at the same time, the penalized team immediately puts a substitute player in the penalty box, and he serves the minor penalty as if imposed upon him. In the case of both a major penalty and a misconduct one, the penalized team sends a substitute player to the penalty box before the major penalty expires since no replacement for a penalized player may enter the game except from the penalty bench.

A *Game Misconduct* penalty involves the suspension of a player for the balance of the game, but a substitute is permitted to replace him immediately. In professional hockey, there is an automatic fine against the offender.

Match Penalties. These mean immediate ejection of the guilty player for the balance of the game. A match penalty is levied for (1) deliberate attempt to injure; a substitute can be used after 5 minutes; or (2) deliberate injury to an opponent, calling for 10 minutes without replacement. In professional hockey, there is usually further suspension and a fine to the offender of a match penalty.

If a goalie is given a minor or major penalty, his time is always served by another member of his team designated by the coach. In the case of a goalkeeper's incurring a misconduct penalty, it must be served by another member of his team (designated by the manager or coach) who was on the ice when the offense was committed. Should a goalie incur a game misconduct penalty or a match penalty, his place on the ice is taken by a member of his own club, or by a substitute goaltender if one is available, and this player is allowed to put on all the goalie's equipment. In the case of a match penalty, any time in the penalty box covered under the rules will be served by another member of the team on the ice at the time of the offense. In professional hockey, the goalkeeper is subject to fine for major misconduct and match penalties

A

B

C

D

Official code of signals: (A) delayed calling of penalty; (B) boarding; (C) tripping; (D) elbowing; (E) cross-checking; (F) hooking; (G) slashing; (H) charging; (I) interference.

E

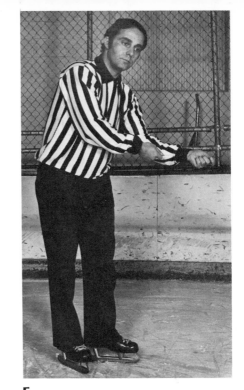

F

G

H

I

as well as for leaving the immediate vicinity of his goal crease to take part in a fight.

When a minor, major, or match penalty is committed by a player of the side in possession of the puck, the referee immediately blows his whistle and gives the penalty to the offending player. The resulting face-off is held at the spot where the play was stopped unless the stoppage occurred in the attacking zone of the player penalized. In such a case, the face-off is made at the nearest face-off spot in the neutral zone.

When a minor, major, or match penalty is called on a player of the team not in possession of the puck, the referee signifies the calling of a penalty by pointing to the offending player. On completion of the play by the team in possession, he blows his whistle and gives the penalty to the offending player.

Completion of the play by the team in possession in this rule simply means that the puck must have come into complete possession and control of an opposing player or has been frozen. This doesn't include a rebound off the goalie or any accidental contact with the body or equipment of an opposing player. If the penalty to be imposed is a minor one, and a goal is scored on the play by the nonoffending side, the penalty is nullified. However, in the case of a major or match penalty, it's imposed in the normal manner regardless of whether a goal is scored or not.

Penalty Shot. This is a free, unopposed shot at opponent's goal with only the goalie defending. It is awarded a player who is illegally impeded from behind when in possession of the puck and with no opponent between him and the opponent's goal, except the goalkeeper.

The player designated by the referee to take the penalty shot may carry the puck in from any part of the neutral zone or his own defending zone, but once the puck has crossed the attacking blue line it must be kept in motion toward the opponent's goal line, and once it is shot, the play is considered complete. (No goal can be scored on a rebound of any kind, and any time the puck crosses the goal line the shot is considered completed.) The goalie must remain in his goal crease until the puck has crossed the near blue line. While the penalty shot is being taken, players of both sides must withdraw to the sides of the rink and beyond the red center line. The offending team doesn't play short-handed after the penalty shot, whether successful or not. If a goal is scored from a penalty shot the puck is faced off at center ice in the usual way. If a goal isn't scored the puck is faced off at either of the end face-off spots in the zone in which the penalty shot was tried.

It is most important for every player—and fan, too—to know the rules of hockey thoroughly. During our fall training camp, Coach Francis spends time carefully going over the rules and any new changes in their interpretations. At our hockey school we do the same thing. In other words, every player must know what he can and cannot do while out on the ice.

Up-to-date rulebooks can be obtained from almost any hockey equipment store or from the National Hockey League, 922 Sun Life Building, Montreal, Quebec, Canada. By the way, except for the colleges, the amateur and professional leagues of the United States and Canada follow the NHL rules. Some of the leagues, of course, have minor differences, but the basic rules are the same. Only the collegiate rules, rules for high schools in the United States, and those used in international competitions such as the Olympic Games and the International Ice Hockey Federation tournament vary to any degree.

In college hockey, icing is called when the puck is shot the length of the rink from inside the defensive blue line; by NHL rules, the center red line is the determining factor. (There is no center red line in college play.) In the colleges, a player can pass from his own end all the way to his opponent's blue line; by NHL rules, that pass over two lines is offside. The colleges also call icing against a shorthanded team, don't permit body checking in the attacking (offensive) zone, and expel a player from the game for fighting.

So much for the basics of the game of hockey; now let's take a look at the equipment with which it is played.

2

Hockey Equipment

THERE may be more physical contact in football than in hockey, but football players aren't moving at the same speed as hockey players at the moment of impact, nor are they smashed up against the boards. And then there are the other built-in risks of the game—a frozen hard-rubber puck traveling over 100 miles per hour, an unexpected fall on a rock-hard surface, and a carelessly wielded hockey stick. Without properly fitted equipment, hockey would be a rather dangerous sport. But with it, the chances of physical injury are minimal.

Dressing for a game or practice is a slow, methodical process. First, we completely remove all our street clothing. We then put on a set of long johns, under which is placed a protective cup for the groin. This is followed by our shoulder pads, elbow pads, shin guards, and thigh pads. A garter belt is employed to hold the long stockings that cover the legs. Pants go on next with suspenders. Skates, the team jersey, gloves, and a helmet (worn by some players) complete the uniform of the game. When ready to go on the ice, we weigh from 18 pounds to 22 pounds more than when we entered the locker room. The only really vulnerable spot on a hockey player is his face.

But, before we take a detailed look at protective equipment worn by hockey players, let's first investigate the two basic tools of our trade: the skates and the stick.

THE SKATES

Since skating in hockey is paramount, the proper fit of your skates is most important. Parents who purchase skates sizes too large to allow for growth are actually doing their children an injustice. While this

When properly laced, there should be a wide space between eye loops.

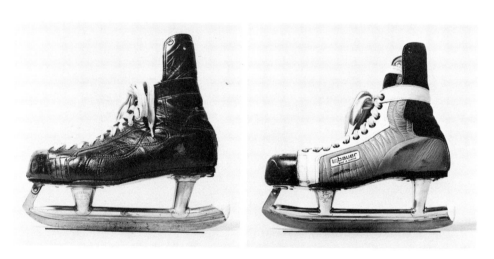

Method of checking radius or rocker of the blades.

plan may be economical, the young player is definitely handicapped. Improper and cheap skates won't give the necessary support. Top quality, stiff leather is needed to give strong support to the ankles. We've all heard this excuse for not skating well: "My ankles are too weak." Let's put that old fallacy to rest for all times. Ankles are seldom "too weak" for skating. In fact, if your ankles are strong enough for you to walk, they're strong enough to skate. The problem of turning ankles, 99 out of 100 times, is the result of poor-quality, ill-fitting skates. Because of this, we strongly recommend that skates be purchased from a reputable sporting goods dealer who has salesmen who are competent to fit skates properly. True, while it may sound strange, many NHL stars learned how to skate by wearing their big brother's skates. Rod Gilbert recalls, "My first skates were my big brother's. You see, Jean-Marie's skates were so big that I could slip my feet, shoes and all, into them. But I don't recommend that anyone learn to skate that way. It's not the best way and, in many instances, can be harmful to your feet."

When skates are fitted, only one pair of cotton socks or light woolen ankle socks should be worn so that a snug, glovelike fit is obtained which will provide good skate control. Never stuff cotton in the skates or use sole cushions. Always consider the skate leather as part of the "skin" of your foot. That is, get the leather of the skate boot as close to the skin as possible without pinching or cramping the foot. Most of us professional players wear skates that are at least a full size smaller than our street-shoe size to assure this necessary close fit.

Select a well-known brand of regular hockey tube skates. (Don't try to play hockey with figure or speed skates.) Hockey skates are usually made of elk or kangaroo leather, lined with heavy duck webbing. A built-up arch support, hard toe caps, firm padding around the ankle area, molded heel counters, and a dependable skate blade are essential. Tendon guards are also a must. They prevent sharp skates from cutting into the Achilles tendon and causing serious and perhaps permanent injury.

When selecting skates, make certain that the fit around the heel is particularly snug and that the heel is *not* able to rise inside the boot. It is because of this need of stiff inner support around the heel area that we usually change into a new pair of skates two or three times during the season. It is important to keep in mind that it is the stiff leather counter, fitted snugly around the heel, that provides the necessary push against the ice to give the power and speed required in hockey skating. In addition, make certain that your toes just reach to the end of the skate boot when the foot is fully extended. A good exercise for your feet is to curl the toes up and grab the sole of the skate boot and then extend the toes. This helps to develop a good feel of the skate-boot sole. Remember that a hockey player should always consider his skates "a part of his foot."

Wide, white cloth laces should be used. (Leather laces are undesirable, since they tend to tighten up when wet and can cut off blood circulation.) The laces should be just long enough to tie a bowknot; laces shouldn't be wound around the ankle.

When properly laced, a good-fitting boot should have a wide space between the eye loops. This desirable condition permits the counters to remain more upright, and thus gives better support. While players' opinions vary on exactly the best way to lace skates, we both follow just about the same procedure; that is, the first four eyelets across the toes are laced fairly tight, the next four at the instep are looser, while the remaining portion around the ankle is snug. But whatever the lacing method employed, remember the important thing is to draw the laces tight enough to give necessary support and yet still feel comfortable.

Care of Skates. Always wipe the skate boots and blades clean with a rag after using them. Then dry them at room temperature. (Never dry skates over extreme heat, such as a hot radiator, because this rapid drying tends to crack the leather.) Polishing or oiling the boot portion of the skates lightly will protect and waterproof the leather, prevent stretching, and resist tearing at stitched seams. Stuff the toes with paper to keep their shape in the off season.

The blades should be kept sharp. Under normal conditions you should be able to get 4 to 6 hours of use from your skates before a sharpening is necessary. (In the NHL, most players' skates are sharpened before each game, and sometimes during the intermission they receive another going over.) To check whether or not your skates are sharp, shave your thumbnail with the blade's edge. Some thumbnail shavings should result if the skates are sharp.

When your skates need sharpening, be sure to use the services of an experienced sharpener, one who uses the hollow-ground method. This process actually gives two edges to each blade, with the middle portion being hollowed out. In effect, the hollow-ground honing reduces blade drag and increases the maneuverability of the skates. It also gives four blade-edges on which to stop and turn. Of course, the degree or depth of the hollow depends on the ice surface. For instance, if the ice is soft, the hollow is generally reduced so that the blades won't cut too deeply into the ice. Cutting too deeply into the ice will reduce speed and can throw a skater off balance when a sudden stop is necessary.

Skate blades are also sharpened to different radii or rockers, depending on individual preference and the position played on the hockey team. To check the radius of your skates, place the blades together and hold them up to the light. The area that touches is the flat—the part of the blade in contact with the ice. While a larger flat permits more straightaway speed, it limits the cutting and turning capabilities. In other words, with greater blade contact you obtain more speed and stability. The smaller the blade contact the better you can start, stop, turn, and dodge. In the beginning, however, don't make the flat too short—anything under 4 inches. You can always lengthen or shorten the radius at a later date. By the way, Rod has about a 3-inch flat, while Brad, being a defenseman, has about a 4½-inch flat to absorb the shocks of body checking and to keep from losing his balance.

When walking off the ice, use wooden or rubber blade guards to prevent nicking the blade edges. Also never put your skates away without blade guards. They will protect the blades from being knocked together, which could result in nicking of the metal. Incidentally, when storing for the summer, oil or grease the blades to prevent rusting.

THE STICK

The hockey stick can best be described as an extension of the player's arm. As such it is important that you select the stick that feels right to you. For instance, the length must be correct for your size, since no player can possibly control either an oversized or undersized stick. To determine the proper length of stick, stand in your *street shoes* and hold the stick in front of you so that the stick rests on the point of its toe. The top of the stick should reach your chin—no lower, no higher. If a stick is too long by this test, saw it off to chin height and file and round off the rough edges. By the way, hockey regulations do not permit sticks longer than 55 inches from the heel (where the stick meets the blade) to the end of the shaft.

Sticks are made right, left, and neutral. Generally, a right shot would use a right stick; that is, the blade is angled so that when a right-shooting player has the puck on his forehand, he can handle it better. Left shots use left sticks. Since the blade of a neutral stick isn't angled, it may be used by either a right or a left shot. Centers often prefer such sticks since they can maneuver the puck on forehand and backhand with

Proper way to tape blade (left)
and knob (right) of a hockey
stick.

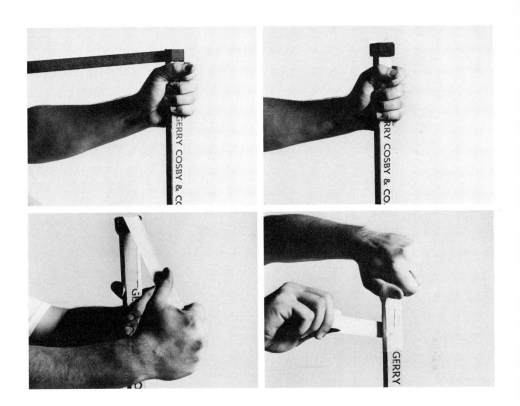

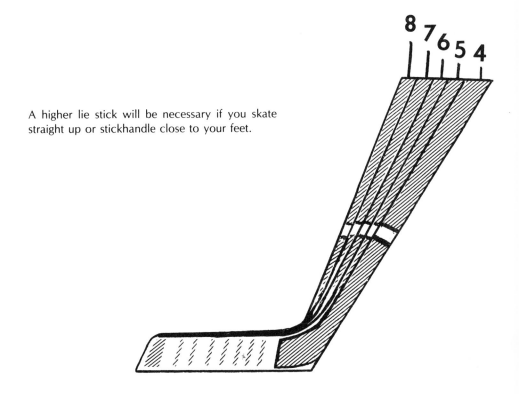

A higher lie stick will be necessary if you skate straight up or stickhandle close to your feet.

equal ease. A neutral stick also helps keep a high shooter's shot down.

The curved, or banana, blade is popular with many of the NHL's leading scorers. We've talked to both of our goalies, as well as to others in the league: they tell us that they can't set themselves as well for a shot off a curved blade as they can against the conventional straight one. The goalies can't tell when the puck will be delivered off the curve. With a straight stick blade it's easier for them to anticipate the shot. In addition, the curved blade imparts a spin to the puck when it is shot that makes it take a tricky drop just before it reaches the net.

While we both use a curved blade, we generally don't recommend this type of stick for the beginning hockey player because he won't be able to make a backhand pass or shot properly. After reaching the junior classification of hockey (see Chapter 10), when a player has learned to pass, shoot, and stickhandle, he has plenty of time to start with the curved stick. Incidentally, if the stick is curved, it may not have a curve of more than ½ inches from the blade out.

Sticks also have different lies; that is, they have different angles between the handle and the blade. The lies most generally used by players are 4, 5, 6, 7, 8, and half points in between. A lie 4 stick has a wide handle-to-blade angle, while a lie 8 has a smaller angle. As a rule, lie 4 sticks are used by players like our teammate Phil Goyette, who likes to skate close to the ice and carry the puck far out in front of him. Lies 5 and 6 are the average lies and permit carrying the puck in a natural nonextended position. Lies 7 and 8 permit carrying the puck closer to the skates, which is ideal for players who skate upright.

To determine if you are using the proper lie for your skating style, take your normal skating stance and note your stick blade on the ice. If the heel of the blade is off the ice so that light shows between the heel and the ice, then you should employ a higher-numbered lie to move the heel down, placing all of the blade in contact with the ice. On the other hand, should the toe of the blade be off the ice, then you should use a lower-numbered lie to bring the toe of the stick blade down so that all of it is in contact with the ice. Also you should examine the blade frequently. If it's worn on the toe, you should try a higher lie. If it's worn on the heel, you should use a lower lie. If your stick wears evenly along the entire bottom of the blade, you are using the correct lie. Experiment with different sticks to find the correct one for you. By the way, Rod uses a stick with a lie 7, while Brad employs a 5.

The weight of the stick and the flexibility of the handle is another consideration when selecting a stick. The sticks usually weigh from 17 to 27 ounces and range from a whippy to a stiff shaft. While Brad uses a light, stiff stick (under 20 ounces) and Rod uses a heavy, stiff one, we both feel that it's best for the beginner to use a light stick with a fairly whippy handle. Always select a stick that has the proper balance, length, lie, and weight for you. In other words, the selection of a stick is a personal thing.

The sticks should also be taped properly. Even with the use of reinforced fiberglass blades, it is wise to apply a thin layer of tape around their centers to preserve the blades and to improve puck control. It is recommended that you start taping from the heel side and wrap toward the toe of the blade. By using black electrical tape, you help to conceal the puck, making it harder for opponents to see a shot coming off a stick. Also the puck won't slide off your stick when receiving a pass and the tape will strengthen the blade so that it won't break when taking a slap shot.

It is also important to have a knob on the end of the handle. Players sometimes will lose control of the stick for a second, and it will start to slide from the hand. If the stick has a knob at the end of the handle, the player will be able to control it before it gets away. In taping the knob, wind the tape around the end a few times and then twist the tape. Continue winding in this manner until the knob is made, then finish it off smoothly. Always cover the knob with white tape since the black electrical tape will stick to the hockey gloves and will cause excessive wear and tear. Rubber knobs, which slip over the end of the stick, are also available from most sporting goods stores.

Remember that professional hockey players treat their sticks with great respect. Therefore, don't bang yours recklessly against the ice or the boards.

PROTECTIVE EQUIPMENT

Earlier in this chapter we briefly described the equipment that made up the hockey player's uniform of the game. The selection of this equipment must be made with a great deal of care. Of course, quality equipment, properly fitted, helps a player to perform with his greatest skill. But more important, such equipment protects him against the perils of games.

In buying protective equipment it should be remembered that you get what you pay for, with better-quality goods lasting over a number

Rod and Brad getting dressed for a game (left to right, top to bottom): After the long underwear and protective cup are put on, they put on stockings, knee pads, and garter belt to hold up the stockings. Skates are the next order of business. Using white adhesive tape, they tape knee pads in place. Next, come pants and shoulder pads. Pants are held in place by suspenders. Rod checks to be sure his elbow pad is properly set. Next come jerseys, and they are ready (except for gloves) for the ice.

of seasons. Fortunately, however, for the young hockey player, most necessary protective gear is available at popular prices. Here's a check list of hockey protective equipment with some essential features of each item:

Underclothing. Weight will depend on the rink temperatures you will encounter. Sets of thermal-knit long underwear are most popular, with cotton T-shirts preferred by some.

Athletic Support. Always—in both practice sessions and games— wear a cup-in-pouch-style athletic support. Ventilated protective cups of metal or plastic should be lined with foam rubber or felt.

Socks. Lightweight cotton or wool ankle socks are needed if the stockings to be worn have no feet.

Stockings. With or without feet, these should be extra-long cotton or wool, with reinforced knees. A garter belt—not tape—should be used to hold up the stockings. It's best to buy a special hockey-stocking garter belt from a sporting goods store, rather than what one of our students once did, borrow his mother's black lace garter belt. While it did the job all right, he had to take a great deal of kidding from his teammates.

Shin Pads. Forwards usually prefer light pads of round fiber or plastic encased in leather and backed with felt. Defensemen usually wear heavier and larger all-fiber pads which cover the sides of the leg and knee. Be sure both types have hard fiber knee caps cushioned with felt or foam rubber.

Ankle Guards. Generally worn only by defensemen, they are hard, circular protectors of leather, plastic, or fiber that strap around the ankles. Remember that every defenseman gets hit at least once a game on an ankle, and these guards prevent broken ankles.

Elbow Pads. Forwards, as a rule, wear either the hair-stuffed "sausage-roll" type or new lightweight plastic guards with hinged fiber pads. Defensemen require large guards and they are usually leather pads built up with foam rubber and covered with a fiber cap. This pad helps to prevent many painful bone bruises and even fractured elbows.

Shoulder Pads. Lightweight quilted pads capped at the shoulder points with fiber and extending just above the elbow are best for forwards. Defensemen need the better protection of the heavier cantilever type, lined with felt or foam rubber. Shoulder pads are usually combined with a foam-rubber chest protector.

Pants. Quilted felt padding inside should cover the hips and spine, with a tail piece of fiber for the latter. Thigh guards of fiber edged with

Defensemen should wear (left) ankle guards. More and more players are wearing helmets similar to the type shown at the right.

felt or rubber may be bought separately to fit into pockets in the pants. Wide "fireman" suspenders are best to hold up pants. Never use a belt for this purpose.

Jerseys. Team jerseys or sweaters should be of serviceable fabric reinforced at the elbows and shoulders. They should fit comfortably over the pads and not restrict the movement of the shoulders or arms in the slightest. The laced-neck type prevents chafing at the throat. Numbers on the backs of sweaters should be at least 10 inches high.

Gloves. In selecting a hockey glove, make certain the thumb is protected. Most good gloves are of heavy-leather construction and are padded with rolled kapok on the backs of the fingers, thumbs, and wrists. The fiber cuffs or gauntlet-style padding should extend to meet the elbow pads. Make certain that the glove's construction permits you to maintain a tight grip on your stick.

Although the stick is held in the fingers, the palm of the glove should be as thin as possible so that you can get maximum feel from your stick. Speaking of feel, don't buy gloves that are too large. They should fit snugly when new because they tend to stretch as they are used. If they're too large, they become too bulky, and you lose the feel of the stick.

Helmets. On the subject of helmets, we both could be considered hypocrites. That is, we both strongly advocate their use, but neither of us wears one. Of course, helmets are mandatory for United States amateur players, while in Canada, under a rule passed in 1962, players in the lower age groups must wear them. When selecting a helmet, choose one that has a webbed suspension system that keeps the outer shell away from the head. It should also be seated firmly on the head so it doesn't wiggle about. The helmet should have air holes for ventilation and, of course, should protect as much as possible without impeding mobility or blocking vision.

The reason most of us don't wear helmets in the NHL is vanity. Players who are wearing them now cannot be regarded as sissies. We're sure that no one in our club—or in hockey—would call Bobby Rousseau, Bruce MacGregor, Pete Stemkowski, or Phil Goyette of the Rangers cowards, and they all wear helmets.

Mouth Guards. We both believe that mouth guards, like helmets, should be worn by young players every time they are on the ice. Most present-day professional hockey players started to lose their teeth when playing in the midgets. When we were youngsters in Canada, a gap between the teeth was a badge of courage. Today, these badges have become bridges, and if you were to visit our dressing room during a game, you would note 18 paper cups on a shelf above the clothes hooks that mutely symbolize the rigors of our trade. Of course, every club has a practical joker, and in ours, Vic Hadfield has the reputation for switching the cups around. Whenever a Ranger unsuccessfully tries to slip a teammate's bridge in his own mouth after a game he immediately yells out, "OK, Vic, where's my teeth?"

Remember always to wear all of your protective gear when on the ice. Some coaches don't insist on wearing all of it during a "light" practice. But we believe it's a good policy to always have that little extra protection; moreover, it gets you more accustomed to playing in the uniform of the game.

Goaltenders have their own special equipment; their regalia is covered in Chapter 8.

Care of Protective Equipment. All types of pads should be hung after use in a well-aired dressing room, where they may dry at room temperature. Avoid hanging pads by elastic straps. Of course, replace broken stitching on straps, fiber pads, gloves, and skate boots before major breaks appear. Stockings and sweaters can be repaired if darned before holes become too large.

3

Skating—
the Name of the Game

WHAT makes a good hockey player? Our Ranger coach, Emile Francis, in the Preface of this book listed things he looks for in a young hockey player. His opinions on this subject follow basically what we look for in our students at Skateland Summer Hockey School. Actually, we feel that to be good hockey players, our students must learn to:

1. *Skate Well.* Power skating is the first necessity. Good hockey players must be able to skate forward and backward and must learn to start, turn, stop . . . fast breakaways, quick turns, sudden stops.

2. *Stickhandle with Ease.* They must learn puck control; learn to carry the puck with their head up, watching for stick checks or body checks. They must be able to rag that puck, to elude defenders, to help their team kill penalties.

3. *Pass and Receive Passes Properly.* Team play is what makes for success in modern hockey, and the basis of good team play is passing. For this reason players must know how to pass and receive passes from both the forehand and backhand.

4. *Shoot Accurately.* The object of the game, as we know, is to put the puck in the net. Therefore, both forwards and defensemen should know how to shoot forehand and backhand and how to use the wrist, slap, and flip shots.

5. *Check Correctly.* All members of the team must know how to check, but it is the defensemen who have to be more accomplished in the art of taking the puck away from the other team—by intercepting a pass, stopping the puck carrier with a body check, or taking the puck off his stick with a stick check. In a game one missed check can mean a goal for the other team!

6. *Be a Team Player.* Every player, forward or defenseman, has two

51

jobs to do. He must share in the attack, and he must share in the defense. No team has room for a one-way player.

But of the six musts for a good hockey player, skating is paramount. You just can't play the game if you can't skate. It's that simple. Skating must become as automatic as walking in order to play good hockey. Fortunately, skating comes naturally at an early age to most Canadian boys. In Canada it's not uncommon to see boys of five and six play an interesting type of hockey. This is because most youngsters are taught to skate not long after they've started to walk. There's no substitute for ice time when it comes to skating, of course. Even when you get to the NHL, coaches have you spend a good portion of the daily workout on basic skating techniques: stopping, starting, turning, etc. It's a grueling routine, but most of us recognize that unless we practice we won't be able to keep up with the other clubs in the league.

POWER SKATING

At the beginning we all tend to skate the way which is the most natural to us. By that we mean that a youngster will learn to move in, say, a counterclockwise direction, and he'll always skate that way. That's all right if you're skating just for fun, but not if you're thinking about playing hockey. You must learn to turn both ways. It has long been the theory of our associate at the school, Allan Eisinger, that a boy of nine or ten could profit a great deal by taking up figure skating. While figure skating and hockey people usually go different ways, the taking up of basic figure skating is bound to make a better skater out of any young hockey player. Therefore, the power-skating methods we teach are very closely related to the techniques of figure skating. In other words, as we teach skating to young players, it combines the stroking and balance of figure skating with the necessary turns, stops, crossovers, and thrusts needed for playing hockey.

In the basic forward power-skating position, the head should be held comfortably up, the chest out, and the stomach in. While you should be totally relaxed, these positions of the head, chest, and stomach can't be overemphasized. That is, learn to skate with your head up so that you can see where you are going and what is happening ahead and beside you on the ice. Also let your chest expand. To power skate you need lots of oxygen in your lungs. Also, practice skating with your shoulders back in a relaxed manner.

When skating, the feet should be at least as wide apart as your shoulders. The shoulders should be slightly ahead of your hips, knees relaxed and slightly bent, in a sort of sitting position. To check for proper knee bend, assume the basic power-skating position and look directly down, sighting over either your right or left knee. If your knees are bent far enough (out in front of your feet), you won't be able to see the toes of your skates. It is also absolutely necessary to keep your knees loose and flexible. You must be able to flex and bend them to get into a good skating position and to absorb the shock of body weight when shifting to various skating positions. Stiff, locked knees won't allow you to become a fluid, smooth skater.

Speed is generated with hip stroking rather than knee stroking. By this we mean power skating results from strong leg action from the hips. For instance, as the left skate turns left for the first stroke on the right skate, the left hip and shoulders are also turned slightly to the left. As the left skate is brought forward, the left hip and shoulder are also brought forward. The same, of course, holds for the right hip and shoulder, working with the right leg action.

While skating, make certain that your body lean is such that it allows enough skate blade to be on the ice to permit proper drive. If you lean too far forward, only the toe of your blade contacts the ice; if too erect, your heel will come down first. Drive off the toe of your forward skate, and push ahead, hard, with the rear leg. Use those leg muscles. Dig that rear skate into the ice and push. The harder you dig in and push, the more power and speed you get. Remember that one of the points of power skating is that you strive to get as much thrust and force from each single stroke as is physically possible.

While you are pushing with the rear leg, whip the other leg forward, with knees bent, and stride. Take long strides, smooth strides, but never stretch beyond the point where you can't maintain your balance. Start with an easy stride, then practice lengthening it. Put your whole body into your stride, swaying slightly, to help you develop a smooth stride. You'll find your stride will lengthen as you find the most comfortable position for your upper body and build confidence with better balance. Incidentally, balance is a different thing to different skaters. To the average player it generally means the shoulders ahead of the hips, but not too far ahead.

Many beginning skaters have a tendency to avoid lifting their feet off the ice. This must be overcome, but it's poor power-skating form to lift your skates high off the ice while stroking. If you feel a jar when your skate goes down on the ice, it's a sure sign that you are lifting your

Learning to skate with a hockey stick in your hands to help maintain balance.

skates too high. Remember that to power skate properly, take low, gliding steps and strides. You've got to keep lifting your legs. It's a lot like running. Skating is a matter of pushing yourself forward with one leg and then the other.

Turning without loss of speed is most important in hockey. When making a turn to the left, for example, turn the head, the hips, and the left shoulder to the left, and transfer the weight of the body slightly to the rear of the left outside blade edge and the right inside blade edge. Be sure the left skate is leading to the left and lean the entire body to the left. Your skating speed forward will cause you to turn the entire body all the way around to the left. Of course, when making a right turn, the weight is transferred to the right outside blade and left inside blade edge. The right skate leads and a change in direction to the right is made. More techniques for changing direction are given later in this chapter.

Keep in mind that success in skating, just as in any athletic activity, isn't dependent on one thing but a lot of little things which when put

With each stride your driving leg is completely extended from the knee. Your arms help by going to the same side as the glide leg and by shifting from side to side with your body weight.

together in a smooth, mechanical whole make for efficiency. Remember, too, that skating style has little to do with ability to power skate —the important thing is to feel comfortable doing it. Usually skating style is determined by the physical makeup of the skater. Bigger fellows generally have longer strides than shorter ones. The latter usually skate with quick, short strides. Neither way is really superior to the other, just as long as it's smooth.

AGILITY SKATING

This important category of power skating is to the hockey player what shift running is to the ball carrier in football, or footwork to the boxer. Once the player has developed the art of agility in his skating, he'll be a tough puck carrier to check on offense and a very hard man to get past when on defense. In other words, excellence at agility skating is what makes a top-flight hockey player. The following fundamental power-skating maneuvers are included under the heading of agility skating:

The Toed-in Stop. The ability to stop quickly is one of the most important phases of power hockey skating. The quicker you can stop, of course, the faster you can get back in the play or the easier you can shake an opponent. For instance, suppose you're going down on the wing with your center carrying the puck, and he gets checked. If you can stop quickly, you'll be able to backcheck your opponent who has stolen the puck.

One simple method of stopping is the toed-in stop. To accomplish this stop, you assume the normal basic forward power-skating position. As you skate forward, simply turn the toes of your skates in, like a snowplow, and let your knees come together. Exert pressure on the inside edges of your skates, to bring yourself to a stop. The outside right and left edges are doing most of the work in this stop. While a toed-in stop is easy to accomplish and is used by beginners, it is not employed in the NHL because of the longer distance required to come to a complete halt.

The toed-in maneuver can also be used to slow down. That is, as you skate forward, turn the toes in slightly, and pressure on the outside blade edges will reduce your speed. Don't turn the toes in too far, just a slight turn inward. The advantage of this slowing down method is that you, as a puck carrier, can approach the defense and slow down while still facing an opposing player. Incidentally, the toed-in stop and slowing down maneuvers can be done by turning in just one of the skates at a time, either the left or the right skate.

The Double-Skate Stop. While this picturesque stop appears to be quite difficult, it really isn't. As you're skating forward, turn both skates, together, to the left (or right) quickly, till your skates are at right angles to the direction in which you were traveling. Bend your knees as you throw all your weight to the front. The edges of both skates will dig in. The harder you then straighten your legs, the faster you stop.

When planting your skates, say, to the left, the body should be leaning to the left, the knees bent, the skates about 6 inches apart with your right skate a slight bit ahead of the left skate. When springing into the double-skate stop position, turn your head and shoulder as well as the rest of the body. Of course, the more you lean to the left, the more the right leg must be straightened to permit the right skate blade to dig into the ice. Try to stop with only the front portion of the blade edge on the ice. When making this stop, keep the hockey stick out in front of your body as a counterbalance.

The Jump Stop. When it's necessary to really stop in a hurry—to avoid body checks and collisions—this is the maneuver to use. To accomplish it, jump a few inches into the air and land back on the ice with skates side by side, both blades digging into the ice, as in the double-skate stop. Practice this again and again. It will perfect your balance and strengthen your ankles.

The One-Skate Stop. This method of stopping is frequently used in hockey and has the advantage that the outside foot can be brought quickly around and forward to start the first return stride. As you're skating forward and desire a stop to the left, lift the right skate off the ice, turn your body tight and hard, and turn the left (front) skate blade at right angles to the direction in which you're traveling. Throw your weight well forward on the left skate and bend your knee. The inside edge of the back skate will dig into the ice and bring you to a stop. The harder you straighten your leg, the harder your stop. Practice one-foot stops in both directions.

The Front Start. In hockey, whenever a stop is employed, the major problem is starting again. The front start is one of the simplest ways to accomplish a quick breakaway.

For the front start, the skates are shoulder width apart, knees are flexed, and the body bent well forward over the skates. The skates pivot outward and the drive leg uncoils like a spring with the thrust coming from the toe of the skate. Short chopping strides are used. The knee

The double-skate stop (left) and the one-skate stop (right).

of the front leg is well bent and the front skate enters with little or no glide. While a few short, choppy, and fast strides are necessary at the beginning of the front start, once under way the skating stride should be lengthened and the stroking should be from the hips in order to be smooth and to obtain the full power of each stroke so necessary for a breakaway.

The Side Start. For the side start we use the basic position—feet apart, knees flexed, and body upright. Now, to start quickly, lean in the direction that you want to go and take three or four running strides on your toes sideways. The thrust is from the toe of the rear skate and the body turns to obtain the forward position in two or three strides. After the start, lengthen the stride and drive the arm and shoulder alternately with the opposite leg. In the stride, the front leg is well bent (at 90 degrees) and the body is well over the front leg. The rear leg pushes to full extension—right down to the toe of the skate. The rhythm of the arm drive and leg extension contributes to the speed and agility of the player.

The Break. In hockey the break can be compared with the first few strides of a running back in football. In a face-off situation, for example, once the puck is dropped by either the referee or linesman, a player must be ready to break quickly and get into the play. Frequently, the difference in controlling a play or losing the puck to an opponent depends on a player's ability to break quickly.

The front start.

The break maneuver is really a refinement of front and back starts and is usually performed from a dead stop. To accomplish the break efficiently, the shoulder, arm, and hip are thrown to the same side and in the same direction as your forward leg. Then, move off quickly with a hard thrust from your forward skate. At the same instant, bring the rear foot forward as quickly as possible. By keeping the weight off the rear foot in the anticipatory position before starting the break, you'll be able to bring it forward rapidly. In other words, be sure to give a hard, explosive push off on the front foot to get going and then get the rear foot forward and on the ice to give another full push as quickly as you can. The rear foot should, of course, be kept close to the ice so that there is no time wasted in getting it on the ice for the second stride. When bringing the rear foot forward, make certain to turn the toe outward so that it will be in a position to thrust hard the moment it makes contact with the ice. The first four to eight strides should be as short as you can make them. From here on you gradually lengthen your stride to normal length. How far you skate using the short, fast strides will usually depend on how the play develops. Don't resume stance too quickly. True, you can move faster over a long distance using your normal stride, but in a quick break from a face-off you're concerned with getting your stick on the puck and controlling the play.

Both forwards and defensemen must know how to accomplish a quick break. Remember that after a face-off the puck can go in any direction, even up in the air. To show how a defenseman uses the break, suppose, for example, Brad Park is in his defense position at the edge of the face-off circle at the left of the Rangers' goal. "My back is to the goal, but I must make sure that I don't block or screen my goalie's view of the play. After the puck is dropped by the linesman, the centermen scramble for it and suddenly I see the puck streak behind me and across our goal crease. Instantly all of my weight is thrown to my right and at the same time my left skate comes over my right for a crossover. While my left skate is in the air the outside edge of my right skate has started to dig into the ice. My right knee is well flexed and when I straighten it the thrust of my thigh pushes me ahead in the direction I wish to go. My shoulders and hips are turned hard and tight until my chest is facing exactly toward the puck as my skate hits the ice. There is another quick shift of weight and the inside of my left skate bites into the ice. Barely clearing the ice, my right skate moves ahead of my left a few inches and I'm off in my quick break. The whole of this pivot—break from the face-off stance—is the swing of my shoulder and the short strides to get my weight moving toward the puck."

The Drag. The drag is a maneuver used to prepare for a break by slowing down without coming to a dead stop. After a whistle, and before a face-off, it is used by most players, when coasting into position, to stop. It's a natural movement all skaters use almost the first time they are on the ice. But it's also a most effective maneuver to employ in play since it can be integrated into many puck-carrying tricks. In addition, it's another way for changing directions quickly, but strong leg muscles are essential for drag to be effective.

To accomplish the drag to the right, place your weight on the left skate and drag the inside right skate edge along the ice surface. As the skate begins to drag, turn your hips and forward foot hard to the right. This body turn plus the drag propels your body around quickly to effect a quick right turn. To do it to the left, merely drag the left foot and turn sharply to the left. It is done, of course, after a stroke forward with the right leg. When dragging in either direction, the knees should be kept well flexed during the entire maneuver.

The Jump. The jump is considered a continuation of the jump stop. That is, after coming to a complete halt by using the jump stop, you then jump sideways in the same direction as you turned to make your stop. The trick is to stop completely and then jump sideways driving hard off the foot farthest from the direction in which you wish to go.

For instance, if you wish to go to the right you push off the left foot. The right foot is lifted off the ice and flung in the direction in which you want to go. Just before you jump the left knee should be well flexed to give you the necessary spring. When you land, the major portion of your weight is on the left leg. Your left knee should, of course, be well bent on the landing so as to absorb the shock and give the necessary balance. When landing, the weight should be quickly shifted on the right leg from which you start any new skating action you wish. If jumping from right to left, it is your right leg from which the drive is given and on which you land. (Eddie Shack of the California Seals and Stan Mikita of the Chicago Black Hawks are two of the best jump artists in hockey.)

Sharp Turns. Sharp turns are very useful when mastered perfectly. The body leans sharply toward the inside of the circle and the inside knee is bent more than the outside one. The interior skate leads the exterior one and the pressure is applied on the back of the blade. The weight of the body is forward to permit a rapid exit from the sharp turn. It's important to keep in mind that the more you lean your body in the direction you wish to go, the sharper will be the turn.

Crossover Turn. To prevent loss of speed in turns, we generally recommend that our students use crossovers. While this is a figure-skating trick, the technique is identical to the power-skating sharp turn except that the outside leg continuously crosses over the inside leg. That is, the weight is placed on the inside foot (for example, the right if crossing over to the right). The knee is well flexed, and then as the outside leg (left if crossing over to the right) is brought around and over the inside leg, another stroke is taken. The body should be leaned toward the direction of the turn. In addition, the outside foot thrust in the same direction as the turn comes from a hard push off from the inside edge of the skate. The faster you're going when you make the crossover, the more you must flex the knee of the inside leg, and put your weight on this leg and to the inside of the half circle you're making. The upper body must lean well in.

Zigzag. The zigzag is actually a refinement of the crossover and is a favorite maneuver of such hockey stars as Bobby Hull. While skating in a straight line, one foot is brought quickly over in front of the other as if starting a crossover to that side. However, just as the foot that you bring across hits the ice, the other foot is whipped back in a crossover step in the opposite direction. For instance, if you go to the right the first time, you bring your left leg over in front of your right leg. Then to put the zag after the zig, you bring the right leg back across the left one and continue to skate ahead.

One of the great secrets in being able to perform the zigzag efficiently, Rod Gilbert has found, is to keep the knees well flexed and fluid and to shift the weight of the upper body rapidly. "When I make the crossover with my first leg, for example, the left one, I move my weight quickly back to the left so that I can push hard with my left skate in the new direction." When properly used, the zigzag will give you a power-skating trick that will improve your puck-carrying capabilities. It can be employed to thread your way through a group of players, or to beat a checker out of position; this is usually accomplished with first crossover.

Single-Leg Swing-Around. This is a technique which enables you to change direction fairly rapidly and to come back down on the ice or to move to either side without actually stopping. It is the best maneuver to employ to get back into play with the minimum amount of time lapse.

To perform this very important power-skating trick you take a stride and then, on a well-bent knee, swing your body around in the direction you wish to go. As the body swings about, the free leg (the one on which your weight isn't placed) should be brought around in a rapid circular motion. However, remember it's not the leg that does the turning. It is the motion of your entire body, particularly the shoulders and hips. When making the swing, make certain that you lean well to the inside and that you keep a forward body-lean position. The moment the turn is completed the foot of the free leg which you're swinging around should be placed on the ice and a hard thrust given. At this point all the weight is transferred from the inside leg to the leg that has been swung around. The thrust of this leg will send you straight off in the new direction. To make the move quickly there must be good coordination of any outward turn of the hips and body in the same direction. Then the free leg swings around.

Two-Leg Swing-Around. This is still another method of turning quickly. It can be employed both as a skating maneuver when carrying the puck or to make a turn when desiring to get back into the play. While it's not quite as efficient for a quick turn as is the single-leg technique, it has the advantage of enabling the skater to keep better balance.

The two-leg swing-around motion is accomplished in much the same manner as the single-leg action. The major difference, of course, is that

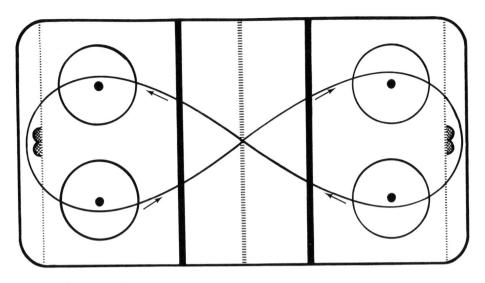

A good drill to practice crossovers.

there's no free leg. Rather than swing this leg around, its skate is kept on the ice and its point is turned in the same direction as your inside skate. That is, it follows the front skate around. Your body is equally divided on both, and both knees are bent the same amount. When the swing-around is nearly completed, your weight is quickly transferred to the forward foot and the rear foot is brought around as rapidly as possible with the toe facing well out. It is placed on the ice to provide the necessary hard thrust to get going in the new direction.

Scooting. When we both played on the same team with Tim Horton (now with the Buffalo Sabres), we really learned what scooting was all about. He could use this technique, which few players use today, to get out of a tight spot most effectively. For instance, with his stick on the puck in the middle of a scramble, Tim could frequently get it out of there by scooting—a glide or a turn to either side prolonged by a series of quick short thrusts on the back foot—far enough to clear the tangle. Most players—including us—try to lunge into full stride and bull their way past the tangle of legs and sticks in the middle of a scramble. Thus, scooting is a trick you should attempt to learn, and you'll find it most effective.

Scooting is performed by taking a stride on the right leg, for instance, and then giving a series of rapid, hard thrusts with the left leg. This moves the skater quickly forward. It's most effective when used as part of a swing-around or other quick change of direction.

The Draw-Away. This is another power-skating trick which is most valuable to avoid a collision or body check. When properly employed, it will frequently enable a player to sneak through with the puck when apparently well blocked out.

To accomplish this maneuver place all your weight on the foot farthest from the obstacle you want to avoid (perhaps a defenseman's hip or the goal post); and move your upper body and hips sideways toward the obstacle. As the body and hips are turned, swing the leg closest to the obstacle back and away from the obstacle in the same direction you move your body. For example, if you're trying to avoid a hip check by a defenseman on the right side, place your weight on the left foot and turn your body and hip to the right, moving your right leg to the right and behind you. The skate of the left foot should continue to go straight ahead or slightly to the left. When the obstacle is cleared, your upper body, hips and the inside leg are then whipped around and your foot placed on the ice for a new stroke. If your weight is on the foot nearest to the checker, as would be the case if you had just taken a stride toward him, you must quickly shift it to the other leg by shoving off on a new stride, and then make your draw-away move.

Slide Glide. Since this is basically a move of a defenseman, let Brad Park describe how he makes this move. "Let's take as an example a slide glide to the right which I may make while skating at normal speed. Then, as my left foot and leg go forward in a stroke, I suddenly turn the point of my skate blade inward, skid a little, push hard against the ice, turn to my right, and stride out with my right leg at a right angle to the direction I was going. The stride on my right foot must be a long one, a sort of glide. My left foot must bite into the ice twice in order to effect a stop, and to thrust hard enough to send my body sideways into a new stride. My weight is thrown upon my left foot (the one that is turned in) as the stop and thrust sideways is made, and then it is quickly transferred on to my right foot as the long stride is taken. When accomplishing this move, I must make certain that my left hip is turned quickly inward as my skate is turned in. As the side glide is completed, my body should be leaned quickly to the left, and the skate on my right foot turned sideways to the left so that I'm going straight again. As the skate is turned, my right foot bites in with a hard thrust so as to complete my second right-angle turn and provide momentum for the forward movement.

Pivoting. This trick is becoming more popular all the time and is a hockey variation of the pivot used in basketball. It's a very effective movement to employ to get free from a checker who is guarding in front of the net. It is also an excellent puck-carrying technique. It does require a high degree of good agility, timing, and balance but can be learned from frequent practice. We believe our teammate Jean Ratelle is one of the best pivot men in hockey today.

The maneuver is performed by placing all your weight on one foot, and then turning your hips and upper body around in a tight circle. The other leg swings around off the ice in the same direction as your body is turned. The knees, especially the knee on which the weight is placed, must be well flexed and a good forward body lean must be maintained. The speed of the pivot is governed by the quickness of the body turn, especially the action of the hips. You must turn the hips around with an explosive whip. The upper body must lean to the inside during the pivot. If it's allowed to move outward, you may easily lose your balance.

Change of Pace. This maneuver, which is most effective for a baseball pitcher or a broken-field runner in football, is also a valuable asset for forwards, especially wings being covered by backcheckers on a rush. By holding back a little speed in reserve you can hit the attack line at top speed, shaking your man by your change of pace. Gordie Howe, of Detroit, was a past master in the art of appearing to loaf, then darting away at top speed to shake his checkers. Actually, Rod Gilbert finds that any reduction or increase in his speed, no matter how small, may be enough to put the checker out of position. The next time you're watching a hockey game—especially from high in the stands—you should be able to notice the change of pace of a good skater if you look sharply.

To change pace, decrease or increase the shove of your back foot. Since the degree of push on the backward thrust of the skate at the end of each stride determines your speed, it naturally follows that pace is controlled by the amount of push you give.

Another change of pace used by many great forwards—and a favorite move of Stan Mikita—is the lunge stride. Oddly enough, the only skill needed to acquire this power-skating trick is to remember when to employ it and to develop especially strong foot, ankle, and leg muscles. The reason for the latter is that it takes a very hard thrust off the back foot to get this maneuver under way. But by practicing it you'll develop the coordination needed. Actually, all a lunge stride consists of is a sudden hard, long stride in the midst of an ordinary skating action. Frequently, you may use two or three lunge strides together to get past a defenseman.

Good backskating form is essential for a defenseman. Here are two basic forms.

BACKWARD SKATING

Many players don't practice their backward-skating technique because they think it is for defensemen only. True, for forwards it's not as vital as it is to defensemen, but there are times in a game when a forward finds it necessary to employ his backward-skating ability to prevent an opponent from scoring a goal. Remember, hockey is a team sport, and a team has no need for a one-way player.

In the basic backward power-skating position, the skates are about shoulder width apart, weight evenly placed on the entire length of the inside edges of the skates, knees are bent and out in front, the buttocks are low, the stomach comfortably drawn in, and the chest held in a natural position. Then with the head looking straight ahead, not at your feet, bend the knees and push one foot away. Bring it back to the original position. Next, push the other foot away and return it to the original position. With practice, you'll learn to bend the knees and push the feet away alternately. With solid pushes you will gain speed quickly and be able to maintain it with little difficulty.

When skating backward, there should be just a slight body lean forward. The back should be almost erect. In fact, the backward skating position is much like the position you would take while sitting in a straight-back chair. Remember that your weight should be placed well forward, not evenly distributed along the entire blade edge or slightly toward the rear of the skate blade. Many beginners believe that to skate backward they must wiggle their buttocks as fast as possible. Never! The only thing this will do is amuse those watching you.

Backward Crossovers. Backward crossovers must be mastered equally well by the forward and defenseman because they are necessary when shadowing or backchecking a player. The procedure of this maneuver is the same as crossing over in forward skating, except that rather than bringing over your outside foot (your left if crossing over to the right) as you would in a forward crossover, you bring the inside leg over in front of your outside leg. For instance, when crossing over backward to the right, you would keep shifting your left foot over in front of the right, pushing off in a twisting motion toward the direction you're turning once the leg has been brought over. Your buttocks should be well out behind you, your knees flexed, and the upper body well into the inside (right if going toward the right).

Backward Side Glide. This maneuver is one of the fundamentals of

good hip check—Brad Park's favorite method of checking. It is funda-
mentally the same as the side glide, but done while skating backward.
"When I do it [he says] I place all my weight on the leg farthest from
the direction I wish to move (the right if going to the left), and push
off hard at right angles to the left side. As I shove off, I swing my
buttocks to the left and place my left foot on the ice in a long backward
and sideways slide. The best time to do this, I find, is when my weight
is shifted to my right foot, after a push off by my left foot during the
backward-skating motion." Make sure, of course, to practice the backward side glide to both sides.

The Double-Leg Backward Stop. Though the average defenseman
must be able to skate backward quickly for short distances, he must also
be able to shift from a backward motion into a break capable of taking
him in a rush from one side or even straight ahead. This move requires
the ability to stop quickly.

Most defensemen prefer to use the two-skate backward stop. This
movement starts with an external rotation of both skates (the toes
rotating to the outside). Your body should lean toward the front while
pressure is being exerted to the front end of the blades. Then this
pressure is gradually distributed over the entire blade. Stability is guar-
anteed if your feet are well separated. To make a quick stop, dig your
skates into the ice and then extend your knees forcefully. That is, the
knees should be well bent at the start of the action but should be
straightened as the feet are pressed into the ice.

One-Leg Backward Stop. Some players prefer the one-leg backward
stop. The technique is similar to the two-leg backward stop, but this
time place all the weight on one leg, turning the toe of the skate. Then,
as you stop, you can shove off quickly for your first forward stride.

Reversing. This means reversing your forward skating to backward
skating (and vice versa) without actually stopping. The best backward
skater in the world would be of little good in hockey unless he could
start moving forward or to either side instantly. The secret of being able
to reverse from forward to backward skating is a keenly developed
ability to shift your weight quickly and with good balance. Actually
there are two types of reverse techniques: the jump reverse, and the
turn reverse.

To accomplish the jump reverse from a forward to a backward
position, for example, you first assume a forward casting position (legs
apart, skates in line), then you jump upward, and spin your body around
180 degrees while in the air so that when you land you'll be skating

The double-leg backward stop (left) and one-leg backward stop (right).

backward. When taking off and landing make sure that your knees are well flexed. This is especially important when landing. The jump shouldn't be high, and proper body lean should be maintained when landing. Keep in mind that this reverse can be a complete flop—and we mean this literally—if your feet aren't spread far enough apart to provide proper balance when landing. But, while the feet must be spread, your knees should be kept close enough together so when you land, the backward skating can start immediately.

While the jump reverse is effective, most defensemen prefer the less spectacular turn reverse. This reverse is made off one leg and when properly executed is surer and just as fast as the jump method. The basic idea of the turn reverse is to take a stroke and then as the stroke starts, swing the entire body rapidly 180 degrees to complete the change of skating position. Let's say, for example, that your last stroke was on to the left and you wish to make a turn in that direction. To complete the reverse, your shoulders and hips should be spun from the right to the left with your weight forward. As your shoulders and hips move, the right skate swings with them. You continue to swing the right skate as far as possible to the left without losing balance. As your body and leg swing around, pivot in the same direction on your left skate. As you pivot, start shifting your weight to begin skating back-

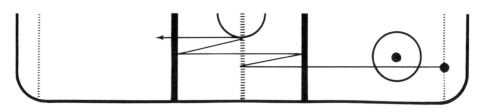

A good stop-and-go drill.

ward. Of course, the secret of turn reverse is to make sure to snap the shoulders and hips quickly around when turning your body. Also, make sure that your knees are well bent, especially the knee of the leg that's swung around. It's wise to practice the turn reverse to both sides.

The only way to master backward skating, like forward skating and everything else in hockey, is through constant practice. Start at one end of the rink and skate backward all around the rink. Then do it going the other way. Always have a stick in your hand when you're practicing. It'll help your balance.

SKATING DRILLS

There are several drills you can use to improve your skating. One is the stop-and-go drill. With another player, take up positions at the goal line. Start as in a race, skate as fast as you can to center ice, stop, skate back to the blue line, stop, turn, and on through the drill as shown in the sketch above. The first player to reach the far goal line is the winner. Try this with the whole team.

This time, divide the skaters into two groups. Each group lines up on a goal line, facing center ice. At a signal both groups start to skate furiously toward center ice. Each stops at center ice in a shower of ice spray, turns, and speeds back to the blue line, stops, turns, and skates, on through the drill.

Another drill we use on the Rangers, as well as at the Skateland Summer Hockey School, is called the "stop and backup." On this one, the coach will blow his whistle and we'll skate out from the end of the rink to around the blue line, where he'll blow the whistle again. We'll stop suddenly and begin skating backward. He'll blow his whistle again and now we'll reverse direction and go forward again, and so on.

It's also important to strengthen your leg muscles, and we do this by lining up against the sideboards, skating as hard as we can across the ice, and pulling up short of the other sideboard. We start this in the training camp and by the end of the season we're still doing this 20 times a day. Remember that endurance is a matter of driving yourself to skate at top speed beyond the fatigue point. Avoid coasting through skating drills. If you want to be able to skate at top speed during the last 5 minutes of the game, you must push yourself hard during practice. Your general physical condition, too, will enter the picture at this often-critical stage of the game. More information on conditioning and the hockey player may be found in Chapter 9.

It is wise to remember that skating is the most fundamental, most important skill in hockey. If you learn to power skate well, you'll be in a position to skate fast without tiring rapidly. You will be a hard man to knock down or steal the puck from, and you will be able to learn most agility hockey-skating maneuvers without too much difficulty. But to be a good power skater, you must work hard and skate often.

The Basics of Offense

THE play of hockey can be divided into two basic phases: offense and defense. When your team has control of the puck and is attempting to score a goal, then your team is on the offensive. But, just as soon as your opponents gain possession of the puck and move toward your goalie in an attempt to score, your team is on the defensive.

The change from offense to defense, or vice versa, is most rapid in hockey. For this reason, both the forwards and defensemen must be well versed in both phases of the game. As we have stated several times, there is no room for the one-way player in modern hockey. True, the forwards are usually the high-point men on the team, but in recent years the defensemen are increasing their output in the point department. Bobby Orr of Boston, a defenseman, has been over the 100-point total (only a very few players have ever reached this milestone) several times in the last few years; in the 1971–72 season Brad Park became only the third defenseman in the history of the NHL to score over 20 goals in a season.

Even the goaltenders are getting into the point-scoring act. Ken Dryden of Montreal and our teammate Eddie Giacomin share the season point record of three. Eddie also holds an unbelievable record for goalies of making two assists in the same game. But, Eddie has said on many occasions that he would gladly give up this record if he could be the first NHL goalkeeper to score a goal.

Of course, the offensive phase has often been called the glamour part of hockey. But just as in the case of skating, the only way one can become proficient in the basic skills of offense—stickhandling, passing, and shooting—is by hard work.

HOLDING THE STICK

Always hold the stick with both hands. (Don't be a one-handed player.) Left-handed players usually place their left hand at the top of the stick (they are called right shots); right-handed people almost always place their right hand at the top and therefore are called left shots. Brad is a left shot, while Rod is a right. At Skateland, we have found a simple way to determine whether a young player is a natural right or left shot. We toss the youngster a broom! How he holds the broom while sweeping tells us which side will be a natural for him.

For the grip itself, remember that the stick is held in your fingers —don't cup it in the palm of your hand. By holding it in your fingers, you get the maximum wrist action into your shot. When the stick is held in your palms, you can't get the necessary whip to get off a good shot. In addition, finger control keeps the stick from turning and wavering. Keep in mind that any wavering you do with the stick's handle is exaggerated when the movement gets down to the blade.

Actually, the top hand controls and guides the stick; therefore, you should never loosen your grip with this hand. Your wrist coordinates inward with the thumb at the back of the handle. In other words, by keeping the thumb at the back of the handle, you keep the blade of the stick closed, which helps to make more accurate shots and passes.

The lower hand is the so-called "power hand." The stick again is held completely by the fingers on the underside of the handle, with the thumb over the shaft. The lower hand can be moved up and down the length of the stick handle, depending on the task being performed. For example, most players find that when stickhandling with the puck it is best to keep the hands fairly close together (generally about 8 to 10 inches apart). This tends to give you a maximum feel of the puck at the end of your stick. But, when passing, it is best to slide the power hand slightly lower on the stick. This still permits the feel of the puck, but provides sufficient power to make a sharp, accurate pass. When shooting, power is most important. Therefore, the lower hand is moved as far down the handle of the stick as is comfortable.

When starting to power skate holding a stick, shift your arms and legs smoothly, and don't hit the ice with your skates. When you walk, your left arm goes out front with your right foot. In skating, with a hockey stick in your hands, it is just the opposite: Your right foot and your right arm swing forward together, your left foot moves ahead with your left arm. It takes plenty of practice to make sure you do it smoothly. Smooth power skating helps your stickhandling.

STICKHANDLING

Stickhandling is the carrying of the puck along the ice by using the stick as a guiding force. This technique is one of the two ways a player can move the puck. The other method is by passing the puck, but of the two, stickhandling is much more thrilling to the spectator. Actually, many fans bemoan the good old days, when it was necessary to carry the puck into the scoring zone or pass it laterally. In those days, the forward pass was illegal. But, if you had to defend, as we do, against the likes of Bobby Orr, Stan Mikita, Bobby Hull, Phil Esposito, etc., you'd quickly learn that the fine art of stickhandling is *not* dead.

The most important feature of stickhandling is the ability to carry the puck without looking down. This lets you see a checker coming at you, a teammate open for a pass, or an opening in the net for a shot. As you'll find it difficult to stickhandle entirely by feel at first, try carrying the puck looking up ahead of you, with frequent glances down to control it. If the natural position of your body lean and stick keeps the puck close to your feet, it is harder for you to develop this "split vision." You may find that using a stick with a lower lie places the puck farther ahead, making it easier to see both it and the ice in front of you. The puck should be cradled in the middle of the stick's blade. In addition, the blade should be kept at right angles to the direction in which the puck is being moved. Sometimes, when skating a very wide pattern, it may be necessary to turn the toe of the blade a little toward the puck so that it won't slide off the end of the stick.

Jean Ratelle is the best stickhandler on the Rangers and possibly the best in hockey today. Let's analyze how he carries the puck up ice: During his first few strides, while gaining momentum, he shoves the puck in front of him. His elbows are about 6 inches away from his body and his hands are from 8 to 10 inches apart on the stick. This position of arms and hands permits Jean to extend his reach so that he can keep the puck far enough out in front of him to gain speed but not so far that he'll lose control of the puck. His hands and wrists are kept fairly loose and easy on the stick. This is the secret of Jean's soft "touch" and great control.

Once Jean has reached his top speed, he pulls his elbows in close to his body. By doing this, his forearms now take over some of the work

The stick is held in your fingers—not your palms—and your thumbs are wrapped around the shaft. The positioning of the hands for stickhandling (upper left), passing (lower left), and shooting (above).

The side-to-side maneuver is the most popular stickhandling technique.

from his wrists so he'll have more power to take a shot or make a pass, while having a little better control of the puck. When he reaches the point on the ice where he must make a move, Jean is in position to pass to Vic Hadfield on his left, to Rod Gilbert on his right, or to shoot himself.

There are three basic stickhandling maneuvers: (1) side to side; (2) diagonal; and (3) back to front. The side-to-side pattern is the most commonly used. There are many times when the puck must be manipulated diagonally, and occasionally it is necessary to move the puck back to front. In other words, which one you use depends on the situation. In fact, hockey is a game of moves and countermoves, and many stickhandling maneuvers are designed to force your opponent to commit himself so you can react accordingly.

Side to Side. In this most popular stickhandling technique, you are, in a sense, passing the puck to yourself. That is, the puck is advanced to one side, then the stick is quickly whipped over and in front of the puck, and then smoothly moved back again. When lifting the stick at the end of the sweep, be sure to allow the puck to move slightly ahead of the blade so that it's not flipped by the stick as it's lifted. Also don't bat the puck along since this may cause it to roll. To keep the puck under control, just "feather" it back and forth with a light, smooth touch in a series of short or long sweeps. In fact, the sweeps may vary in width from 3 to 4 inches to as wide as you can reach, depending on the play of the man who's checking you.

As you approach a checker with your side-to-side sweeps, for example, pass the puck wide to your backhand (to the left for a right shot). At the same moment, break sharply to your left around him, placing your body between the puck and the checker. Don't make this move too soon, or your opponent will be there to meet you. If you wait too long, of course, he will poke the puck from your stick. To know when to go around him you must notice whether he is backing up, stationary, or moving toward you. See how necessary it becomes for you to have your head up. Practice this maneuver both ways; then you can keep your opponent in doubt until the last moment, and prevent his anticipating your move.

Sometimes, to increase the width of side-to-side sweep pattern, it's necessary to release the lower hand and use only the top hand on the stick. As soon as the puck is started back, the bottom hand is placed on the stick again. However, it's generally best to move the puck only as is needed to avoid a stick or some other obstacle since any unneces-

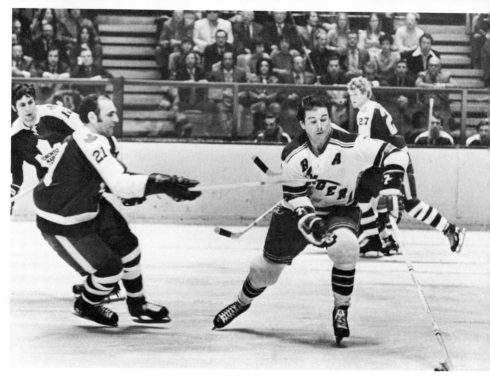

To get around a checker, it is sometimes necessary to release the lower hand to get the wide sweep pattern.

The back-to-front stickhandling technique.

sary movement slows up your forward propulsion and makes it more likely that you'll lose control of the puck.

Diagonal. In this stickhandling maneuver, which is Phil Esposito's favorite, the player moves the puck forward in the direction he wishes to go, at the same time patting it back and forth in front of him. When this maneuver is accomplished by a good stickhandler, the stick hardly seems to move as he streaks down the ice, but each time he touches the puck, either on his forehand or backhand side, it travels ahead at an angle.

Diagonal stickhandling is considered an advanced phase of the art. It requires the proper touch to keep the puck from getting too far ahead of you. That is, you must know just how hard to pat the puck and must have the stick's blade at the proper angle. Keep in mind that the flatter the angle the farther ahead the puck will move.

The best way of determining the proper angle is to experiment at slow speed. Remember that your shoulders should be turned so that they are as square as possible to the path of the puck while it's moved back and forth. For instance, if you're a left shot and if the puck was being moved from a spot just outside your right foot to a location well out in front and to the side of your left foot, the shoulders would have to be turned around to the right.

Back to Front. This is usually considered the most difficult stickhandling maneuver for young players, but with regular practice you can develop a fair amount of puck control. Let's again analyze how Jean Ratelle moves the puck using the back-to-front technique: As he moves up ice patting the puck back and forth, Jean, who shoots left, keeps his stick at his right side, and the blade is at right angles to the direction of his motion. He pats the puck ahead with the front of the blade, stops it with the back, and then pats it backward. Then he stops it again with the front of the blade and so proceeds, alternating with backward and forward moves. (Actually, the whole secret of this stickhandling maneuver is to develop backward and forward rhythm so that control of the puck is never lost.)

When Jean comes to the point where he must either pass or shoot the puck, he generally pivots his entire body to his right, putting the puck on the front of the stick blade, and either shoots or passes to Rod Gilbert on his right side. But if a defenseman rushes Jean while he's stickhandling back to front, he has the choice of either bringing the puck back in front of him and switching to the side-to-side maneuver; or, if the defenseman has made his move, Jean can do one of the

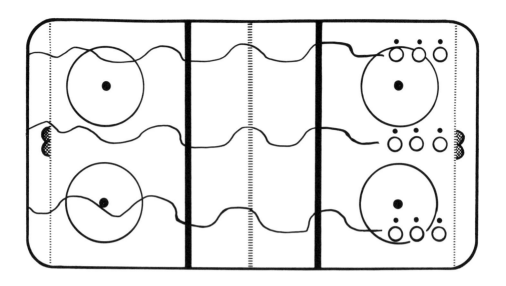

Two stickhandling drills we use at Skateland Summer Ice Hockey School.

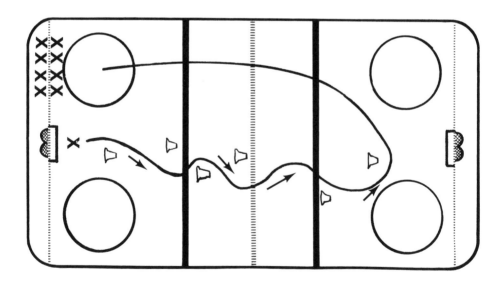

following: (1) put the puck through the defenseman's legs, skate around him, and pick it up again; (2) throw the puck off the boards on a backhand and go around the defenseman in the hopes of regaining it; (3) pass off the backhand to Vic Hadfield on his left, or to Rod Gilbert on his right; or (4) if in close enough to the cage, shoot for the goal.

While there are several variations of these three basic stickhandling maneuvers, once you master them and have good control of the puck, you can develop your own refinements. To help your stickhandling, we have illustrated here several drills that we use at Skateland Summer Ice Hockey School. But when faced with a stickhandling situation, here are four points to keep in mind:

1. The puck will travel faster by passing than you can carry it.

2. Stickhandle as little as possible in your own end; save your skill for around the opponent's net.

3. The easiest man to stickhandle around is the one who rushes straight at you.

4. Make your opponent commit first, then go around him (especially if it is the goalkeeper).

How to Deke. As previously stated in this chapter, hockey is really a game of moves and countermoves. This is especially true when you are stickhandling your way down ice. In fact, you always attempt to force your opponent to commit himself first. Then you'll decide on your countermove depending upon the opponent's definite move. Of course, sometimes you can fake, or "deke," your opponent into a commitment before deciding the countermove.

There are two basic types of dekes:

1. *Body deke.* Drop your head, shoulder, or hips one way, then move the other.

2. *Stick deke.* Hold the stick as if you're going one way, leave the puck, then quickly shift the stick and pick up the puck, and quickly move the other way.

Frequently, it's possible to combine these two basic dekes into one deking move. For instance, in deking right, dip your head and shoulder in that direction, carry the puck to that side, shifting the weight to the slightly bent knee. Then quickly swing the puck to the left, drive off the right skate, and break sharply to your left. Use short strides throughout to make it easier to cut, making your break when the opposing player commits to your fake. He'll be easier to beat if standing still or rushing at you. If he's backing up as you approach, be ready to pass or shoot to avoid being checked. Knowing that it is easier to cut around the side on which the player holds his stick as he faces you, make your fake to his "off-stick" side. That is, when you want to stickhandle past a defenseman who is facing you, between you and the other team's goal, you have to move him out of your way. To do this, fake a move in one direction that will fool him. It may be a movement of your eyes, head, shoulders or hips that indicates to him that you plan to go to one particular side of him. If he reacts and makes his move to that side, you must be ready to move quickly around him on the other side.

Your feet are most important in deking. You must be able to pivot back and forth. Fast feet are necessary when an opposing player has caught your deke. You must be ready to skate in the opposite direction. It's also important to remember not to slow down when you approach a man who is trying to check you—keep your speed up. Don't give him time to figure out which way around him you really are going. Here you can see how the deke is used in typical game play: The player gets the puck and streaks for the other team's goal. Their closest defenseman moves to meet him. The player with the puck suddenly cuts to meet the defenseman . . . looks him in the eye, and fakes to one side. If the defenseman makes a move to one side, the puck carrier moves around him on the opposite side. The important point is to get the defenseman to make the first move; if he doesn't follow the first fake, be prepared to fake to the other side and try to trick him into making a move. In a situation in which the other defenseman is also able to come in on the play, the puck carrier goes through exactly the same move and dekes the second defenseman too.

In deking, like everything else, only practice makes it near perfect. Get another player on the ice and practice one-on-one faking and deking until you have it worked in as a part of your stickhandling technique. Remember that when deking you have the big advantage that only you know which direction you really intend to go!

PASSING

Good hockey is fast, and its speed can only be maintained through effective passing and alert receiving. Poor passing and receiving are perhaps the major weaknesses among hockey players. Because passing and receiving are the real basis of coordinated team play, a player must realize the importance they play in a team's success.

Before you pass the puck, there are several things you must consider.

Always head-man the puck whenever possible. Here Rod Gilbert head-mans a pass to line mate Vic Hadfield.

For example, how fast are you moving? How is your intended receiver moving? Should you pass it across the ice, or is there an opponent close enough to intercept the pass or get his stick in the way and deflect the puck? Most passes will have to lead a player skating up the ice. To be accurate you must be able to watch the receiver, and gauge his distance and speed while controlling the puck. Your head must be up to do this. Split vision can be developed to enable you to see the puck on your stick from the bottom of your eyes, and the moving player at the same time. You must judge the speed and the distance the puck is to travel to determine the "lead" required and the speed of the pass. Your target won't be the receiver's skates, but a point ahead of his stick.

Knowing when, and when not, to pass is essential. The "blind" pass made without looking for a receiver is a serious mistake in a game, and usually results from not playing with the head up. Rather than risk a blind pass, you should stickhandle for better position, freeze the puck for a face-off, or shoot on the net. Never pass blindly when you're about to be checked.

When bringing the puck out of your defensive zone, remember that the fastest way to advance it up ice is by a pass to a teammate breaking out ahead. Always give it to the "headman." While all NHL teams attempt to pass the puck to the headman as much as possible, the Montreal Canadiens actually incorporate it into their style of play.

As previously stated, it's not wise to stickhandle, except on rare occasions, in one's defensive zone. You'll need to pass often when clearing out of your own end. But don't pass directly in front of your defensive net unless a fast relay from an open teammate is being employed to beat a would-be forechecker. Of course, once in your opponent's end, use a pass to a teammate in better scoring position than you are. At rare times, when right in on the goalkeeper, a pass to a teammate flanking you will leave the latter an open net for a goal.

One mistake many young players make is to confuse passing and shooting. They aren't the same thing. A pass should be laid out with the intention that a teammate will pick it up, and be able to do something with it. A shot is made with the intention that the opponent's goalie won't be able to stop it. Never mistake passing for shooting—they are not the same!

There are eight basic passes: (1) the sweep, or flat; (2) the snap; (3) the slap; (4) the flip; (5) the lift; (6) the clearing; (7) the drop; and (8) the board pass. The forward pass, the back pass, and the lateral pass are all straight passes that travel along the surface of the ice. Each one can be delivered forehanded or backhanded. Forward, back, and lateral refer to the direction in which the pass travels.

The Sweep or Flat Pass. The sweep pass is usually employed when deception isn't an overly important factor or when the puck carrier has sufficient time to make the pass. In the forehand sweep pass, keep the puck in the middle of the stick and watch the target—not the puck. When you pass the puck, transfer the weight from the rear foot to the front foot. The stick blade should be flat on the ice and tilted slightly over the puck. For accuracy, follow through in a straight line toward the target, keeping the stick low. There should be a slight spin on the puck, and at the completion of the follow-through, the face of the blade is low and closed. For a good sweep pass, whip the puck off the toe of the stick to a point just ahead of the receiver's stick. If the blade of the stick follows through along the ice after the puck, the puck can't lift off the ice. Many good play possibilities are lost because the puck is lifted unintentionally. A full follow-through will help assure an accurate pass, but when you follow through, keep your stick as close to the ice as possible. This motion will also help the puck to spin off your stick.

In fact, a flat pass sometimes lacks the momentum to reach the target and tends to go away if it hits a rough on the ice. But a pass with a little spin isn't as likely to be sent astray by a chip in the ice.

The backhand sweep pass is executed in a similar manner. Look at the target and sweep the puck in a straight line to the target. Get a good forward push of the lower hand and follow through with both hands. Because it is mainly the arms that perform the backhand sweep pass, there is no rotation of the upper body.

Don't sweep pass the puck—either backhand or forehand—too hard. It should go across the ice at a good speed, but the receiver should always be able to handle it. A bullet-type pass is more liable to jump over the receiver's stick blade than one that moves flat on the ice, smoothly and quickly.

The Snap Pass. This pass, which is also called the wrist or push pass, is used mainly when there is little time in which to make the pass or if the puck carrier wants to make a quick, unexpected pass in the midst of a stickhandling pattern. To execute the snap pass, the stick is brought back about a foot up and behind the puck. Use a short snap of the wrists which brings the stick blade to and through the puck. The follow-through of the lower hand is required for accuracy. Since there is no sweep it's very easy to loft this type of pass if you don't remember to let the stick blade follow through a short distance along the ice. Also tilt the blade slightly over the top of the puck and release it near the toe of your stick. You can get real zip into this pass, but guard against banging the puck.

If you can whip a pass accurately across the ice in this manner, it is a big advantage since you'll be able to make the pass without giving away your intention. For most players, the snap pass should never be used if there's time for the more accurate sweep pass, but hockey is the kind of game in which there is often little time for the more considered movement. Therefore, it's important for every player to have a snap pass that is fast, accurate, and on the ice.

The Slap Pass. This is a quick pass that is used when the puck comes to a player in the midst of a scramble or when the man receiving a pass wishes to get the puck to a teammate without first stopping. The technique is similar to that used for a slap shot. The blade of the stick is slapped at the puck with a forward whip of the wrists and a firm grip on the stick so that the blade won't rebound from the puck. The important thing is to make certain that the blade of the stick follows through along the ice after the slap so that the puck isn't lofted. Also be careful when making a slap not to roll or bounce the puck. The blade of the stick, as in any other type of pass, should follow through in the direction the pass is going.

The Flip Pass. This pass is used when you plan to lift the puck over an opponent's stick or when you intend to flip it between two defensemen. It's also the pass usually used to center the puck in front of the enemy's goal when the puck carrier has possession in a corner or behind the opponent's net.

The flip pass is executed with a quick upward and forward flick of the wrists with the weight on the forward foot. The blade is tilted open and the puck rolls off the toe of the blade. Keep your eye on the target, shift the weight to the forward foot, use an easy flick of the wrist, and follow through high with your stick. Remember that spin is more important in the flip pass, for without spin the puck bounces wildly. A slight spin makes the puck lie flat when it hits the ice.

The backhand flip pass is the reverse of the forehand flip and is performed with an upward and backward twist of the hands. Again, not as much body is used as with the forehand flat pass.

The flip pass is a most useful one. It can be used to clear an opponent's stick and it's especially good for pass-outs from behind the opponent's net. Also, in your defensive zone, if you can't see an open teammate, employ a flip pass into the boards near the blue line to get the puck into center ice. Raise the puck when making any doubtful passes in this zone; if intercepted, they'll be difficult to handle cleanly. In the attacking zone, if you cannot see an open teammate, work behind the net to gain time, or force a face-off if you're unable to stickhandle. Remember that blind passes in either end of the rink can be disastrous.

The Lift Pass. While the flip is employed primarily when the receiver is fairly close, the lift is used when the puck is to be sent some distance and has to pass over a stick, or a player on the ice in the way. It is accomplished in the same manner as the flip pass, but the amount of lift depends on the amount of twist to your wrists. The direction of the pass is controlled by letting the blade of the stick follow through toward the target.

The Clearing Pass. This pass is nothing more than a long lift shot and it is used to get the puck out of your defensive zone by flicking it high over the heads of any opponents. The weight starts on the rear foot and is transferred to the front as the puck is lifted. The blade of the stick is wide open and the follow-through is high.

The backhand clearing pass is usually easier and is more frequently used. Be sure that the weight starts on the back foot and transfers to the front foot. The hands are well apart and the arms end up in a high follow-through.

The clearing pass is an effective weapon to use in a penalty-killing situation. There is no better way to move the puck out of your end and down the ice as far as possible. There will also be times in every game when your team has a letdown, and the other team is pressing. Icing is one call that can give your team an opportunity to substitute players. However, there are times when it is important to be able to clear the puck without being called for icing. This is when you should be able to clear the puck in such a way that it results in a shot on the other team's goal. This is a particularly important play in the last moments of a game when the other team pulls its goalie and sends six attackers up front. And, although this action is called a clearing pass, remember that in the true sense of the word, you're not passing the puck, you're shooting it at the other goal. Thus, when making such a clearing pass, put some steam and power behind that pass (shot).

The Drop Pass. The drop pass isn't really a pass. It is a play or maneuver where one player comes across his opponent's blue line and finds one or two defensemen between him and the goal. He knows one of his teammates is coming in behind him. He simply leaves the puck just inside the opponent's blue line for the trailer who is coming up behind. For example, if you're the centerman, carry the puck in and leave it just across your opponent's blue line, toward the center of the rink. To throw the defenseman off stride, fake a shot just before you drop it. Try to leave the puck motionless. Then move in on the defenseman and try to take him out of the play so your winger, who is trailing you, can pick up the puck and skate right in on the goal. More on the strategy of this maneuver is given in Chapter 6.

When making the drop pass, move the puck forward by stickhandling following your normal maneuver. Then, when the drop is to be made, quickly move your stick blade ahead of the puck and give it a sharp, backway, choppy slap, so that the forward progress of the puck is stopped dead. The important point here is to place the blade just in front of the puck to stop it dead—don't bat it back. Also, if this chop stroke is done lightly, or too carelessly, the forward momentum of the puck won't be stopped, and the puck will continue to slide forward and away from the intended receiver. Remember that you don't want to leave the puck rolling or bouncing; the puck must lie dead.

The Board Pass. A puck passed off the boards rebounds away at the same angle, that is, the angle onto the boards equals the angle off the boards. This pass is useful when a defender is between you and your receiver. Another common version of this pass is the pass behind the goal from one defenseman to another.

The board pass has another good use. For instance, when you're carrying the puck, and bearing down on an opposing defenseman—if you are near the boards, he'll usually try to steer you toward the boards and into the corner. That's when you can use the boards to your advantage. He has one thought in mind, to move you into those boards. If none of your players is behind him, he won't expect you to pass the puck ahead of you. This is the time to give him a shoulder shift, as if you are going to try to go to the side and get between him and the boards. On this maneuver, lay a pass onto the boards. Deke suddenly and break to his left and around him to pick up your own pass and move right in on the goal. If the other defenseman is moving over to you, and you have a trailer coming up on the play, you can block out that second defenseman. Your trailer can then pick up the pass off the boards, and skate in on goal.

This passing play is particularly good if you know the rink well and have regular opportunities to practice bouncing the puck off the boards. Whenever your team plays on foreign ice, make certain you know the rebounds of the rink. All rinks have their own peculiarities. Question others who have played there before. Rebounds from the wire or glass that are used to enclose the rinks differ, as do rebounds from side, end, and corner boards.

RECEIVING

Receiving a pass in hockey is similar to catching a baseball. Your stick must "give" with the puck at the moment of contact, and the blade should be tilted slightly to form a pocket to trap the puck. That is, receive a pass on the center of your stick blade, with the blade flat on the ice at right angles to the direction from which the puck is coming. Your hands, arms, and wrists should give at impact. Then, as your stick gives, the blade should tilt over the puck as contact is made. More give is necessary on fast passes to prevent the puck from bouncing away. But in all cases, nurse the puck as it comes to the stick. This cushions the blow, prevents the puck from rebounding off your stick, and gives you control of the puck. Never stab or poke at it or try to receive it with a hard stick, since the puck will rebound from it or slide off the end of the blade. (By a hard stick we mean a stick that is held in a tight hand grip which doesn't permit the stick to give when the puck contact is made.) Also don't reach out for the puck, but let it come to you. This common fault is caused generally by overeagerness and tension. Keep calm and let it come to you, don't fight it.

When a pass is a little ahead of you, keep your elbows high when reaching for the puck and move your hands together at the end of the shaft in order to obtain maximum reach. By raising your elbows, it will be easier to keep the blade of the stick flat on the ice as you reach out. If the elbows aren't raised, the toe of the blade will be up and the puck could easily slide under.

If the pass is well ahead of you, it frequently can be reached by bending your forward knee and reaching out with your stick flat on the ice, the toe of which is facing the direction of oncoming passes so as to form a hook, as in a hook check (see Chapter 5). Your stick, in such cases, should be held in one hand with the grip completely at the end of the stick shaft. By employing this technique, you can get many passes that would otherwise go free or slide off the end of your stick because you can't reach far enough forward with your two hands on the stick and your body upright. By bending your knee, you increase your reaching ability and prevent overbalancing. Incidentally, backhand passes are received the same way as forehand passes.

When you are about to receive a pass, to your forehand or backhand, make sure the blade of the stick is on the ice. This gives the passer a target and also enables you to control the puck better.

Skate Deflections. Bad passes can sometimes be turned into scoring opportunities by using your stick, which is on the ice ready to receive the puck. Move the skate so that the puck, when it hits the skate, will deflect toward your stick. Do not kick the puck.

A pass on the back skate is more difficult to control and the deflection will probably not be in line with your stick. Therefore, keep your stick ready to move toward the deflected puck.

Receiving Airborne Passes. Receiving an airborne pass may be done with the glove—direct it down in front to the stick. If the pass is too far in front, use the blade of your stick to knock it down. Sometimes a hard, chest-high pass may be bunted to the ice with the stick; however, the glove would be easier and safer to use in this instance.

The Don'ts of Passing and Receiving. Here are a few common hockey faults to avoid when passing and receiving:

1. Don't skate with your stick in the air. If you are receiving a pass, keep your stick on the ice. Your stick gives the passer a target to shoot at. Also, you won't waste time getting that stick down when the pass does come at you.

2. Don't pass the puck unless you know where it is going. Never pass the puck just to get rid of it. Always pass to a teammate or away from an opponent. Be aware of what the result of your pass might be before you release the puck.

3. Don't pass in front of your own net. It is an open invitation to the other team to pick it up and score a goal against you.

4. Don't throw a pass from beside your net out to center ice unless you see a teammate in position for a clean breakaway. Try to carry the puck out over your blue line, or pass it directly to one of your own players who is in the clear.

5. Don't, in the other team's half of the ice, try to pass the puck the width of the ice if they have a player in position to reach that pass. That's how breakaways start.

6. Don't hold your stick too rigidly when you receive a pass. Tilt the blade a little so the blade lies slightly over the puck to help trap it.

7. Be sure that the blade of the stick is always facing the direction from which the puck is coming. Should the blade not be facing the direction from which the puck is coming, there's a very good chance that the puck will slide off the blade as soon as it makes contact.

8. When handling a pass directed at your feet, be sure to bend your knees and take a low grip on the stick so that the heel of the stick is closer to the ice.

9. Don't be afraid to use your skates to catch a pass. Sometimes a pass is a little late and you have to take it on a skate and kick it up to your stick.

10. Don't skimp on practice. Practice every aspect of passing and receiving and keep on practicing; day after day and year after year. The pros don't stop practicing—don't you!

SHOOTING

The ultimate play in hockey is the scoring of a goal. Whether the player is a beginner or a superstar, it is important to have a hard, accurate shot. But, to score a goal you must get the puck past the

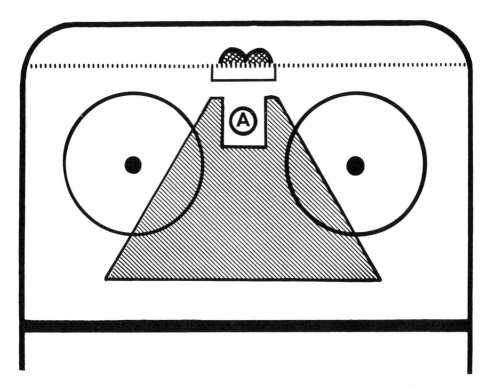

The prime shooting area, also called the slot, is the small rectangle marked A. The shaded area outside the rectangle is also good, but other places are not considered good.

goalkeeper. A survey conducted a few years ago indicated that scoring shows some interesting patterns. Here are a few of the facts the survey indicated:

1. Most goals scored were shot from directly in front of the net.

2. Most of the successful shots were below the level of the goalie's knees.

3. The best shots were down around the goalkeeper's ankles.

4. The majority of goals were scored on the side of the goaltender on which he held his stick, not on the side where he wears his catching glove.

If we translate this into on-ice action, you should pick your scoring attempts in this order:

1. The best chance to score comes from a low shot on the side opposite the goalie's catching glove.

The shots to shoot for.

2. Second best chance is from a shot that's high on the side opposite his catching glove.

3. Third best chance is a low shot 4 to 8 inches off the ice on his catching-glove side.

4. Fourth best chance is a high shot on the goalie's catching-glove side.

As the survey pointed out, the best shots are made directly in front of the goal, about 10 to 25 feet out. From this position, which is known as the slot, the shot can be made to all corners. As the player moves away from center to the side, he is left with only one side of the goal at which to shoot and the goal opening gets smaller until in the extreme angle little exposed goal is left. Practice cutting in to the center to get the best angle. The great goal scorers cut in toward center whenever possible. Remember that when the goalkeeper is deep in his crease the shooting angles are at their best and players should usually shoot. If the goalie comes way out to cut down the angle, more of the goal is open, so deke the goalie. Always work at getting the puck, not the goalie, in the best angle possible for a shot on goal. More on this aspect of shooting is given in Chapter 6.

Shooting a puck is like hitting a golf ball. In both cases you are working with a round object. So, the blade of your stick, like the face of your golf club, must be tilted forward—not back—to get the maximum power and accuracy from your shot. Actually, one of the biggest mistakes young players make in shooting is that they aim the heel of their stick at their target. What this does is open the blade of the stick, or bend it back, and the shot loses steam and usually goes off target. So try this: Aim for your target with the toe of your stick. That is, finish up your shot with the toe pointing right at the spot you were aiming for. If you're shooting low, aim the toe low. If you're shooting waist high, aim the toe waist high. If it's a high shot, aim it high. You'll find that by doing this you will be "cupping" the puck, so to speak, and it will leave your stick with surprising power and precision. But, before going any further let's look at the five commonly used hockey shots: (1) the wrist, (2) the snap, (3) the slap, (4) the backhand, and (5) the flip.

The Wrist Shot. This shot, often called the sweep, or power, shot, is the most common, and Rod Gilbert's favorite. It is performed with a sweeping action of the stick along the ice, with a snap of the wrist at the last moment. Once the wrists are strong enough, little or no

The Gilbert wrist shot in action.

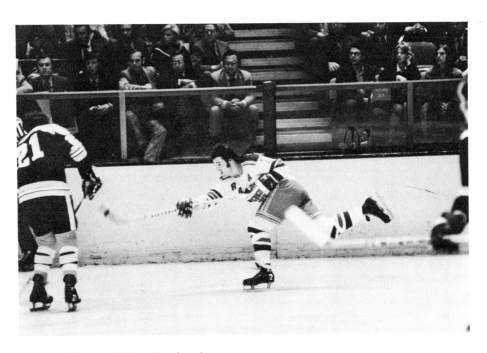

The completion of a slap shot.

lowering of the lower hand is needed between the handling or passing and the wrist shot. Here are the important considerations when taking a wrist shot:

1. Your weight should be transferred from the back leg to the front leg as the puck is swept along the ice. That is, when the sweeping action starts your weight should be on your rear leg and then placed on your forward leg as the puck is snapped forward with that all-important explosive effort. After the puck has gone, make sure you allow your stick to follow through smoothly. Don't stop it with a jerk. Let the blade of the stick follow through until it is pointing at the target you aimed for. Remember that the speed of the shot is dependent upon weight transfer, while the follow-through determines the height of the shot.

2. Your grip must be firm and your thumbs should be well over the shaft. The back of your lower hand should face back, with the back of your upper hand facing toward the direction in which you're planning to shoot. Your wrists should be cocked at the start of the shot, the hands turned back from your wrists. To get the wrist snap when you shoot, whip them forward again. Keeping the wrists stiff all through the shooting action is a common fault that makes it impossible to get maximum speed and accuracy.

3. The weight of your body should be well over the puck, and the puck shouldn't leave the ice before reaching the front skate. Your wrists are then snapped at the end of the sweep.

4. Use split vision to see the puck on your stick and to watch the target. Incidentally, the puck should be about halfway between the heel and the toe of the stick blade. When going in to shoot get in the shooting position (puck to the side) as quickly as possible. Align the puck, not the body, with the middle of the goal to get the best shooting angles.

5. To keep the shot low, roll your wrists to close the face of the blade and keep the stick low to the ice. That is, lean your body well over the stick, keep the shaft of the stick well ahead of the blade, let the puck go with the wrist snap a little sooner, and follow through after the shot with your stick on the ice or just a little above it. It is your follow-through that counts most.

6. For high shots, snap the wrists upward and follow through to the height of the determined shot. That is, to lift the puck, let the blade of the stick come through until it is ahead of the shaft and then snap the wrists and let the puck go. To control the height of your shot let your stick follow through to the height required. If, for instance, you

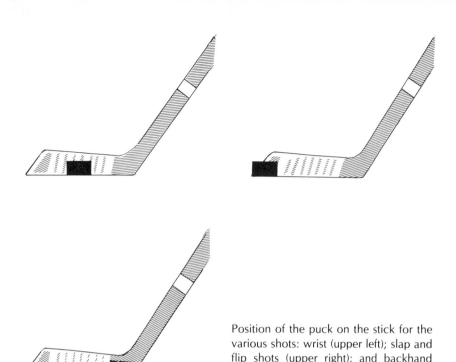

Position of the puck on the stick for the various shots: wrist (upper left); slap and flip shots (upper right); and backhand (lower left).

want to shoot shoulder high, follow through to a shoulder-high position. Don't try to scoop the puck up with an upward scooping action of the stick blade. Let your follow-through do the work.

The Snap Shot. The snap shot is excellent for quick, accurate shots in front of the goal. Vic Hadfield has used it with great success. Actually, it's just a type of wrist shot that is used to get the puck away quickly. There is no sweeping action, and the weight of the body can be on the front, the back, or equally on both skates. The weight is usually on the leg closest to the puck. Accuracy can be improved by driving the top hand in the intended direction before the snap of the wrists occurs. The major differences between the wrist and snap shot are as follows:

    1. The bottom hand is lower on the stick than in the wrist shot.

    2. The stick moves back 12 to 18 inches, the wrists are cocked, and the blade flattens parallel to the ice—the arms move forward, the wrists uncoil and snap the blade into the puck.

The Slap Shot. This shot has been clocked at over 100 miles an hour and is a surprise shot. It's also the shot that brings the "oohs" and the

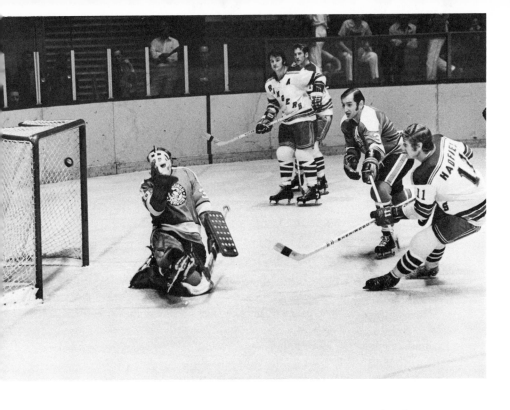

The result of a flip shot can be good (top). Backhand shots come in handy, too (bottom).

"ahs" from the crowds, but it has a very low scoring ratio when compared with the wrist shot.

In making the slap shot, the lower hand is dropped farther down the shaft to stiffen the blade. The stick is swung so that the blade comes down in an arc like a golf club. Try to hit the puck with the center of your stick blade. Keep the back swing low, bend well over the puck and transfer the weight from the back to front foot. The wrists are cocked in the backswing by turning the toe of the blade slightly downward. The blade should contact the puck closer to the heel than the toe, and should be kept perpendicular to the ice. Keep the puck between the skates at contact.

Look at the target first, then keep your eyes on the puck for contact and follow through to the spot aimed at. The hand grip is tightened just before contact is made so that there is no give on the part of the stick when the puck is hit. The position of the puck on the ice as it is slapped should depend on how high a shot is desired. If you wish to shoot low, place it slightly behind you. To shoot higher, place it further ahead. All the other principles of controlling the shot such as following through, keeping over the puck, not pulling away, and so on as listed for the wrist shot also apply to the slap shot. It's important to keep in mind, however, that if you get off a good, powerful slap shot, the puck will usually pull in a few inches—to the right for a left shot, to the left if you're a right shot. Allowance must be made.

By the way, the slap shot can be made by stopping the puck first, then teeing off on it, or the slap may be made at a soft pass-out without stopping the puck. The latter is more difficult, requiring better timing. When you do get all your power into the slap shot, you'll find that your stick shaft will bend and the whip will help you get a sizzling shot away.

The slap shot is Brad Park's favorite. "I have what is called a 'heavy shot.' No one that I have ever talked with could tell me exactly why, but my shot seems to rip the goalie's pad more easily than say Rod's slapper, although his is traveling faster. Of course, a heavy shot is fine when playing the points on power plays. I think a heavy slap shot is good for any defenseman to develop if he can." Incidentally, you don't have to have a slap shot to be a big scorer in the NHL. In all his years with the Rangers, Jean Ratelle probably has never scored on a slap shot. In fact, he receives a great deal of kidding about it—"Ratty, you *almost* scored on your slap shot."

The Backhand Shot. The backhand is probably one of the most neglected shots today, yet it is a terrific weapon that all goalkeepers

Always be ready to put the puck in the net.

fear. And most goalies agree that Jean Ratelle and Red Berenson of Detroit are about the best in this department.

The technique is similar to that of the wrist shot. Transfer the weight, sweep the puck, and then snap the wrists. Follow through high or low depending on the shot. But you may find this shot always goes high since your wrists will tend naturally to lift the puck in this move. Counteract this by decreasing both follow-through and wrist action. Usually the backhand is best executed during a sharp turn.

The Flip Shot. The flip shot is a technique used to hit the upper corners of the net from close in, or to lift the puck over the sprawling goalkeeper. The lift is given by tilting the blade so that only its bottom edge contacts the puck. The shot, like the flip pass, is delivered from in front of the plane of your body, with a scooping action of the stick by the wrists. That is, with a quick snap of your wrists and a high follow-through you can direct the puck to the upper part of the net. Start the puck off the toe of the stick blade and near the front skate. The blade should be slightly tilted behind the puck. Keep the movement sharp and drive the blade through the puck directly upward with a long, hard follow-through. Have the weight on the rear foot throughout the shot. When shooting over the goalie or defender in the goal mouth, keep the shot hard and fast; never make it an easy flip.

The backhand flip shot is identical to the forehand except that the puck should be further back, so you can get better action.

There's another type of flip shot that some players use called the lob shot. It's really a high arching flip shot that travels a considerable distance. It is used in hopes that the puck will take a fluke bounce when it lands and go past the goalie. It sometimes works.

Tipping the Puck. Experience and practice are the best teachers in the art of tipping the puck. Experts like Phil Esposito and Dave Balon have learned to get away from their man in front of the goal, giving them freedom to tip the puck into the goal. Learn to direct the blade into the path of the oncoming puck. Keep your eye on the puck until it touches the stick, and keep the shot low whenever possible. Learn to tilt the blade for higher tips. It is important to remember that any time you take a shot, get your stick back down on the ice. You may be able to get another shot.

The most important feature in scoring goals is being in the scoring position. You must be prepared to shoot on goal once you cross the blue line. Stickhandling the puck from side to side does not allow you to get the shot away quickly. You must first bring your stick along to the side. Therefore, try to stickhandle on your shooting side. Being in a shooting position also means that your stick is on the ice ready to receive and shoot the puck. Scoring goals involves knowledge of shooting angles and using all shots well. To be a great scorer, you must have a hard, accurate shot, and this requires hard work and practice. More details on scoring goals are given in Chapter 6.

5

The Basics of Defense

"A good defense is the best offense." We have all heard this statement uttered numerous times and pertaining to all forms of sports. While we both don't agree wholeheartedly, certainly the importance of a superlative defense is very clear. A good example of this was a Chicago Black Hawk team of the mid-1950's. They had nine players in one season with 20 goals or more. And back then, a 20-goal man was like a .300 hitter in baseball. But in spite of this powerful offensive, they finished last in the league. Reason: Their defense was the worst in the league.

The basis of defense, of course, is to keep your opponents from taking a shot on your goal and goalie. To do this, it is the duty of all the players—both forwards and defensemen—to prevent an opponent from coming in on the goal and to try to take the puck away from the opposing players. The best way to accomplish these objectives is by checking.

ELEMENTS OF CHECKING

Often you'll hear words in hockey jargon that can be confusing for people who aren't directly involved in our game. The two most common ones are the two basic forms of checking: (1) forechecking and (2) backchecking.

Forechecking. The forechecking form of defense takes place while your team is still in its attacking zone and just after your opponents have gained possession of the puck. The major purpose of forechecking is to pin the opposition team deep in their own end of the ice and make it difficult for them to get an offensive play under way. Of course,

Forechecking (top) and backchecking (bottom) are important positions for forwards.

sometimes a forechecker may steal the puck and get his team off defense and onto offense. But, generally the big feature of a good forechecking unit is that it gives the defense time to organize.

Much of the success of forechecking depends upon mobile, aggressive forwards using good position play to swarm over the puck carrier, catching him in a corner or just as he comes out from behind his own net. On most teams, the centerman initiates the forechecking by attempting to harass the puck carrier. Should the puck carrier try to skate to his left to avoid the forechecking center, the right winger will then move in against him and almost double-team him. On the other hand, if the puck carrier attempts to go to his right, the left wing must skate in and try to force him back. You'll note that only two forwards—the center and either of his wings—should forecheck at the same time. In other words, if the left wing moves in to help the center, then the right wing should remain near the blue line, ready to skate toward his defensive zone should the opposition team break away from the forechecking and start their rush up ice. When all three forwards get themselves caught forechecking too deep in their attacking zone, disaster can result.

When forechecking, Rod Gilbert never faces the puck carrier head on, but rather approaches him at an angle. "Then he must maneuver away from me, and I have found that my angled position gives me a much better chance of taking the puck away from him. Also, when forechecking it is important to play the man—not the puck. If you can take out the puck carrier, then your teammate who forechecks with you most likely will be able to pick up the loose puck and start your team's offensive effort. Dave Keon, Bob Nevin, Derek Sanderson, and Chico Maki are some of the better forecheckers we must face."

Backchecking. Frequently a team can't get into position to utilize its forechecking type of defense. When this occurs, the forwards must then resort to backchecking. That is, the forwards, skating side by side with an attacking player, must be ready to intercept a pass or make any other defensive play necessary to prevent a shot on goal. But, when backchecking, make certain never to skate too far ahead of your man; if you do, he can cut behind you and slip into position to receive a pass. Never turn your back on the man you're backchecking.

When backchecking, always try to keep your stick out in front of you. Often the attacking player may try a pass, but with your stick out you can block it. If your opponent happens to get the puck, force him into the corner and take him out of the play. Here are some other important points to keep in mind when covering an attacking player:

1. Stay between your man and the puck; in your own end stay between him and your goal.

2. Know where the puck is at all times when covering an opposing player.

3. When the attack breaks out, pick up your man as early as possible; stay no more than a stride in front of him.

4. Don't coast while you check; most holding, hooking, and slashing penalties are caused by not being able to reach the puck carrier.

5. The closer your man is to your goal, the closer you must cover him.

6. In your own end, never leave your man while his team has the puck. The only exception to this rule is to cover a more dangerous man left open.

Defensemen are, of course, engaged in the task of covering their men at all times when the puck is in their defensive zone. Before going on to methods of checking we want to say a word about defensemen. Two major factors are of foremost importance for a great defenseman; first, the willingness to sacrifice, and second, the enthusiasm for contact. To play defense properly you won't receive the credit of the high-scoring forward, but certainly you'll receive your share of bruising physical punishment.

It is important that a defenseman assumes the proper stance while waiting for the play to come into his defensive zone. While most defensemen vary their stance slightly from the so-called "ideal," usually the best one is with the feet comfortably apart and parallel, knees bent slightly, the arms relaxed, and the stick held out in front with the blade on the ice. The stick is usually best held in the inside hand (left hand if right handed) so that if the play goes to the side, you can go with the puck carrier because your stick is always ready for any cut-back attempt.

As the puck carrier approaches, move the stick out in front of you and keep your body between the net and the attacking player as you skate backwards. Don't lunge into the attacker, or commit yourself, until he has made the first move. Remember that hockey is a game of moves and countermoves; therefore, when on defense always try to have your opponent make the first move. Then you can counter.

Most likely you've heard the expression "bad penalties." As a rule, these penalties happen as a result of poor checking techniques. Let your man get free and you may have to resort to an illegal move, such as tripping or hooking to stop him. That's a bad penalty, because alert defensive play could have prevented it. Another bad penalty occurs when you do something illegal in the other team's end and get caught. There's no way the other team can score on you if they're still in their own zone. If you trip a guy just as he's about to break in on your goalkeeper, that's one thing. It's a last-resort move. But taking a run at an opponent when you're attacking is just plain foolishness. Thus, to prevent bad penalties, it's important to know how to check properly.

METHODS OF CHECKING

There are two basic methods of checking (getting the puck away from the opponent or causing him to lose control of it): (1) with the stick playing the puck, and (2) with the body playing the man.

When checking an opponent, you must always guard against the deke. The best way to do this is to keep your eyes glued on your opponent's chest. While players can move their shoulders and heads in one way and go the other, their chests have to ride with the rest of the body. By watching your opponent, you're set to take him over, use a sweep check, and come up with a poke check.

STICK CHECKS

There are four basic ways of taking the puck from the attacker's stick: (1) the poke check, (2) the sweep check, (3) the hook check, and (4) the stick-lift check.

The Poke Check. In the poke check, a quick thrust or poke of the stick is aimed at the puck on the blade of the attacker's stick. To make this thrust the lower hand is released from the shaft. The stick must be whipped out smartly and at just the right moment. The poke check is one of the most useful of the checking maneuvers, but when using this defense, you shouldn't apply too much body. Hold the stick in one hand with your arm bent; keep the upper arm in, next to your body. Whip the arm straight out and knock the puck from the attacker's stick, but don't lunge forward and be caught off balance. Keep your head up.

When planning to poke check a puck carrier coming directly at you, it's not a good idea to take a step toward him because it puts you off

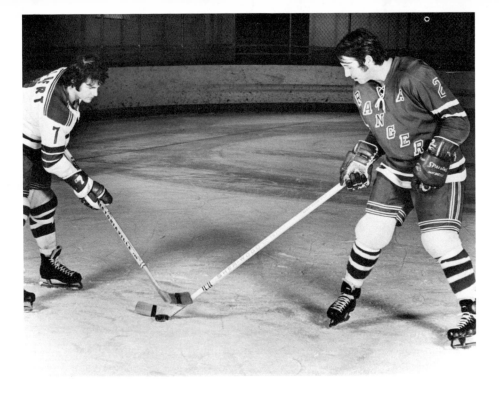

The poke check.

The sweep check.

balance. Since in all probability he expects a poke check, he will continue to skate in on you until he is too close to avoid such a check. At that time, like a fencer bending forward for a quick thrust, move your stick in on the puck. The surprise element involved will usually completely fool the puck carrier and will make the poke check successful.

If the poke check is missed, always be in a position to start over again. You'll be surprised at the number of times you can steal the puck with your second motion because what usually happens is that the puck carrier, after he has avoided your poke check, thinks he has passed you for good and may try to pass the puck behind your back to a teammate. If you suddenly wheel around and lay your stick flat on the ice, you'll be amazed how often you will intercept such passes. If a poke check is successful, stop quickly and go for the puck.

To stop an opponent from scoring on a breakaway, a last resort may be the diving poke check. The check should be used carefully, and only as a last desperate move. To perform it, dive headlong with your stick flat on the ice and knock the puck away from the attacker.

The poke check is also used by the forward when forechecking. Again, don't lunge at the puck carrier; stay out in front and allow him to get close; then flick your stick out and go for the puck. Always end up in a balanced position so that you can repeat the check if it is missed the first time. Remember to keep your head up, watch the puck carrier, and try to look at the puck with split vision.

The Sweep Check. This stick check maneuver is similar to the poke check. It is made by sweeping the stick in a half circle toward the oncoming puck carrier, with as much of your stick flat on the ice as possible. The hand not holding the stick is out and cupped, ready to stop the puck if your opponent shoots. Just as in the poke check, you should get down with lots of knee bend, but not so far down that your balance is affected.

The sweep is also most effective used from the side when the checker is skating with the puck carrier. At such a time, the stick is swept around in front of the puck carrier. Actually, the major advantage of the sweep check is that it covers a great deal of ice surface and, as the stick moves rapidly, the puck carrier has difficulty in avoiding it. The sweep check is also useful when your man has gotten ahead of you, since you can reach behind him and clear the puck aside. Unfortunately, the main disadvantage of the sweep check is that, even when the puck is contacted, possession isn't obtained because the puck will be knocked

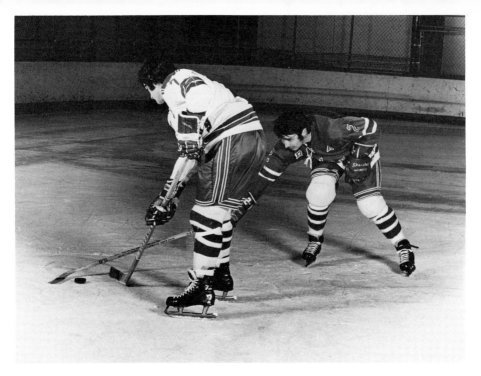

The hook check.

The shoulder check.

some distance away. Another problem with the sweep check is that it must be started early, thus giving the puck carrier warning.

The Hook Check. The hook check is considered by most professional players and coaches to be the most effective of all the stick checks. It is employed usually when checking a puck carrier from the side or rear.

To accomplish the hook check, the stick held in one hand is snaked out as far as you can stretch your arm. Bend low to get as much of your stick as possible flat on the ice and cradle the puck on the blade. Then sweep the puck away to the side. In other words, the whole idea of the hook check is to get your blade ahead of the puck as it comes off your opponent's stick during his normal stickhandling action.

Since the hook check, with the stick held in the top hand at arm's reach, covers more ice, the checker can fake a poke check, then use a hook check. For example, a stickhandler approaches Brad Park. "I can favor my left (remember I'm a left-shot) by a step sideways as though to poke check. This will invite the puck carrier to veer to my right. Then I step in with my right foot, quickly whipping my stick far to the right and low to the ice to take the puck away."

Remember that a stickhandler can easily get by you if you're rushing straight at him. All stick checking will be successful if you can wait for the puck carrier to commit either to your right or left. A left-shot checker then uses a poke check if the attacker swerves to his (the checker's) left, and a hook check if he goes to the right. Defensemen especially must be either stationary or backing in as the attacker approaches. At the moment the latter commits to either side, the checker strides forward in that direction to check him.

Stick-Lift Check. This check, sometimes called skate-off checking, is made simply by lifting the puck carrier's stick from the ice by hooking it at the heel with your own stick. The stick lift, properly executed, can stop passes and shot attempts. It's particularly effective in front of the net, where it may prevent an opponent from shooting.

Another trick when chasing an attacking player—especially if you're not gaining on him—is to reach forward and with the toe of your stick blade jab the back opening of his glove. This jab may jerk his stick and force him to lose control of the puck.

BODY CHECKS

Of the two basic methods of checking, spectators seem to prefer the body check. Nothing—except a score—brings the crowd to its feet

The hip check.

The Park hip check in action.

faster than a good crunching body check. But there's a right and a wrong time to throw a body check.

A good time to body check is when your opponent is passing or receiving the puck. Being occupied, his guard is usually down and that's the ideal time to hit him with a solid body check. Also when a puck carrier is skating with his head down, that's the perfect time to level him onto the ice. The wrong time to body check is when you are the final man remaining in the line of defense protecting your goalkeeper. A missed body check in such an instance usually leaves the path open to a goal.

The best body checkers in the league, such as Bobby Baun, Bob Plager, Don Awrey, and Doug Jarrett, like to establish themselves in a game in the hopes of intimidating certain players or even the whole team. Frequently, such action forces opponents to respect the defensemen more at the defensive blue line and in the defensive zone. Sometimes the mere threat of a vicious body check forces the puck carrier to swerve or stop at the blue line and force his teammates offside, to panic-pass to covered forwards, to pass inaccurately, or to take a harmless long shot. Remember that a team intimidated is a team defeated. The Boston Bruins have long tried to use intimidation as part of their strategy. But remember that intimidation alone never wins a hockey game.

The most important thing to remember in body checking is to play the man, not the puck. This sounds easy, but it isn't. The urge is always there to go for the puck. But if you've ever had Bobby Hull or Frank Mahovlich skate around you when you're trying to take the puck away, you learn pretty fast.

Since hockey is a contact sport, every player should learn to take and give a body check. Body position, timing, balance, strength, and weight transfer determine the force and effectiveness of the check. But, keep in mind, a body check should only be used when it has been mastered, since a missed one can be disastrous. And, in addition, according to the rules of hockey, a body check is permitted only with the torso and can be preceded by no more than two steps toward the puck carrier. If the body checker does take more than two steps, he can receive a penalty for charging. The use of elbows and legs can also draw a penalty. In other words, body checking must be done cleanly.

The Shoulder Check. The most frequently used body check is the shoulder check. You generally use it along the boards. You let your man get a slight lead on you—not too much, just so he thinks he can get by—and then you squeeze him into the boards with your shoulder. That is, you drive your shoulder and hip into your opponent's body, pinning him against the boards.

To assure a solid shoulder check, you should concentrate 100 percent on the chest of your intended victim—never watch the puck or stick or legs or eyes. Remember that there are no "chest dekes" in hockey. You should have a good wide stance for stability; your torso should be leaning forward about 45 degrees. But while the upper body is bent forward at the waist, the back should be straight. Keep the head up and aim your shoulder at the center of your target—your opponent's chest. As contact is made, push upward and through the attacker with an extension of the back leg. After contact, continue to drive through the attacker. That is, at contact your skates are dug in, one skate in front of the other in order to push up and through the attacker.

To set up a good check, the proper shoulder should be employed. For example, if the puck carrier is swerving toward your left shoulder, the left shoulder should be used for checking. If the right shoulder were used in this case your head would swerve as a lever, your body would be spun by the force of the check, and the attacking player would continue on his way. Remember that if you're too erect or limp when applying a shoulder check, you may find yourself flat on your back after contact has been made. Always prepare yourself for a jolt.

Shoulder-checking range is usually considered a stick's length away from the puck carrier. If he penetrates this range straight on or from a side-front position toward you, the two steps permitted in the rules will make it possible to contact him with a shoulder check. If the puck carrier skates outside the stick-length arc, shoulder-checking contact is rather difficult and it's usually best to turn with him and attempt to skate him away from a good shot.

The Hip Check. The hip check has more or less become Brad Park's trademark as a defenseman. While it is the most difficult check to throw in hockey, it also can be the most effective. It's not wise to try to throw a hip into your man unless you're absolutely sure you can connect. So many players can skate so well nowadays that they can speed right by you and leave you there looking foolish. The best time to throw a hip is when the attacker tries to go around you.

Bending low at the waist, make the hip check when the opponent is immediately beside you. Keep your eye on the man. As timing is so important, learn to judge his distance and speed. Then, when the puck carrier is just about beside you, turn sharply into his committed path,

and direct your hip into his body. Even a grazing blow, putting him
off stride momentarily, may be enough to cause the puck carrier to
lose control. But remember to keep low to the ice as in the shoulder
check.

Hip checking should be employed when the puck carrier has swerved
beyond the poke-checking and shoulder-checking range and has
reached a point just off your hip. This check is used very effectively
along the boards when an attacker attempts to go between you and the
boards or when he tries to split the defense. But, don't use a hip check
on an attacker if by doing so you leave another opponent completely
open. That would be playing right into the opponent's hands.

The Board Check. If you don't or aren't able to body check your
opponent, then your next duty is to turn quickly and skate alongside
the puck carrier, keep him between yourself and the boards, make sure
not to give him a cutback angle, and eventually force the puck carrier
to a bad shooting angle. The success that you attain in carrying out this
important assignment depends entirely upon the speed of your turn.
If you turn slowly or too late, then the puck carrier as he goes around
you will have at least a stride lead and no matter how much you try,
after you have given the puck carrier this handicap, you can't fulfill your
duty properly and it will be impossible to force the puck carrier into
a bad shooting angle. Of course, when successfully carrying off this
maneuver, a good board check may come in handy.

The purpose of the board check is to squeeze your opponent on the
boards with the arms and body. Try to arrive at the boards slightly
ahead of the attacker. Push, with your arm, down and across his chest
and move your body in front of him to block his path between you and
the boards. Some coaches prefer two hands on the stick when forcing
an opponent on the boards. With this move, keep the elbows bent and
place the stick across the opponent's hips, pushing downward and
toward the boards. After contact, keep the body low and well balanced.

In scrambles and some rush situations, a body block is effective. This
maneuver is the same as a body check, but there is no hard contact.
Its intention is usually to hold up the attacker for a moment or two,
or to force him to the side. When Brad Park uses a body block he uses
a combination of hip and shoulder checks, much the same as a cross-
body block in football. "That is, with my knees and body well bent over,
I hit my opponent with the side of my body between the shoulder and
hips. If he tries to go past, I move forward or backward with a series

The board check.

of short strides to stop him." But when performing a body block, be sure that you don't leave yourself open for an interference penalty.

If you're trying to move an attacker away from the puck during a scramble, go in low, getting your shoulder into your opponent and driving down. The leg on the same side as the shoulder you're using should be as close to your opponent as possible; the other leg should be held behind about 18 inches to 2 feet and spread laterally from the other leg approximately the same distance. When expecting pressure from the front, or when trying to apply it forward, never allow your feet to move into a parallel position or else you'll be easily pushed off balance. When checking and battling for the puck close in, remember that one leg should always be in front of the other. This will give a much better foundation to move your opponent.

Watch the play in the National Hockey League and you'll notice how much checking is done with the arms. And watch the duels that take place in front of the net as a defenseman tries to fend off one of the opposition as he waits for a pass-out. If you're the defender, the thing to do is stay near your man's stick hand. That way you can lift his stick or push it away. You've got to be careful of drawing a penalty here but you can jostle your man around with little pushes and shoves. The thing is to keep him off balance while keeping your own balance. Again, this goes back to what we said earlier—play the man, not the puck.

Brad Park is a great believer in the theory that it's a good idea to throw a few good, hard checks early in the game. If you can catch one of the opponent's faster forwards with a solid check, it'll give the other team something to think about and may even slow them down. But don't go out of your way to try to get this advantage or you're apt to wind up in the penalty box. Of course, you must guard against retaliation. As a result of body checking, Brad has had to mix it up with most of the tough guys of the league. "Actually, I learned my lesson in retaliation early in my NHL career. Just after having joined the Rangers in my rookie year, I was sent out to check Detroit's Gordie Howe, who sometimes used his stick to effective advantage in ways other than for goal scoring. Since the guys told me to watch out for his elbows, I went in low under the elbows and caught him with a good solid hip check. Howe, the career goal-scoring leader of the NHL, went down to the ice. However, only a few seconds later, his stick found its mark and I fell to the ice like a ton of bricks. After being revived, I learned that retaliation can be quick in the NHL."

Single-knee drop (top) and double-knee drop (bottom).

TAKING CHECKS

Whenever a body check or collision is inevitable, its effect can be lessened by lunging forward into your opponent first, before he has the opportunity to start his drive into you. By gaining this important forward body momentum, it is possible to hit him harder than he hits you. As you lunge, lean your upper body forward, hit him with your shoulder, and drive him off that back leg, straightening it out, and bending your forward leg as you go into the checker. In this way, your balance is improved, and you'll be able to absorb the shock of contact a great deal easier.

Good balance is, of course, important in giving and taking checks. It depends upon several factors, including the flex of knees, the upper body position, the spread of feet, and the general relaxation of the muscles. That is, the knees should be well bent, while the upper body should be forward so that the shoulders are positioned above the knees. The feet should be comfortably spread apart and the entire body relaxed as much as possible. In this way you'll be able to take a check much better.

All players, of course, must learn to protect themselves against the boards. When being checked, distribute the force on as large a surface as possible. Place the forearm and upper thigh against the board and keep the feet well apart and the body low. After impact, recoil by pushing upward and outward with the forearm and inside leg on the one closest to the checker. In the corners where the screen or the glass may become a dangerous hazard, the glove can be used as a cushion for the head when being body-checked. Never fully extend your arms toward the board when cushioning a body check, because serious injuries may occur.

Expect checks when playing the puck on the boards. Get a good stable position, feet apart, knees flexed, body bent from the hip, and forearm and hand on the boards for protection. When you are stickhandling the puck along the boards and an attacker is in close checking you, push back to the left and then go right or vice versa. Protect the puck with your skates and try to drag the puck forward. More on getting around a checker can be found in the next chapter.

The baseball slide.

BLOCKING SHOTS

The defenseman must know how to block pucks. The secret is to know when the shot is coming. Here are some good indicators of when a shot is coming: the attacker drops his head, he slides his hand down his stick, or he drops his shoulder or arm on his shooting side. When the attacker is about to shoot, you have a choice of three methods of blocking shots: (1) a single-knee drop; (2) a double-knee drop; or (3) a baseball slide.

When making the *single-knee drop*, say onto the left knee, transfer your weight to the right skate and drop the left knee to the ice. While doing this extend your stick flat on the ice and out to the side of you ready for a poke or sweep check. Be sure to keep your body under control as you execute this move and make certain to recover early from knee-drop position to move quickly for the loose puck. To make the drop on the right knee, transfer weight to the left skate, drop the right knee to the ice, and extend your stick out to the side of you. With only one knee on the ice, you can get back up much faster than if you were blocking on both knees.

When making the *double-knee drop*, you drop both knees to the ice simultaneously and in effect throw your body directly at the player shooting. While keeping your arms close to your body to present the largest blocking area possible, extend your stick flat on the ice on the same side from which the attacker shoots (the right side if the shooter is a right shot and left if he's a left shot). Your other hand is kept on the opposite side. The reason for keeping the stick on the side from which he shoots is that you'll generally be in a better position, once you go down, to check him if he fakes a shot and tries to go around you.

If you're careful to select your dropping position between the player and the goal, the shooter won't have a chance to lift the puck over your body; and because of your glove and stick, there is no angle the shooter can choose that will put the puck in the net. But, it's most important that you don't commit yourself too soon. If you do, the attacking player can easily pass to a teammate. Wait until the shooter's stick starts through in the shooting action, and then take a stride forward, drop to your knees, and get as close to the take-off spot of the shot as you can. To recover your normal skating position, place both the inside-left and inside-right skate-blade edges on the ice and snap up. You can also rise to the normal skating position by placing the left (or right) inside skate-blade edge on the ice and getting up one leg at a time.

The *baseball slide* may be made either to the left or to the right. To make the slide to the left, for instance, lean your body to the left, pick your left skate off the ice first, and quickly follow by lifting the right skate. Then the body slides into the puck to the left with both legs extended behind the body. To make the slide to the right side of the body, lean to the right, lift the right skate off the ice first, then the left skate, and the slide is made. The move may be done while skating forward or backward.

In either of the three methods, the blocks should be made at the opponent's stick and puck, not at his body. Don't commit yourself too early or the puck carrier will easily skate around you. Remember, if you're too close to the net, in the 15- to 25-foot range area, let the shot go through unless you're absolutely certain of blocking the shot. While all three methods are very effective to block shots, they have several disadvantages. For example, if you drop or slide too soon you're out of the play and it's no problem for the attacking man to move around you. Also, if the shot gets past you, chances are good that your goalie won't

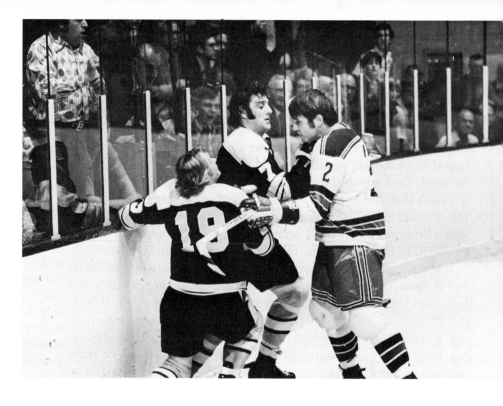

You can have slight disagreements (above), but sometimes it ends up in fighting. But remember that fighting isn't part of the game.

see the puck coming, which could mean a goal. Or even if you make the stop, the puck might bounce off you at an angle and set up the advancing shooter for another shot. In addition, after the shot has been made, it takes time—especially in the case of the baseball slide—to get back on your skates and into the play. Also the puck may get tangled in your knee pads, forcing a face-off in a poor position for your team. But worse for you, unless wearing a mouth guard, you may catch the puck right in your mouth.

Remember that if any player other than the goalie closes his hand on the puck, a minor penalty is imposed on him. You are permitted, however, to stop or "bat" a puck in the air with your open hand. You may also push it along the ice with your hand and the play won't be stopped unless, in the opinion of the referee, you have deliberately directed the puck to a teammate. A penalty is also imposed on a player other than the goalkeeper who deliberately falls on a puck or gathers it into his body. But when dropping to your knees to block a shot, you aren't penalized if the puck is shot under you or becomes lodged in your clothing or equipment, but any use of the hands to make the puck unplayable is illegal.

If you should lose or break your stick, remain in the play, particularly if the puck is in your own defense end. (Remember that playing with a broken stick can draw a penalty, so drop it immediately.) Freeze the puck if you can, or get in position to stop the puck with your body or skate. Body check your opponents if possible. As soon as the puck is frozen or cleared and there is no immediate danger, get a new stick from the bench. Arrangements should be made before the game to have a new stick available if such an emergency arises.

For forwards and defensemen, checking requires good backward and forward skating agility. Practice skating off to the side in both directions and skating the circle both forward and backward regularly.

FIGHTING

Before leaving the subject of defense, we'd like to say a word about fighting. In this hard contact sport, it seems to be a necessary evil. While neither of us has ever backed away from a fight, we both know that they can be most costly—both in time in the penalty box and possible injury. Brad Park missed three games because of a leg injury received in a fight with John McKenzie of Boston. Of course, if a teammate of yours is involved in a fight, be sure to hold the nearest opposing player near you. This is to prevent any ganging up on your teammate. There's also a sort of unwritten rule in hockey that players must drop their sticks and gloves and go at it with their bare fists. Unfortunately, there are times when this rule is not always observed. There are a few players in our league who have a reputation—and not a good one—for fighting with their sticks, and we're pretty sure they justify their reason for doing so on the grounds that they're not good fighters. As far as we are concerned this is no justification at all.

Fighting on ice is a difficult task because of the problem of retaining your balance on skates while delivering a blow. For this reason, most hockey fights are inconsequential affairs. Of course, if there is any secret to winning a hockey fight it can usually be found in the first punch. The surprise element, landing the first blow, puts the opponent off balance, and once this occurs, it is difficult to regain balance in a fight. Another trick used during a fight is that of pulling the opponent's jersey over his head, so that he can't see, and then trying to pound him with the free hand. Still another is to get a bear hug on the adversary and wrestle him down to the ice.

Nobody can deny that fighting is seemingly part of the game. Yet, we don't consider fighting a major aspect of our game, and we'd like to repeat, don't start fights—it won't improve your hockey-playing ability.

The Offensive Game—
a Team on Attack

To win, a team must score at least one more goal than its opponent. Everyone likes to get into the scoring act and it's one of hockey's greatest thrills to score your first NHL goal.

Rod Gilbert remembers his first one vividly: "In 1962, I was playing with the Kitchener-Waterloo team of the Canadian Eastern Professional League. Then, one Friday, during a game against Sault Ste. Marie, I got the surprise of my life. About halfway through the first period, our general manager came over to the bench and told me that I was going to New York. I almost ran to the airport.

"I arrived in New York in time to work out with the Rangers for game No. 2 of their Stanley Cup series against the Toronto Maple Leafs. I never expected to be put on a regular line, but they put me with Johnny Wilson and Dave Balon. I got an assist on a goal by Wilson. Two nights later before more than 16,000 spectators in Madison Square Garden, I scored two goals in our 4–2 victory. On the all-important first one, Allan Stanley made a bad pass. I picked up the puck and walked right in on Johnny Bower. I saw an open corner and slid the puck across the ice into the net. I was then twenty-one, and the two goals and three assists in four games of that Stanley Cup playoff still rank as my biggest thrill."

The big thrill for Brad Park came on February 23, 1969, in a game against the Boston Bruins in New York. "The Rangers were leading 8–0 midway through the third period when I drilled a 50-foot slap shot past Eddie Johnston in the Bruins' net for my first goal in the big league. I threw my arms into the air and jumped and then I landed . . . on my face. Right on my puss!"

While it's a thrill to score goals, it should be remembered that

The first time Brad Park did his goal-scoring war dance he fell flat on his face.

The G-A-G line strikes again!

hockey is a team game, and the most important factor in a team's success is how well it functions as a unit. Even in a game as fast as ours, every team has a plan of action, and the winners are usually the guys who carry out that plan best. Take the Montreal Canadiens. It's well known that for years the Canadiens' battle plan has been to head-man the puck. That means that when Montreal is on the attack, the puck carrier will always try to pass to a man ahead of him. That strategy prevents many offside calls and keeps the flow of the attack moving forward.

The Rangers favor an attack that places a man in the slot, cruising in that area about midway between face-off circles. We'll send two men in after the puck—for example, Jean Ratelle and Vic Hadfield if it's on the left side or Jean and Rod if it's on the right side—and leave the third guy back in the slot. The advantage of this strategy is that the two players on the puck always know where the third one is. If they win control, a quick pass to the slot can often lead to a goal. If they lose control, the man in the slot can always get back in time to prevent a clear breakaway.

INDIVIDUAL ATTACKING TACTICS

Offense is a team effort. But a team is made up of individuals, each with a slightly different style of play. It is up to the coach to put these various player styles together to make an effective offense. For example, on our G-A-G (goal a game) line, Vic Hadfield is considered bullish, Jean Ratelle is the graceful member, while Rod's style is usually called slick. The blending of these three different styles has made a successful line.

Players should choose the style that best takes advantage of their strong points (such as rugged physique or skating speed), and protects their weak points (such as lack of size). Look around the National Hockey League. Guys like Henri Richard, Mike Walton, and Dave Keon aren't big bruisers. But they can fly on that ice and their style of play is based on their speed and agility. Though we all can't help admire the player who, in spite of his lack of weight and size, plays a rugged contact style, we can't hold the same admiration for his intelligence. Therefore, when considering the style of play and adapting the tactics you're going to use, keep in mind your physique and special talents. In this way you'll be able to get best results for the energy expended and perhaps avoid

It can be quite difficult to get past a good poke-checking defenseman.

many unnecessary injuries and disappointments.

Beating the Checker. Since hockey is a game of moves and counter-moves, your individual attacking style must be based on your talents as well as those of an opposing player. In determining what technique you're going to employ to beat a checker, for instance, you must ask yourself such questions as: Am I faster than he? Does he play the body or the puck? Can he be deked easily? What is his favorite type of check? Does he back up? Does he like to hit hard?

When bringing the puck up the ice, of course, you don't have time to perform such a mental quiz. However, spend some time when on the bench or while talking to your teammates trying to analyze the style of play of the opposing players. By developing such an analytical attitude, you'll have a fine mental book on your opponent and you'll be able to react instinctively whenever he approaches. For example, if the guy is big and rough but on the slow side, you'll know the more you make him move and maneuver, the better your chances of getting around him. On the other hand, if he's a fast player, you should try a move that will make him come to you and then use body deception or a stickhandling trick to get you by. Here are some other general suggestions on how to cope with the various types of checkers:

1. If the checker is strong on one side (for instance, if he has a good poke check, like a J. C. Tremblay), fake to that side. Chances are good that he'll probably be only too willing to employ his best weapon.

2. If he likes to body check, fake as if you're going straight at him. Then as he starts to move for a check, deke him by changing direction or pace. A man who prefers to play the body often can be beaten by such power-skating tricks as zigzags, cutbacks, shifts, and stops and starts because they spoil his timing. Stickhandling tricks and other deke maneuvers in which you get close to the checker are less effective against a good body checker.

3. If he plays the puck, invite a check and then deke him. Such a player is also sometimes fooled by stickhandling tricks.

4. If a checker has the habit of backing up, slow down and let him. Always try to force him into making the first commitment, and then make your move to go around him. If he's close to the goal, let him back up as far as he wishes within the time at your disposal.

5. If he's a headlong checker or a charger, use power skating tricks and shifts to turn his aggressiveness against him. Don't try maneuvers that take you too close to him.

6. If a checker likes to come at you from the side, make sure to keep your body between him and the puck. Use an outside carry when bringing the puck up ice.

7. If a guy likes to cling to you or go with you rather than make a check, employ changes of pace and stops and starts to throw him off. Remember that the player on the attack should generally be able to obtain some free ice on his opponent since he knows what he's going to do, and the checker must wait to react until the move is undertaken.

While it's wise to compile a book on each checker you face, it's important to keep in mind that he's probably doing the same thing about you. Therefore, don't always follow the same skating pattern and stickhandling maneuver as you go up the ice. Move from side to side one time, and straight the next. Never get in a groove. Also, if your dekes and other stickhandling techniques are not working, perhaps you're using the same trick too often. But if a checker has your number, find out why and then correct your fault. Of course, there are some checkers you just can't seem to beat no matter how hard you try. Bob Plager of St. Louis, Don Awrey of Boston, and

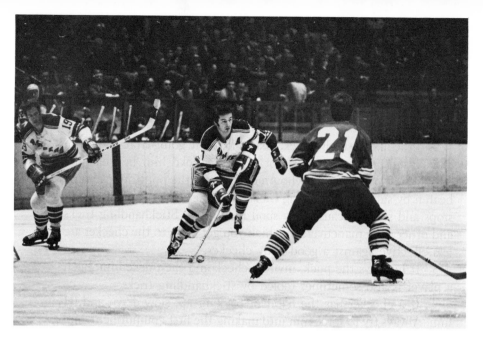

A good deke can frequently get around a defenseman (top). Some defensemen stick very closely to their man (bottom).

Bill White of Chicago give Rod all kinds of fits.

There are times in a game, of course, when you may have to face two checkers. The basic principle in such a situation is to maneuver so that you take the defense pair one by one. For example, if the defense pair is composed of players who like to body check, a good trick is to skate toward a spot between the checkers as if you're going to attempt to split them. Then, as they move together to lower the boom on you, slip the puck between them and swing around the pair, or deke as if going through after the puck and then swing around.

Another good maneuver is to skate directly at one of the checkers and then veer to the inside so as to fake the other player into getting ready to give you the works. At this point, quickly veer to the outside and you have only one checker to beat. Another good move is to skate as if you're trying to swing around one side and then, as the defenders start to spread out, cut back quickly between them.

A fake shot between the defensive pair or between the legs of one particular checker is another good move. After faking the shot, stick-handle the puck out and around opposing players. Frequently, by faking a shot aimed at one defender, you can neutralize both men. The player at whom the shot is aimed usually will tense in a protective reaction, giving up the split second needed to get around him, while his partner most likely will move toward the goal to clear a possible rebound. Of course, another trick is a fake shot followed by an actual one. This is especially good when the defenders are fairly close to the net.

Frequently you may be standing still with the puck, waiting for a teammate to break for a pass, or you may arrive at a loose puck at the same instant as an opponent does, and in either case the opponent may jab at the puck to knock it away. A simple but effective move to prevent this from occurring is to hold the blade of your stick over the front edge of the puck so that it forms sort of a shield of protection and any jab at the puck by an opposing player will merely contact your stick blade and not touch the puck at all.

Beating the Goalie. A question we're both frequently asked is, "Which NHL goalie do you find easiest to beat?" It's a reasonable question, and our answer is simply that they're all tough. National Hockey League records show that in a penalty-shot situation, when an unguarded player skates in alone for a play, the odds are with the goalie. (The record book also reveals the interesting fact that Wayne Connelly, when he was with the Minnesota North Stars, is the only

Once you get past the defenseman your problem is the goalie.

player to score a penalty shot in a Stanley Cup playoff game.)

Theoretically, the goalkeeper always has the last word. You may notice a bit of space on the right side and decide to shoot for it on the assumption that the goalie is unaware of its existence. But the goalie may have left the space just to lure the shot to that spot. Then he'll suddenly cover it up and block the shot. Another time the forward aims for the open space, which the goalie hasn't left deliberately. Still the goalie has the final say because he has the opportunity to thrust out his skate, stick, pad, or glove to cover up the opening. That's why we'd never say a goalie is easy to beat.

However, there are a few tricks we've found that make it easier to beat a goalie. For instance, sometimes it's possible to make the goalie move first by heading for a spot just outside one of the goalposts, as if you're going to shoot the puck in from that side of the net. This action will bring the goalie over to that side of the goal. Then, when you're fairly close to the goalkeeper, cut quickly at a right angle across the net toward the other goalpost. This forces the goaltender to shift again since he must go across with you in case you shoot it suddenly into the far side of the cage. While moving across the goal, watch the goalie carefully. If he starts quickly across with you, shoot low and hard at the side of the cage the netminder has just abandoned. If the goalkeeper is slow in moving across, shoot at the open net on the side of the net to which he's heading. Often the goalie will slide across to stop the shot. If he does this, you can shoot high over him.

Another good trick is the so-called backhand to forehand shift. Carrying the puck in front of you, shift the puck, when nearing the goal, to your backhand as if you're planning to shoot for the far corner (to the left of the goalie if a right shot). Start the shot but rather than letting the puck go, slip it quickly to your forehand side and shoot for the other side of the cage. Of course, this maneuver can also be accomplished forehand to backhand.

The fake shot is an effective deke because often it makes the goalie move first. As you come in on him and are about 15 to 20 feet from the goal, slow down or come to a dead stop, and fake a shot to either side of the netminder. If he slides out to cover the shot, you can step back and shoot over him as he goes down or slip the puck under him as he goes down, or shift to either side and fire the puck behind the goaltender as he comes sliding out. If the goalie remains on his feet but moves to cover your deke, you can shoot to the other side or any spot he may leave open by his action. If the goalkeeper glides out on his feet, attempting to stop the shot by cutting down the angle, you can veer around him and slide the puck behind him into the open cage.

The goalkeeper who comes out and cuts down the angle gives Rod the most trouble. It may sound paradoxical, but all goalies will tell you that the closer you come in on them the easier it is for them to prevent a goal. As the puck is advanced closer, it boils down to a battle of wits between the netminder and you, and if the puck is carried close to the net the goalie has an even chance of fooling you because he may make a sudden dive, or sprawl, or smother that will take you by surprise and upset your plans before you can pull any of your tricks. Most forwards agree that the ideal distance seems to be 10 to 15 feet out from the goalie. Also it's best to shoot from directly in front of the goal because from this position you can shoot to either side of the netminder. When you come in from the side, you usually have only one side to shoot at and this gives the goalie the advantage of knowing where the shot is going. When the shot is coming from directly in front of him, he has no choice but to wait to see which way you're going to try to put it in.

One of the major causes of missed goals is indecision on the part of the shooter. If you shoot too soon or get in too close, the goalie has the advantage. But when shooting from the slot—10 to 25 feet out in front

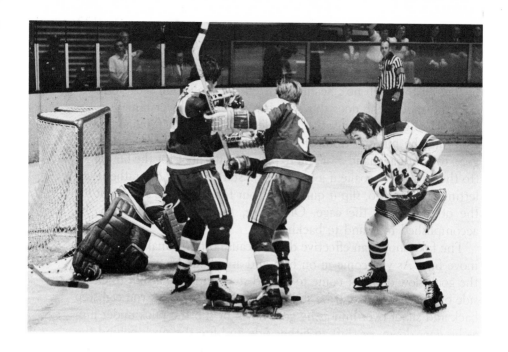

In both instances faulty play by the defenseman helped lead to a score.

of the net—the tables are turned. Also, always try to add new tricks to your scoring repertoire. Remember that the player who gets lazy about developing additional scoring tricks will suddenly find his goal-scoring average dropping off as the opposition gets a "book" on him.

Screens and Scrambles. During the average game there are many chances to shoot on goal from behind a screen formed by either one or more players (opponents or teammates). In such cases, the goaltender's vision is usually obscured completely or partially. When making a screen shot, keep the puck low and aim for an open spot that appears between the players.

Sometimes you can force an opposing defenseman into creating a screen for you. As we stated earlier in this chapter, some defensemen have a habit of backing up too close to the goal. When up against such an opponent, let him back up as far as possible, in front of his goalie, and then snap a low shot through their legs, or between them. Such a shot will frequently get by the netminder without his catching even a glimpse of it.

Many screen-shot opportunities present themselves during wild scrambles in front of the net. Keep alert for such chances. In fact, there are two important points to keep in mind when playing in a scramble: Keep your eye on the puck and keep your stick on the ice. If your stick is on the ice, you'll be ready to sweep a pass out into the net. But if your stick isn't on the ice, the puck will pass by before you have a chance to slap it. The next time you watch a game, count how many loose pucks and pass-outs are missed because a player didn't have his stick on the ice.

Another thing to note while watching your next game is the number of players who will fan on close-in plays or will slap the puck wildly, yards past the goal. Or you'll see a player stop the puck and then attempt to shoot only to be knocked off the puck or checked because he took too long in setting up the shot. Being able to intercept a fast-moving puck and deflect it toward an open spot in the goal area demands a high degree of skill that doesn't just come to a player. It must be practiced.

OFFENSIVE TEAM PLAY

The organization and coordination of the forwards and defense into a unified attack is known as offensive team play. The center in general will set the pace and give direction to the attacking unit. All five men

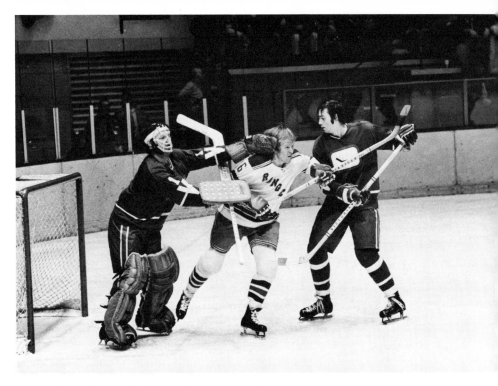

Play in front of goal mouth can get rough.

Brad Park and his defensive partner move up the ice on attack.

should work as a unit, however, and each position must be readily interchangeable in order to fill all of the gaps. But, since the puck will rarely remain in either team's possession for more than 30 seconds, forwards and defensemen must switch instantly, and often, from attack to defense. This makes for a fluidity that defies set play patterns, such as in football and basketball. It is difficult to say "in such a situation, you do this or that," because the speed of play gives the player little chance to recognize static situations. But the hockey player can help himself by thinking of his play in these two phases: "What am I to do on attack?" "What are my duties on defense?" In this chapter we'll cover your duties on attack, whether forward or defenseman.

FORWARDS ON ATTACK

The attacking strategy can usually be divided into two parts: (1) from the defensive end to the attacking blue line; and (2) inside the attacking zone.

From the Defensive End to the Attacking Blue Line. Here are some general rules of play the forwards should follow when starting on an attack:

1. Move the puck up the ice and out of your own end as fast as possible. This should result in the opposition's forecheckers being left behind.

2. Always pass to a man ahead in the clear, rather than stickhandle. When a lead pass is made, follow up as a trailer.

3. If there are no receivers in the open, it is better to lose the puck to a forechecker than to have the puck intercepted in a dangerous pass. If the forechecker steals the puck, you at least have a chance to recover it or to tie him up. If necessary, freeze the puck and force a face-off. Or, fire the puck off the boards and out over your blue line, but try not to ice the puck.

4. In a pass situation, the receiver is as much responsible for getting the puck as the carrier is for getting it to him. In other words, potential receivers must work to get into the open but must not get out of position.

5. When the wingers go back into the corners they should turn always toward the puck, but preferably they should stop, then start back up the ice.

6. An unbreakable rule should be: Never carry the puck in front

of your own net. This shouldn't ever be done in the National Hockey League, but it is. It is extra-perilous for younger players to skate in front of their net with the puck. Too many things can happen to it; it can be poked away, it can start to roll, or you can just lose control of it. It's far better to stay behind your net and look for someone to pass to instead of trying to sneak out in front of your goaltender.

7. Attack on as wide a front as possible; widen out nearly to the boards when flanking the puck carrier. The man in the center carries the puck in on the defense, since he presents a threat to either side.

Inside the Attacking Zone. Here are general rules of play the forward should follow when inside the attack zone:

1. One forward is at all times in scoring position in front of the net. Ten to 15 feet is ideal—closer than that is too easily covered by a defenseman.

2. Always take a shot on goal if you have the puck within the slot, the prime shooting area, unless there is an open partner closer to the net.

3. Be ready to shoot immediately. When you receive the puck in the scoring triangle, your stick should be at your side, on the ice and ready to shoot.

4. If unable to pass to an open forward and not in position to shoot, pass back to your own defensemen who have followed up the attack closely to the point positions (just inside the attacking blue line).

5. Passes are made only to uncovered or open teammates.

6. If no teammate is open and a shot is impossible, stickhandle for position. If you can get around your check, shoot, or draw another check, freeing a teammate for a pass.

7. Never turn your back on the puck.

8. Don't bunch up or one defender will be, in fact, covering more than one attacker.

9. Players without the puck move around to avoid checks and get in the clear for passes.

10. When possession is lost in this zone, the closest man pounces at once on the opposing puck carrier. If this fails and the opponents start out, the two forwards nearest their own goal swing immediately into backchecking roles.

We both are great believers in position hockey—that is, avoidance of roaming all over the ice. Rod, as you know, is a right winger. "That means I'm responsible for the right side of the ice, both on offense and defense. And that's where I stay if I can help it. Sometimes I'll go into the left corner if I'm the first man in after the puck, but generally I keep on my wing. Sure, you'll notice that some crisscrossing is done by the wingmen in the National Hockey League. You can get away with this if your name is Bobby Hull. But generally, it's a wise practice to stay on your side of the ice . . . especially for younger players. If you're a right winger, stay on the right wing. There's less chance of a mix-up in assignments."

Another important thing about playing wing: When you make a run at the net, don't circle behind the cage after you've taken your shot. It may look good but you'll lose 10 or 15 strides in getting back down the ice. And, if you're behind the net, there's no way you can be ready for a rebound off your shot.

We can't say enough about anticipating where the puck is going when a teammate takes a shot. This, to us, is one of the most important aspects of playing hockey. Make a real study of your line mates—their types of shots. You'll be able to tell after a while whether their shots will be on the net or whether they'll go wide. Then, the thing to do is to skate to the spot where the puck will go, whether it's in front of the net or around the boards.

The whole line shouldn't chase the puck into the corners, so we've got a system on the Rangers which works pretty well, we think. Say the puck goes into the opposition's right corner. It's the duty of our center, Jean Ratelle, to go into the corner and dig for the puck. Rod Gilbert will help him, while Vic Hadfield stations himself, as sort of an anchor man, halfway between the blue line and the net and in the center of the ice. That way he's ready to take a pass out or he's ready to break back to help the defense in the event we lose the puck in the corner.

If the players on the same line practice and work together, they'll soon develop a play sense and will often coordinate their thinking and actions very well. While skating and shooting are the most important phases of offensive hockey, don't forget talking. You've got to talk all the while you're on the ice. Help your line mate. Let him know what you're doing and where you are. If he's breaking up ice, you might yell to him, "I'm with you," or "You're all alone." Or you might yell, "I'm covered." Rod is sure that's why our G-A-G line has been so successful. (It is only the second line in the history of the NHL to make over 300 points in a season.) "Of course, the experience of playing for a number of years together helped. Vic Hadfield joined the line in the 1965 season, while Jean Ratelle and I have been playing together for over 20 years. We both played on the same line as fourth-grade students in our home town of Montreal."

In forming an attack, you'll have to use your own judgment when to try to carry the puck in and when to shoot it in ahead of you. A good rule to follow is this: Never throw the puck in when you've got a manpower advantage—say, three on two, or two on one. Try to work it in. However, if your two line mates are covered and there are two defensemen back to make a play on you, then the thing to do is fire the puck in and go after it. That way the defensemen will have to turn to make their play and this is the best time to take the puck from them.

DEFENSEMEN ON THE ATTACK

Very often the defense starts off the attack in their own end by checking an opponent.

From the Defensive End to the Attacking Blue Line. Clearing the puck out of their own end is one of the most important functions of the defense in hockey today. Here are some principles to follow:

1. Once you get the puck in your own end, move speedily away to avoid a check. You may have to use fast reverses behind the net to gain time and space enough to look for a breaking teammate.

2. The pass up to an open teammate is the quickest method. Such a pass must find the teammate open, and must be a crisp pass.

3. The puck-carrying defenseman stickhandles *only* when no teammate is open. Your partner backs you up from his position in front of the net.

4. Both defensemen follow up the ice once a successful breakout has been started.

Inside the Attack Zone. It is important for a defenseman to know how to carry the puck into the offensive zone. But it's even more important to know when. Basically, the forwards should do the attacking. By that we mean never try to carry the puck up the ice when you can pass it. The puck obviously can travel faster than you can. Of course, a defenseman who *can* carry the puck is a vital asset to any team —but as Brad has said, "He must know when to make his move. The best time to stickhandle is after you break up a play and you've got a couple of rival players trapped in your end. If you've got an opening, it's important to move out quickly. When I'm carrying the puck, the forward farthest back on our team takes a look around and if there are three players ahead of him, he usually takes my spot on defense. Or our other defenseman will call to the last forward to hold back until I've completed my play at the other end. It's just as important not to get trapped in the other end. As long as you've got a chance for a goal, stay there, but once the play is broken up, get back to your defensive spot as quickly as possible."

If the puck is in your team's possession deep inside the attack zone, both defensemen move quickly to the point positions. If the puck is in the left corner, the left defenseman moves just inside the blue line at the left boards; his partner is just inside the line at its center. Their positions move quickly to the right when the puck goes into the right corner. From these points, the defensemen may receive passes back from their forwards. With these passes, they have three alternatives: (1) to shoot at the net; (2) to return the pass into the corner if there is any danger that the shot at the net may be blocked by a close opponent; and (3) to pass across to the other defenseman (often used when the other team is short-handed, but dangerous otherwise).

A defenseman must know how to shoot from the blue line. It is a mistaken idea that the best shot is the hardest shot. True, when you're young, that hard shot banging off the boards carries a lot of prestige with it. But in the NHL the only shots that count are the ones that go in the net. It doesn't matter how hard or soft a shot is. Usually, when you're shooting from the point, you'll have to shoot around a player who is charging at you. Try to get it by or past him. That's the first thing to think about. Even if it means your shot will be a little off, it's better to get it past him rather than risk the chance of the puck hitting him and bouncing out to center ice . . . which could lead to a breakaway. The best shot from the point is a low shot since there is less chance of its being blocked.

VARIOUS RUSH SITUATIONS

There are two basic types of attacks in hockey: (1) the spontaneous or rush attack, and (2) the planned or pattern attack. The following are some of the various spontaneous or rush situations that frequently occur when a team moves up ice on attack.

Brad Park (top) waits on the point for the play to develop, while at bottom he takes a slap shot on goal.

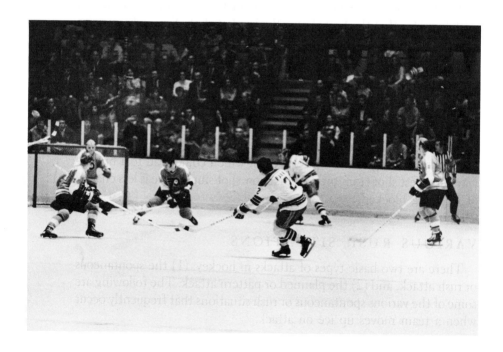

One on Two. Because of the mobility of hockey, there are times during a game in which you may find yourself in possession of the puck with no opponents ahead except a pair of defensemen and no teammates at hand at that moment to help. When this situation arises there are three things you can do. First, you can maneuver until a teammate gets there to give you help. Second, you may work the puck in as far as possible without endangering its possession, take a shot, and fall back. Or three, you can attempt to set up a scoring opportunity by carrying the puck in on your own. Which of the three you do will usually depend on the score of the game, the position of your teammates, and your own individual skills.

If your team is well ahead or is behind and needs goals, you should attempt to set up a scoring play either on your own by working the puck in as close as possible and shooting, or by trying to maneuver into a position from which you can make a pass to an approaching teammate. If your team is ahead by only a goal or two, or the game is tied, you should either shoot and fall back or stickhandle around, keeping possession of the puck near the attacking blue line until a teammate can get close enough for a safe pass. The reason for this is that if you attempt to carry the puck far in past the defense, you may well get checked and give the defense pair a chance to break down the ice with an odd-man advantage.

Breakaway. This situation involves an attacker coming alone on just the goaltender—no defensemen in the play. In this case, as you approach the netminder you should shoot for the corner—either corner from about 15 feet out. When approaching from the wing, you usually have two alternatives (provided you cradle the puck on the stick along your side and not in front of you): (1) shoot on the goal; or (2) fake a shot, pull the puck in front of the goalie, and then slide it into the net. Don't attempt to fake the goalkeeper head on, because you'll then have only about one-third of the net to shoot into by the time you've completed your fake and moved to one side. The secret of the breakaway, as on most scoring plays, is to have the goalie commit himself first. But, one of the major mistakes most players make—and this includes us at times—is that they concentrate so much on how to beat the goaltender that, as a result, they outsmart themselves and never even get off a decent shot.

One on One. When there's one defender against you, there are three alternatives open, depending on how the defender plays you:

1. If the defender doesn't back in, fake a shot and stickhandle around him.

2. If the defender backs in slowly, carry around him into the corner or behind the net, looking for a chance to work out in front to shoot.

3. If the defender backs in fast, or very close to the netminder, shoot a low, ankle-high shot for either corner of the net.

Note how these three alternatives stress the importance of stickhandling with the head up to see what the opponent is doing.

Two on One. How two attackers can get by one defender is a very basic concern in offensive hockey. Remember that the defense alley is the defenseman's strongest playing position. When two attackers move on one defenseman, they should attempt to maneuver him out of the defense alley. Also keep in mind that the defenseman is trying to force you to shoot from outside the alley and preferably from a bad angle. Every effort must be made to shoot from within the alley—the best scoring angle.

In the two-on-one situation, the following plays are effective:

1. A drop pass to your trailing partner may enable you to skate around the defenseman and await a return pass, or a rebound if the partner elects to shoot on goal.

2. If the defenseman stays in the alley, a pass over or under his stick to your teammate may afford him a clear shot at the net or allow you to get into the clear for a return pass.

3. The puck carrier can stop and pass to the other forward who is breaking toward the goal.

Two on Two. When two attackers find two defensemen facing them, they can always be safe in shooting on goal and driving in for the rebound. Of course, in the two-on-two situation, the attackers should try to isolate one defenseman to create a two-on-one advantage. (In hockey, remember that all plays are designed to get a one-man advantage.) The defensemen will try to keep their slightly staggered position; therefore, try to force one defenseman out of position. Use a change of pace to go around the defender on your side. As he forces you into the corner, look for a trailing teammate. If none appears, work behind the attacking net, trying to draw the defender covering in front. If he moves to you, your partner will be left open in front of the net. If in danger of being checked at the blue line, shoot low at the goal, and break in for the rebound.

Three on Two. When three men rush together down the ice after a play is made, it is a common mistake for all three to continue skating straight in almost to the goal line. This is serious because it means that all three are in danger of being trapped if the opponents break out. Furthermore, the two men without the puck are too far in to be in good scoring position. To correct this, whenever three men rush abreast, it should be a rule that one man (either the passer or the wing, whichever one *doesn't* receive the pass) slows down to trail the play, getting into good shooting position approximately 20 to 25 feet from the goal line. He can pick up rebounds, get second chances, and often be in position for a clear shot on goal. All alternatives of the two-on-one situation are applicable here.

Frequently in a three-on-two situation it is possible for a member of the attacking line to isolate one of the defensemen so that there are two on one. For example, as right wing, Rod will frequently try to isolate one of the two defensemen, and thus make the situation actually a two-on-one play for Vic Hadfield and Jean Ratelle. On the ideal three on two, the centerman should carry the puck, and he will dictate the play.

PLAY PATTERNS

Hockey teams don't have elaborate offensive plays as do football and basketball teams. This doesn't mean, however, that you can't set up an offensive pattern in hockey. But, because of the speed of the game, it does mean that an offensive pattern may disintegrate rapidly and a team must quickly adjust. Of course, should a team lose the puck, it shifts from offense to defense at once.

Breakout Patterns. Usually, a team begins its offensive attack from within its own defensive zone. Every hockey team has its own type of breakout plays that are planned by the coach.

Our first breakout pattern, which the Rangers use and which is similar to the one employed by Montreal, has one defenseman with the puck behind the net and one defenseman in front. The wings come back deep into the corners close to the boards and the center circles well out in front of the net. From this basic pattern four options are possible:

1. The defenseman can carry the puck out himself if unchecked. The wingers turn, and the center turns into the slot and moves up the ice with the defenseman.

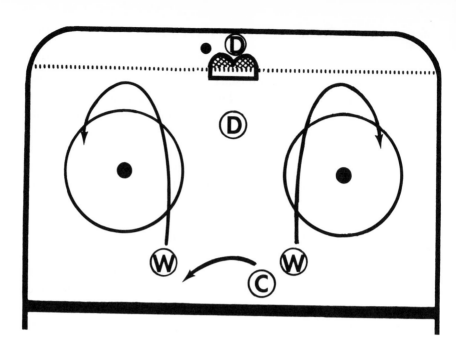

Three basic breakout patterns.

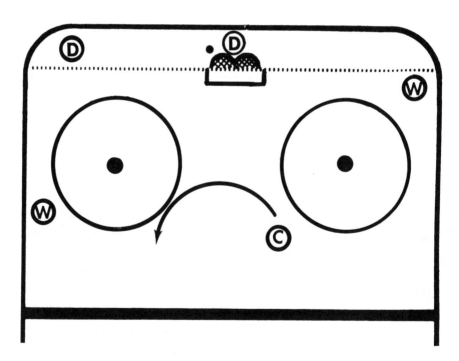

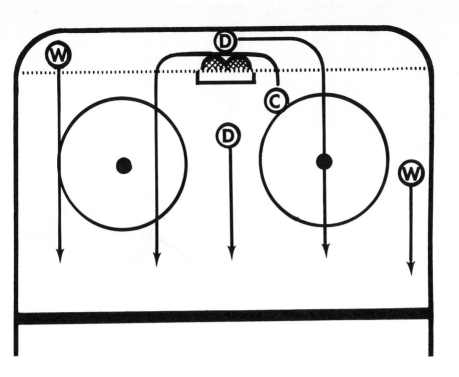

2. If the forechecker moves toward the defenseman, the pass can be made to the winger on the side to which the defenseman is breaking. The centerman swings and is ready to take the quick lead pass while breaking down the ice.

3. The defenseman can pass to the centerman who is circling in front of the goal.

4. The defenseman can also start out on one side, attract the forechecker, then stop and pass off the boards behind the net to the unchecked opposite winger. The center is again ready to take the lead pass if necessary from the winger. When carrying the puck out from behind the net, the puck carrier should cut as close to the goal as possible. This will force any forechecker to stay close to the puck carrier. If the puck carrier goes too wide, the one forechecker will be in essence covering two men, the puck carrier and the winger or defensemen along the boards near the corner.

The second breakout pattern, frequently used by Boston, uses one defenseman behind the goal and one in the corner. The wingers are in their positions by the boards with the one on the opposite side of the defenseman, deeper in the corner. The center circles well out in

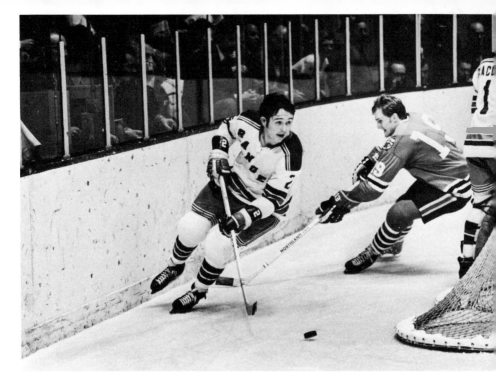

Brad Park beats a forechecker and starts the Ranger breakout pattern.

front of the net. From this basic pattern, the options for the defenseman behind the net are very similar to the previous options:

1. Carry the puck out himself if unchecked.
2. Pass to the winger on the side to which the defenseman is breaking.
3. Break out and pass to the circling defenseman.
4. Pass off the boards behind the net to the opposite, weak-side winger.
5. Pass off to his other defenseman, who has moved from in front of the goal to the corner. If the puck is passed to the defenseman in the corner, he has these breakout options: He may *(a)* pass back to the defenseman behind the net; *(b)* pass to the right or left winger, who are waiting at their positions by the boards; *(c)* pass to the swinging defenseman; or *(d)* carry the puck out himself.

The principle of the second breakout pattern is to overload one side of the ice so that you have at least one extra man against the opposition's forechecker.

On some teams the breakout is started in the corners rather than behind the net. In the two examples illustrated, both start with the puck in the corner, controlled by a defenseman. Of course, all the breakout plays shown represent a few of the many maneuvers that can be employed. However, it's not wise to make your attack too complicated at this point. Remember that the more the puck is passed around in the defensive zone as the attack is being formed, the greater the chance of losing control. For instance, as we said earlier, headmanning is good strategy, but before doing so, make sure you get the puck out of your end. In other words, head-man the puck behind your own blue line only if the receiver is well in the clear. Head-manning is more applicable when you're outside of your own blue line.

Blue-Line Techniques. Blue-line technique involves getting the puck into the offensive zone after you have it out over your own blue line. Here are some of the common ways this is accomplished.

1. One method has the center move the puck over the blue line, stop, and then pass to a breaking winger. If the breaking winger can't get around the defenseman, he can back pass to the following center. Or, if the defensemen fall off toward the wingers when the center carries over the blue line, then he moves in himself and takes the shot.

2. The drop pass is one of the most effective moves in hockey and can be made by the center or winger after crossing the blue line. The puck carrier moves in on the defenseman and the teammate cuts in behind to pick up the drop pass. The original puck carrier breaks for the goal to screen the goalkeeper from a shot on goal and to pick up any rebound in front of the net. When the trailing forward picks up the drop pass, he should be heading directly toward the goal so that he can shoot immediately.

3. One of hockey's most difficult pattern plays to defend against is the double drop. It is started with the centerman carrying the puck across the other team's blue line. A good center will slow down through the center ice zone, backing the other team's defensemen into their own zone and giving his own wingers time to skate up and position themselves for the play. The centerman drops the puck near the middle of the rink and then skates in to take one of the defensemen out of the play. One winger swoops in, picks up the puck, and pretends that he is going to shoot on goal. But he, too, drops the puck and skates in to take out the other defenseman, or screen the goalie's view. The third man, the other winger, is the trailer. He bursts in after them, picks up the puck, and usually has a chance to swoop right in for a good shot on goal. The crossover of wingers that happens in the double drop helps

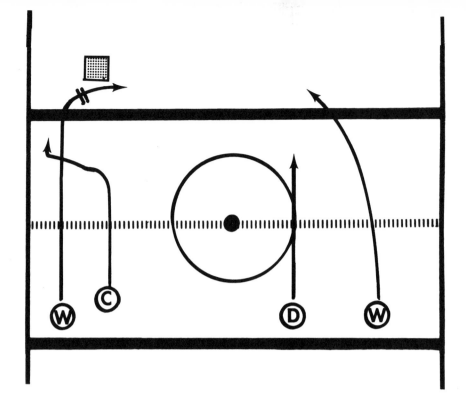

Basic center ice attack patterns.

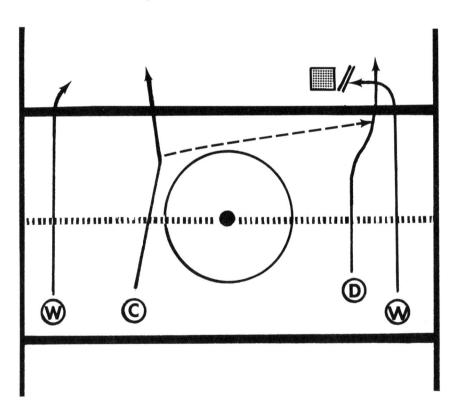

confuse the defenders and draws the defense out of position.

4. The fake drop pass is also very effective and follows the same pattern as the drop pass, only in this case the puck carrier fakes as though he is going to drop to the trailing forward, keeps the puck, and goes around the defenseman.

5. The back pass can be used effectively when the winger is carrying the puck in and the covering defenseman drops back deep. In this case the winger passes the puck back to the trailing center or he may also pass to the other winger who might be free in front of the net.

6. When moving the puck over the blue line, the center may shoot the puck into the corner for a fast-breaking winger who retrieves the puck and then passes to the center or the other winger. The center may also shoot the puck off the boards so that it rebounds to the breaking winger for a shot on goal.

The puck is often shot into the corner by the centerman when his wingers are ahead of him and he can't make the pass at the blue line. In any case, the center trails to the puck side. Remember to shoot the puck in only if you can't carry it across the blue line or in order to avoid an offside play.

Not everyone can chase the puck into the corners, so we've got a system on the Rangers which works pretty well, we think. Say the puck goes into the opposition's left corner, it's the duty of the center to go into the corner and dig for the puck. The left winger will help him while the right winger stations himself, as sort of an anchor man, halfway between the blue line and net and in the center of the ice. That way he's ready to take a pass out or he's ready to break back to help the defense in the event we lose the puck in the corner.

The secret of strong offense is organization. There will, of course, be many situations when you must ad lib, but if you have practiced a number of basic pattern plays such as those just given, you'll have developed a play sense and will probably come up with a variation of one of the plays you have been practicing. This is why time spent practicing pattern plays is always worthwhile even though the situation for the pattern play may never quite happen.

OFFENSIVE STYLES OF PLAY

Before getting into the so-called special offensive situations such as face-offs and power plays, let's take a quick look at styles of play. We said "quick" because style of play is completely up to your coach, but

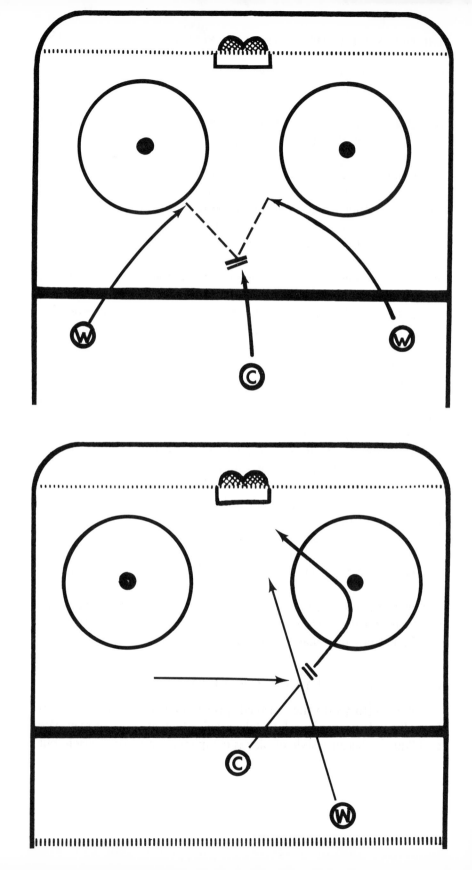

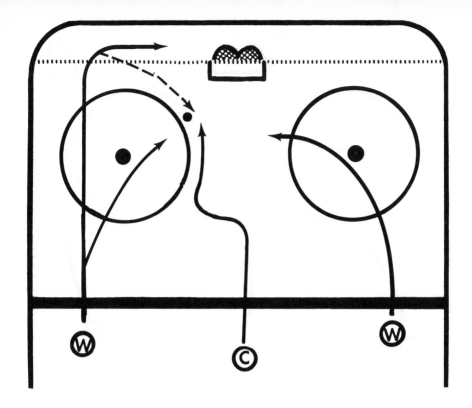

Six basic methods of bringing the puck into the attacking zone (see also p. 154).

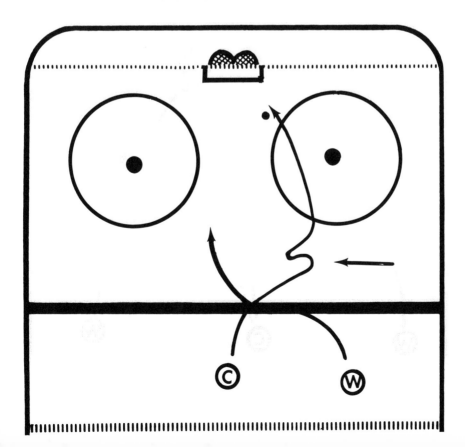

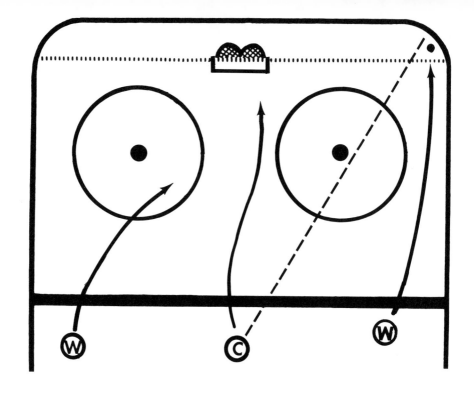

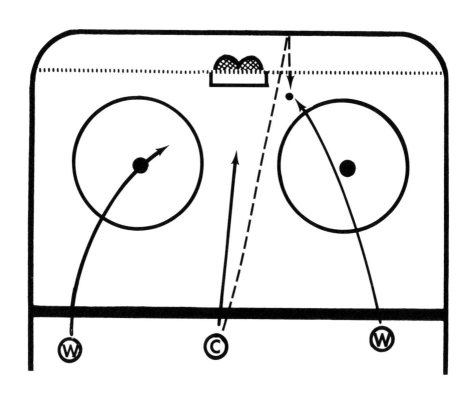

remember that he, by employing carefully planned strategy, tactics, and player personnel, can often defeat a team superior in actual individual playing skill.

The style of play for a team depends generally upon the philosophy of the coach. In many cases, his philosophy is based on the way he played as an individual or the way the team of which he was a member played. Another important factor is player talent available. Coaches in the NHL do their best to trade for, select, or purchase players who will provide a balanced team that can play any style of hockey. But a minor league or college coach has to make do with the material given him.

Here are three offensive styles of play generally used today. They are:

The Rushing Game. The basis of the rushing game is to overwhelm the opposition by disorganizing them and forcing errors in the opposing defensive zone through constant application of offensive pressure. To accomplish this, a team must employ aggressive forechecking and must resort to every possible tactic to keep the puck in the opponent's portion of the ice. Both defensemen play well up with the forwards, but all players must be able to skate at breakneck speed back down the ice into their own defensive zone if play shifts in that direction. It's most important for the team using the rushing game to keep the pace of the play at fever pitch.

To play a rushing game, a team needs fast, strong skaters who have the physical makeup and temperament for aggressive play. All the members of the team must also be good at both forechecking and backchecking and they mustn't be afraid to use their bodies when necessary. Strict position play isn't too important. And while passing plays are a significant part in the success of such a style of game, the paramount factor is to get the puck inside the opponent's defensive zone and keep it there. This means that the puck will be shot rather than carried in and then followed in by all five players. There are, of course, variations of the rushing game, such as increased use of definite play patterns.

The Tight Game. This style of play is basically a conservative one —few offensive chances are taken. This doesn't mean, however, that teams playing a tight game throw away any goal-scoring chances. Rather, they don't force opportunities by taking great risks. For example, when playing a tight game, only two forwards make up the rush into the attacking zone. It can be the center and one wingman, or both wingers, depending on the position of the puck as it crosses the attacking blue line, but one forward always trails on the lookout for loss of the puck. The defensemen only move up to join attack if there's a clear opportunity for a goal. While the team does little or no forechecking, the ability of the players to backcheck is vital to a tight-game style of play. Because of need for this close checking, positional play is important, too. The ability to break fast is also of great value if full advantage is to be taken of any loose play by the opponents. In other words, the tight game is really an opportunistic style of play. For this reason, it's very important that every player on the team conform to the tight style at all times and not try for goals unless a definite opportunity exists.

The Pattern Game. The basic principle of this style is that by passing the puck in play patterns, scoring opportunities will present themselves. It is based on clever passing and well-planned maneuvers. Positional play is important, too. But a pattern game style is, more or less, strictly a team game with each player playing an equally important role. That is, there's no place in it for the individualist, no matter how talented he may be. The whole idea is pass, pass, and pass. Such a system isn't usually geared at a very high pace and should concentrate on setting up passing play patterns.

The team style of offensive hockey in the NHL can change almost as quickly as the puck can travel down the rink. In other words, all NHL teams have the personnel to change the type of play almost at will, depending, of course, on the score. The best example of this that we know involves the Maple Leafs when playing at home. They usually start the game playing patterns. If they get a goal ahead, they play tight; but if they get behind, they play the rushing game.

FACE-OFFS

Winning face-offs is important to the success of any hockey team. Since, during face-offs, there is little or no movement of players, a team can get organized to set up for certain plays. In fact, sometimes a team will force a face-off by lobbing the puck into the stands, holding it against the boards, or causing a deliberate offside, just to get a play underway. There's an old adage in hockey that says that the team that wins face-offs wins the game. The reason, of course, is quite obvious: Since most hockey games have at least 50 face-offs, the team that controls the puck from the majority of them has the better chance of winning.

There are some excellent face-off artists in the NHL. We have Jean

Ratelle, Pete Stemkowski, and Phil Goyette on the Rangers. Others in the league include Pit Martin and Stan Mikita of the Black Hawks, Phil Esposito of the Bruins, Norm Ullman of the Maple Leafs, and Alex Delvecchio of the Red Wings, to name a few. While the center is usually the person involved in the face-off, every player should know how to take a face-off because in case of a face-off violation, an official may order you to take it.

If you're the player taking the face-off, remember that in most instances you'll be playing your opponent's stick, not the puck. That is, the winning of a face-off generally depends upon whether you can manage to bat his stick out of the way and get yours on the puck. To do this successfully, both skill and strength are important.

To obtain the most power from the stick, concentrate your weight and muscle on the bottom hand. By increasing the leverage at this point, you'll be able to resist your opponent's effort to knock your stick away and still have enough power left to get the puck back to a teammate behind you. This can usually be accomplished best by using a quick snapping motion of your wrists, much like a scissors movement. For example, if you're a right-handed shooter and wish to make a backhand pass, your left hand is at the top of the stick and your right is well down on the shaft to provide leverage. Your weight should be straight ahead. Then, to bring the puck around and away from your opponent's stick after it has been dropped, pull the right hand toward you as the left comes forward.

Advance knowledge of your face-off opponent and of the official who will be dropping the puck is most helpful in gaining the draw. For instance, some players will always go after their opponent's stick, while a few, such as a Stan Mikita, like to go for the puck as soon as it hits the ice. While most players favor their backhand on the draw, some prefer their forehand and will even go backward on their forehand. Keep in mind, however, that experienced face-off men will change their style on occasions.

Before the puck is dropped, of course, you must decide on what you're going to do. Are you going directly after the puck or are you going first for your opponent's stick? Are you going to tie up his stick and play the puck with your skates as you move forward? Are you going to your backhand? Are you going to your forehand? Whatever you decide, here are several tricks that may help to win face-offs:

1. Check your opponent's stance. Usually if he's leaning away from you, he's going to go backward with the puck. If he's

One of the most important things to do in a face-off situation is to watch how the official drops the puck.

leaning the other way, he probably will go forward.

2. Watch the official from the corner of your eye to anticipate the exact moment when the puck will be dropped. Move with his hand.

3. As the puck is dropped, quickly slap your stick against your opponent's to knock it away, and then sweep the puck back. Aim at a spot about 4 inches above the heel of his stick, using your stick blade.

4. If your opposing face-off man generally resorts to the slapping of your stick, just lift your stick off the ice when the puck is dropped, and when he slaps at your stick it just won't be there. Then after you have lifted your stick you can either bring it down quickly and pass the puck backward to a teammate or you can bring it down quickly, pick up the puck, and advance it yourself.

5. Another good trick is to block the opposing player's stick by quickly placing your blade between his and the puck, holding your stick with a firm grip and leaning on it to make your stick difficult to move. Then, when his stick is stopped, flip the puck quickly back to a teammate.

Jean Ratelle wins a face-off and passes to
Rod Gilbert to get the attack in motion.

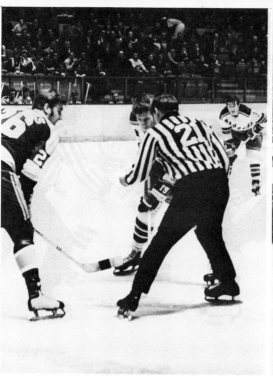

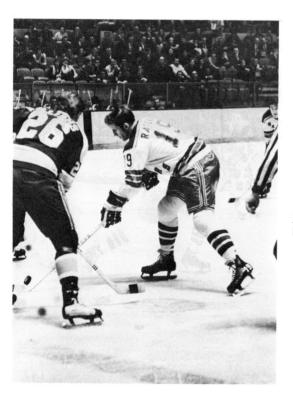

Jean Ratelle wins a face-off and uses a backhand pass.

6. When the puck is dropped, give your stick a quick quarter turn so that the entire blade of the stick is flat on the ice in the form of a hook. Then, taking a sudden, pull-away, backward-skating stride, simultaneously pull the puck sharply toward you with the hook of your stick blade. This trick is practical only when the official drops the puck gently, and remember that you must have sufficient weight on the stick so that the puck can "yank" in your direction.

7. As the puck is dropped, move the blade of your stick quickly forward and then turn the toe of the blade of your stick toward the side (to the right if right shot) and pull the blade quickly backward.

8. Another good face-off pass trick is to tilt your stick blade to one side, cocking the wrists just before the puck is dropped. As the puck hits, the blade can then be whipped across to flick the puck either ahead or aside.

9. When the puck is dropped, quickly rotate in a half turn so that you'll be actually facing your own goal and will have the stick blade parallel to the sideboards. As you make this move, slap the puck through the skates or by the skates of the opposing face-off man to a teammate who moved up the ice for this pass as soon as the puck was dropped by the official.

10. As a change of pace, reverse the grip of your lower hand on the stick to increase speed and power for a quick draw.

11. A left shooter draws best to his left, a right shooter to his right. To prevent your opponent from drawing to his best side, drive your stick to that side of his stick and hold it forcefully there.

12. If you don't win the face-off, create a stalemate; this is the next best thing to winning. Frequently, if you've alerted a teammate to come in and pick up the loose puck, it's wise especially in the defensive zone to tie up your opponent's stick.

13. A face-off must *start* evenly for both players with neither having an unfair advantage. Therefore, if the opposing face-off man is "cheating" by not staying square with his skates before the puck is dropped, or if he is interfering with you before the puck is dropped by skating into you, back off from the face-off; don't stay in ready position and attempt to bring the fact to the official's attention. Frequently, before this can be done, the puck is dropped and won by your opponent. The only way you can insist that he face off properly is by backing off and waiting until your chances are even.

14. As a rule, it's not wise to use the same face-off trick each time. Vary it depending on where the face-off is and with whom you're

facing off. Of course, if you find a face-off technique that beats an opponent regularly, stick to that method until he gets wise.

Once you have control of the puck at the face-off, be ready to get moving immediately to a specific position. In fact, once the puck is dropped, every player on the team has a specific position and task to perform whether his team wins the draw or not. If your team controls the puck on the face-off, you and your teammates must be ready to go on offense; if the other team wins the draw, your team must be prepared to play defense. The face-off formations or plans vary slightly from team to team, depending primarily on the particular strategic thoughts of a coach and the talent of his players. But one fact that doesn't change is that regardless of where the face-off takes place—in the attacking zone, neutral zone, or defensive zone—each player has a specific position and duty. On page 164, we've shown the basic formations used by the New York Rangers in the attacking zone.

Face-Offs at Center Ice. Play is started here at the beginning of each period and after each goal. When taking the draw at center ice, the best move is to try to bring the puck back to one of your defensemen. Since the opposing players must stay back of the center ice line until after the puck is dropped, your chances of obtaining control of the puck are excellent if the draw is back. Most centers prefer to take the draw on their backhand. For example, if you're a left shot, you would generally get the puck back to your left defenseman. As a change of pace, of course, you could take the puck on the forehand so that you move it backward to the right defenseman.

Just after the face-off has been taken, the forwards must screen off their men until the defenseman safely has control of the puck. By screening, we don't mean to interfere with the opponent, but rather keep your body in between your opponent and the puck until your side gets it. Rod remembers a game recently against Toronto in which Dave Keon, their center, sent the puck back as he was supposed to, but it took a crazy bounce over their defenseman's stick. "Because the opposing winger hadn't screened me, I was able to break in from the face-off, grab the loose puck, and skate right in on their goalie and score the only goal of the game. Unfortunately, for us, this has happened a few times to the Rangers, too." In other words, it's most important that the forwards screen their men until your team has possession of the puck.

Once your team has the puck, there are several ways the center or face-off man can start the attack. For example, after your defenseman has the puck in his control, you can permit your opponent to skate by you to forecheck the defense. Then your defenseman can wait a few seconds and simply pass back to you in the face-off circle. From there, you can take off for the attacking zone. Another possible maneuver is for you to skate off the opposing winger to the side on which the defenseman has the puck and have your winger break in the face-off circle to take the pass from the defenseman. Of course, it is sometimes possible for you to tie up your opposing face-off man on the draw and have either of your wingers break into the circle behind you to pick up the loose puck and start the attack.

While feeding the puck back is the most common procedure in center-ice face-offs, there are a few occasions when you may wish to shoot the puck quickly into your attacking zone and hope that by vigorous forechecking your opponents will commit an error. To accomplish this, you should shoot the puck ahead on your forehand from the draw, and the winger on that side should break quickly into your attacking zone in hopes of recovering the puck.

Face-Offs at Your Blue Line. When the face-off is in the neutral zone, but near your blue line, the draw should always go back to your defensemen so that your team can move to the attack.

Face-Offs at the Attacking Blue Line. Again the draw can go back to the defenseman, who can then either carry the puck or dump it into the attacking zone. Or, the puck can shoot ahead on the draw to a forward breaking into the attacking zone. Frequently when Dale Rolfe and Brad Park are defense in this situation, "One of us will move up fast before the puck is dropped to screen off an opposing forward. Then our winger on that side moves wide to the boards. Either Dale or I then moves directly behind our center. Once the puck is dropped, our centerman attempts to get it ahead to our wide winger, who has broken into the zone. If he's successful, we'll usually have a good shot on the goal."

Face-Offs in the Offensive Zone. When taking a face-off in the attacking zone, there are five basic maneuvers you can make:

1. Take a shot on goal. When the puck is dropped, you can take a quick shot on goal while the two forwards break for the possible rebound.

2. Draw back to the defenseman who has moved up in the slot for the shot. The forwards screen the shot.

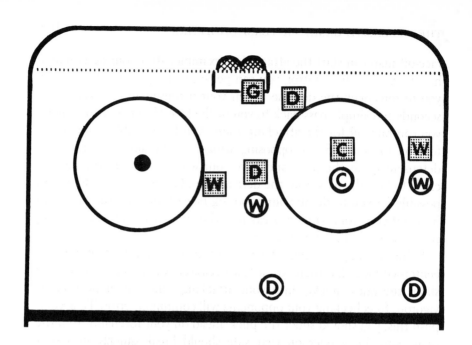

Face-off position for left-hand shot centerman (top) and right-hand shot centerman (bottom).

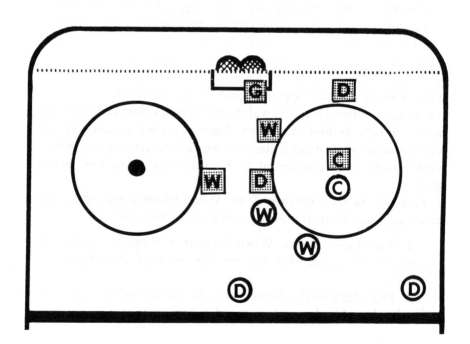

3. Draw back to the winger, set back near the top of the face-off circle. From there, he can take a quick shot on goal.

4. Draw back to the defensemen on the point, who may shoot or pass off.

5. Draw to the winger who has remained at the boards. He, in turn, passes back to the defenseman for the shot or pass.

The main principle to follow on face-offs in the attacking zone is to set up a position pattern and take quick advantage of possession. Which of the maneuvers should be employed will generally depend on which face-off circle is to be used for the draw and the type of shot the face-off players have. For instance, if you're a left shot, facing off in the right circle, the most normal for your use would be maneuvers 1, 2, and 3. On the other hand, if you're a right shot, facing off in the right circle, maneuvers 1, 4, and 5 will generally be best. The illustration here shows the usual player position patterns for both face-off circles and the type of shots.

Information on how face-offs should be taken in the defensive zone and during short-handed situations are given in Chapter 7.

THE POWER PLAY

Very few hockey games are played without penalties being called. Frequently a team's ability to score goals when the opposition is short-handed will decide the final outcome of the game. During the 1971–72 season, the Rangers scored 60 power-play goals in 257 attempts while our opposition had 44 in 282 tries. Of our 60 goals, Brad scored eight and Rod had six, while Vic Hadfield set a Ranger record of 23 power-play goals.

The attacking team makes one major change on a power play; it usually puts out only one defenseman. That is, most teams on power plays will use their highest-scoring regular line—center, left wing, and right wing—up front, one defenseman who has a fairly accurate power shot on one side, and a forward with a strong and accurate shot on the other. The latter two players are called the point men—the guys who'll station themselves just inside the attacking blue line and set up the plays. The typical power-play combination for the Rangers is the G-A-G line, with Bobby Rousseau and Brad on the points. This unit scored 46 of our 60 power-play goals during the 1971–72 season.

There was a time when teams could score three or four times on one

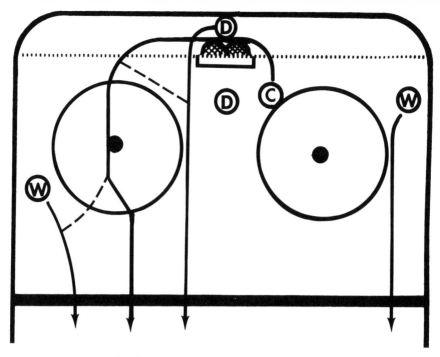

A typical power-play breakout formation.

penalty. That was when a penalized player was kept off the ice for the full 2 minutes on a minor penalty. But the Montreal Canadiens of the early 1950's became so proficient at using the manpower edge that a decision was made to let the penalized team return to full strength as soon as the team with the extra skater scored. Of course, Rod, a little older than Brad, remembers very well the team that forced that change. "They were my boyhood heroes: Doug Harvey and Bernie Geoffrion on the points; Rocket Richard, Jean Beliveau, and Dickie Moore up front. They made the puck do tricks, and in two minutes it was nothing for them to score two or three goals and turn a game completely around. Now, of course, as soon as one goal is scored, the penalty is terminated and the power play is over."

When on a power play, take full use of the penalty time and employ precise and accurate puck control in order to get good shots on goal. Our coach, Emile Francis, always stresses that we must get at least one good, clean shot on net when we have the manpower advantage. It doesn't matter to him whether we score in the first 10 seconds of a penalty or the last 10 seconds, as long as we do it.

The object of successful power play is to gain control in your attacking zone. Once that's accomplished, there are five attackers to four defenders, so somebody is always going to be free. The basic fundamentals of offensive team play apply to the power play.

Breaking Out. When playing with a man advantage, most teams break out by sending their defenseman (now considered a point man) with the puck behind the goal. The center (or the team's best puck carrier) then circles behind the goal, picks up the puck in front of the defenseman, swings wide, and turns up the ice. If the forechecker goes at the center, he flips the puck back to the defenseman, who will in turn break up the ice. The centerman should swing as wide as possible, allowing himself plenty of space to pass back to the defenseman, who in turn will have ample room to break up the ice.

If the center is forechecked after his swing he may also pass to his winger, who will return the puck to the centerman as soon as possible. If the forechecker is moving in quickly to cover the center who is about to sweep behind the net, the defenseman will signal his center that he is going to keep the puck and will reverse behind the goal. He can then pass to the second point man, the winger, the center, or carry the puck out himself. The second point man should be playing in front of the goal for protection.

When a penalty-killing unit doesn't forecheck, the attack should be made with four men in as straight a line as possible. The second point man can move into a corner just before the center picks the puck up behind the net. He can then slip down the side with the winger. The defenseman who started the play behind the net with the center should trail the play behind the puck carrier in the middle of the ice and can act as a "safety valve" in case the puck carrier is checked or loses the puck.

On the Rangers, we take our time forming the power play. For instance, often our defenseman will take the puck behind our own net and stand there, waiting, for what seems like hours instead of seconds. The fans boo, but the defenseman knows what he's doing. He's sizing up the play, waiting for the moment to start the rush up ice. Those few extra seconds are a worthwhile investment if you get a goal as the dividend.

Incidentally, if the opposition ices the puck—remember that they can do this when they're shorthanded—your offensive rush should always be organized in your end of the rink. This will ensure that every member of your team is in position.

Moving into the Attacking Zone. To take full advantage of the extra man it's imperative to maintain possession of the puck when moving

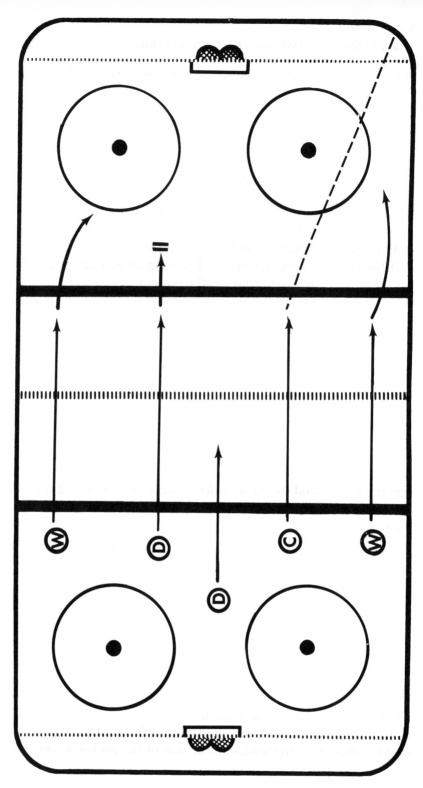

A typical power-play attack as it moves up ice.

into your attacking zone. The following are three maneuvers that the Ranger power-play unit uses for moving the puck into our attacking zone:

1. While the center carries the puck, the winger may break along the blue line in front of the opposing defenseman, thereby screening him. The rushing point man moves toward the hole just inside the blue line which was vacated by the breaking winger and receives the pass from the center. This technique requires good timing and is most effective when the winger, who breaks along the blue line, is closely covered.

2. In a similar manner the winger can break, straddling the blue line in order to screen the opposing defenseman, and the centerman carrying the puck cuts to the open area near the boards. He can carry the puck in from there or pass to the winger who has moved into the slot.

3. The center shoots the puck into the corner and the winger breaks in at full speed to recover the puck. The center tries to have the puck cross the blue line just in front of the breaking winger. The point men move up quickly to take their point positions. This controlled "shoot-in" is most effective when the opposing defensemen are standing up at the blue line. In this situation the breaking winger has a good chance of beating the defenseman to the puck in the corner. It should be noted that puck possession is of the utmost importance during the power play, so the attackers should carry the puck in unless forced to shoot it into the corner.

Of course, other patterns can be used to move the puck into the offensive zone. Earlier in this chapter, the section on blue-line technique of the offensive-team play outlines other team patterns.

In the Attacking Zone. Most teams use the box system when they are one man short and the play is in their zone. They will allow you to move the puck around quite freely outside the box. Therefore, it's important for the attackers to move the puck quickly to force the box out of position. In this way the puck can be fed to one of the attackers who has moved into the slot for a shot.

The attackers must be set up properly in order to take full advantage of the extra man. The puck should be passed accurately and the attacking players must move quickly in the hope of creating a four-on-three or three-on-two situation. Here are some plays when enjoying a man advantage:

1. There are several ways to break down the box zone. For example, let us say that the puck is passed from the left point man to the left winger in the corner. The center in the slot breaks to the goalkeeper's right, leaving the slot open. This leaves three possible maneuvers: *(a)* the right winger may move into the slot for a pass; *(b)* the left point man may move into the slot for a pass; and *(c)* the winger with the puck may move into the slot.

2. The attacking players move the puck quickly to load one side of the ice. This will often leave the point man or winger free on the opposite side. There are plays that develop from the overload on the side of the zone. For example, if the point man has the puck, he can move toward the opposing player at the top of the zone. If this player commits himself to the point man, he passes to center on the side and if the opponent then turns with a pass, the point man breaks into the middle of the zone for the return pass. Meanwhile the deep winger on the overloaded side of the zone should keep his defender occupied so that he can't help out the player at the top of the zone. The other two offensive players not involved in the overload spread out and keep away from the slot area. This, of course, keeps the other two defenders away from the immediate action.

One of our best-scoring power plays on the overload involves Jean Ratelle and Vic Hadfield. Let's say Vic has the puck in the corner and he passes to Jean at the side of the net. Then, our centerman skates out in front of the goal. If the defender goes toward Jean, he can throw the return pass to Vic out in front of the net for a shot on goal. If the defender stays with Vic as he comes in front of the goal, Jean can simply skate out in front of the net himself for a good shot. If the point defender comes out of position to check Jean, then he can pass the puck back to the point for the shot on goal.

3. Another way to break up a defensive box is to keep a player in or running through the box continuously. The maneuvers should eventually get an extra man free in front of the goal. But the simplest way this can be accomplished is to keep the puck around the outside of the zone. Eventually, these quick passes will draw one of the defenders out of position so that the puck can be slipped into the middle of the zone. Of course, this can often be facilitated by having the attacking player with the puck move at a defender, faking either a shot or pass. When a defender moves toward him, the puck can be slipped more easily into the center of the box zone for the shot on goal.

The point men are most important to the success of any power play.

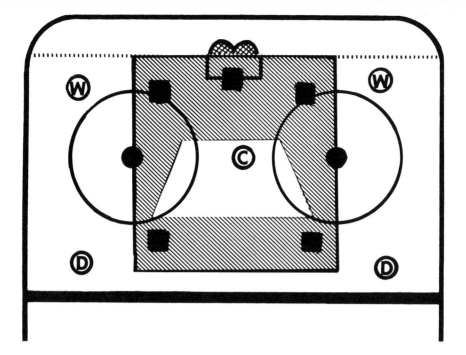

Typical power-play formation in attacking zone.

In most cases, they organize the attack. For example, suppose the left point man has the puck along the boards. He can slide the puck across the ice to the other point man on the right side or pass to the wing in the corner or to a player moving in the slot. Or, of course, he might choose to take a shot on the net, hoping that the slot man can deflect a rebound.

In shooting from the point, it's always best to shoot the puck on the net. But if there's a man blocking the way, then it's up to the forwards in the corner to get free for a pass from the point man. The lower you shoot, the harder it is to stop. All the legs are in the way. With all the players crowding the net it's difficult for the netminder to see. He can pick off a high shot a lot easier than he can a low one.

When you're in front of the net, the defensemen will rough you around. So Rod tries to back off the net a little, toward one of the corners, "until I see the point man ready to make his shot.Then I try to hit the net at the same time as the puck. That way the defender can't do two things at once—he can't watch the shot and watch me at the same time. So then you're in position to jump on a rebound. It's all a case of your own timing.

"You'll see a lot of tip-ins in power plays. A lot of these goals will

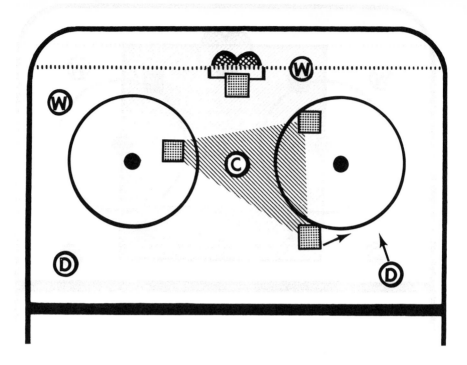

Three typical moves when there are five skaters against three.

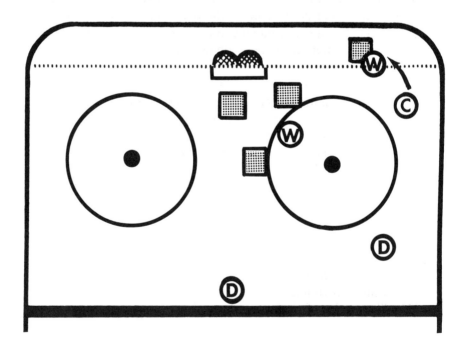

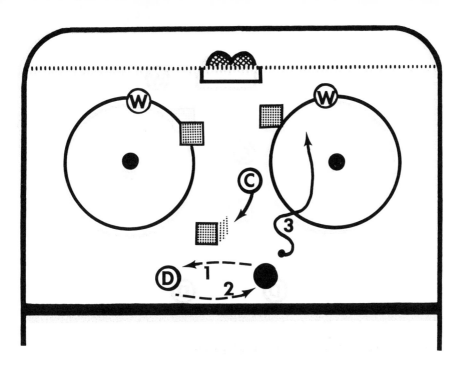

look accidental, but they're not. It's possible to develop a tip-in shot. For instance, Brad and I will often stay out an extra five or ten minutes after practice to work on it. He'll get twenty pucks or so and fire them from the point. I'll practice tipping them toward the net. It's a tricky maneuver—you've got to bend the blade of your stick and steer the puck toward the net—but it can be perfected."

When possession of the puck is lost during a power play, aggressive forechecking by all forwards is the keynote. By getting to the puck carrier before he has time to look up, they can force him to make blind passes. If the first forward misses him, the second man should be close enough to swoop in on him at once. The third man, meanwhile, covers the nearest open pass receiver; he, too, may have to take a crack at the puck carrier. The point men stay at the points ready to intercept passes coming out. In fact, point men are sometimes referred to as offensive goalies because of their most important task of stopping the puck from being shot or flipped out of the attacking zone. Accordingly, they should know how to use their hands to stop the puck, as these are their best tools, as they are the goaltender's. If a puck carrier gets by the forwards, the nearest point man should try to stop either the puck or the man. In this way, at worst only a one-man break should develop.

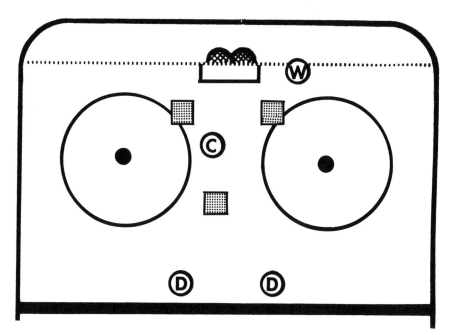

A typical four-skater-versus-three attack pattern.

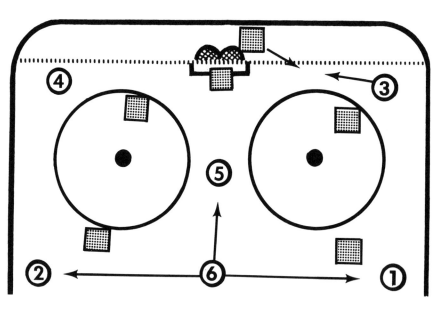

A typical six-skater-versus-five attack pattern.

The other point man (farther from the puck carrier on such a breakout) moves outside the blue line to act as a safety man if the puck does get out into center.ice.

It's most important to remember that power plays can't be carried out with total disregard for defense. A careless or lazy pass between the point men can be intercepted and result in a breakaway for a penalty killer. Also a shot by a point man into an oncoming penalty killer can bounce off him past the point man onto neutral ice. Since the penalty killer is underway, he can move in a breakaway and often score a shorthanded goal. You can't be careless about your defense on power plays. We know. Our Ranger power-play unit holds the ignominious Stanley Cup record, established in the first game of the 1972 finals, of permitting two shorthanded goals in the same 2-minute penalty.

Two-Man Advantage. With a two-man advantage, the power-play unit should have little difficulty in bringing the puck over the attacking blue line since most shorthanded teams won't bother to forecheck with only one forward. All NHL teams defend against the two-man advantage with a three-man triangular zone.

When attacking a triangular zone, move the puck around quickly, especially to the points, until a clear shot is available on goal. Spread the attack to take full advantage of the two extra men. Break into openings but keep the attack balanced. If your point man moves in for the puck, the center or a winger must move out to cover the point. Try to get two men on one directly in front of the goal.

One method of assuring a good shot on goal is the so-called center screen. In the diagram on page 173, the puck is passed from the right point man to the left point man. The center moves out and establishes himself between the opposing top man on the triangle and his right point man. The puck is then returned to the right point man and the defender can't get by the centerman screen to check the right point man, who then moves in for the shot. When recovering the puck on a two-man-advantage situation, try to organize the attack from your own blue line. This will save valuable time.

Six-Attacker Power Play. In the closing seconds of a game, when a team is one goal behind, the coach will almost always pull his goalkeeper out of the net and replace him with another attacking player. While this move may appear risky, it makes little difference whether you lose by one or two goals—you lose!

The fundamental strategy of the six-attacker power play is to make full use of the extra offensive man. There should be a definite pattern play attempted instead of just a haphazard scramble hoping the extra man will pay off. Let's take a look at how the Rangers' six-attacker power play is set up and how it should function.

One player is placed at each point at the boards (1 and 2); there is one man in each corner (3 and 4) to dig out the puck. Each man in a corner should be checking any opponent who tries to carry the puck behind the net and out his side. The man in the corner should try to get that puck and pass it back to the point—or to the player (5) who is in the slot directly in front of the net. The sixth man (6) has a big job to do. He is on patrol just inside the blue line across the whole distance between the two point men. The sixth man is out there for two reasons, like every other man on the ice. He is there on defense —to stop the puck if the other team tries to clear it or carry it out. He is also on the offense. If the man in the slot misses the pass back, the sixth man should pick it up and blast on goal if he has a good clear shot. In this case he can use the man in the slot (5) as a screen. If the sixth man doesn't have a clear shot on goal, he should try to work the puck to one of his players who does have a clear shot.

Frequently the goalie is removed when there is a stoppage at the other end of the rink. The possession of the puck from this face-off is vital to the attacking team. When positioning the players for the face-off and play if possession is gained, make certain that your extra or sixth man is free in open ice and keep the puck going to him until you break an attacker free in position to shoot.

If possession of the puck is lost, the team without the goalie must react very aggressively, checking furiously, and trying to regain. The extra man, or the player closest to the open net, should retreat at least to the center line the moment the puck is lost and attempt to keep directly in front of the cage. He then will be in a fairly good position to stop a long shot or get to the puck if it's flipped out in an attempted clearing play.

7

Defensive Play— Everyone's Game

Good defensive team play is *not* only the responsibility of the defensemen and goalkeeper; it is a duty that must be shared by all players. As one of our goalies, Eddie Giacomin, always says, "The netminder usually makes the final mistake by giving up the goal, but at least one other player on his team earlier made one that set up the goal-scoring situation."

On the other side of the coin, the netminder gets the credit for a shutout. His teammates must share in the glory because it is their defensive effort that cuts down the attacking team's effectiveness. We feel rather strongly about this since we've frequently seen goalies cheered by hometown fans on nights when their team was winning and booed off the ice when they were losing. Sure the goaltenders are vitally important in any team's success or failure, but every member of the club must share his victory or defeat. Hockey, as we have stated several times, is a team game, and this is especially true of defensive play.

FORWARDS ON THE DEFENSE

The swing from offense to defense is made the moment the opponents gain possession of the puck.

As the Attack Breaks Out. When the opponents gain possession and start out of their own end, there are two general styles of defensive play for the forwards in the other team's end. As we stated earlier, these are called forechecking and backchecking and are used by forwards at different stages of the defensive play. It is important for defensemen and forwards each to know what the others are doing in this regard.

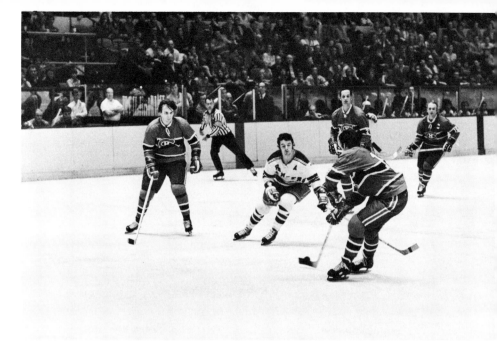

Sometimes quick forechecking movements can win back the puck.

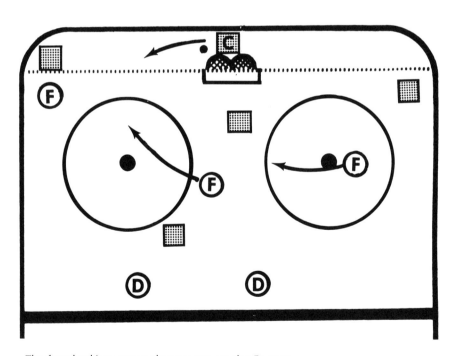

The forechecking system that we use on the Rangers.

The big thing in forechecking, of course, is to get to your man before he gets set to make his run up the ice. In other words, get to him before he is organized. Of course you've got to know when to pass the play and when to play it safe. The score of the game generally will dictate this. If you're behind, naturally you take more chances. Of course, the best spots to forecheck, in order of decreasing effectiveness, are: (1) behind the net; (2) the corners; and (3) the attacking blue line. But each team has its own method of forechecking.

On some teams, the nearest forward hounds the puck carrier before he has a chance to make a breakout pass. The deeper in the end of the rink this can be done, the better. If two men are near enough, they both go after him, while the third man covers the closest open opponent. On the Rangers, if the puck is behind the goal, the forechecking center never goes behind the net after the puck carrier unless he stands an excellent chance of stealing the puck.

When the puck carrier comes out to one side, the forechecking center moves across in front of him, cutting off his angle to center ice and forcing him toward the boards. The forechecking winger moves to cover the middle-zone area but is always between the puck carrier and any potential receiver on the weak side of the ice. The point men move to the strong side and look for passes up the middle.

There is a slight variation to this system whereby the man closest to the puck becomes the forechecker rather than having the center man always assigned to this responsibility. When this happens the center automatically moves to cover the vacant position.

When forechecking, don't skate after the puck at full speed. Try to approach the puck carrier from the side and force him toward the boards while trying to poke check or sweep check the puck away from him. But, in trying to steal the puck by means of a sweep check—or even a poke check—the important thing is to turn with your man as he starts up the ice. If you go straight at him, your chances of getting the puck are remote. By turning with him, you can stay in stride with him, look for an opening—and, if you miss, you won't be trapped in the opponent's zone. As soon as the puck is knocked free, be ready to go immediately on the offensive. Good and vigorous forechecking has a tendency to confuse and demoralize the opposing team.

If the opposing team breaks out, your two wingers should backcheck by skating between the puck and their opponent, trying at all times to keep one stride ahead of the opponent. Forechecking can be a gamble, but very few teams ever win by being *too* cautious. Of course, it helps to study the opposition. Get to know which players can work the puck out from behind their own net and which ones have trouble. Learn which ones like to stickhandle their way out and which ones like to pass their way out. This will help your percentage in taking the puck away from them.

Backchecking. One of the most backbreaking jobs in hockey for forwards is backchecking. It's easy to skate down the ice with the puck, but it's hard to come back and get it. You've got to be in condition to play all positions, but you've got to be really strong to be an effective backchecker. On the Rangers, the forward lines work as a unit. In other words, when we're pressing in the attacking zone, one of the wingmen always lays back a little in the event the opposition breaks out with the puck.

When you're backchecking it's best to keep the man you're playing on the outside of you. That's so if he's going to get a pass, that pass has to go through you. Let Rod Gilbert give you an example of how it's done on the Rangers: "Say I'm on the right wing and we've got the puck in the enemy zone. Now they break out with it on the left side. Well, I don't chase over to the left wing to try to get the man. I stay on my wing. Even if there is no one on my side of the ice at the moment of the play, I stay on my wing. We'll have two defensemen back and it's their job to stop the puck carrier. By staying on my side of the ice, I'm ready to pick up a trailer or anyone else who may come into the play.

"It's important to talk to your defensemen. I might say to Brad, for instance: 'I've got this man.' Then he doesn't worry about him. He concentrates on the puck carrier or picking up someone else. If I make a mistake and the player I'm supposed to cover gets in for a goal, then it's definitely my fault.

"On my side I play against some of the strongest skaters in the league, like Bobby Hull, Frank Mahovlich and Johnny Bucyk. What I try to do when they turn and begin to wind up is to skate in front of them. It throws them off stride and takes away some of their momentum. By the time they recover, I'm going at the same speed as they are. I've found that if you're skating stride for stride with your man, he won't go in most of the time but will let up, figuring there's no sense in wasting his energy."

In backchecking, make certain you carry the stick in both hands, and use it as a psychological weapon. Tap your man on his stick with it— it doesn't have to be more than that—just to let him know that you're around. Again this can throw him off stride and even if it's only a step, it can be enough to spoil the play.

In the Defensive End. Regardless of how far behind the play they may be when the opponents break from their own end, all three forwards must skate hard to get back. Other factors to remember when playing forward inside your own blue line are:

1. The first two forwards back help the defense in checking and covering opponents around their own net.

2. No opponent in good shooting position is ever left uncovered.

3. In checking a man in the corner, the checker ties up the man, never letting him stickhandle out into the open.

4. The last forward to return (usually the forechecker) circles out near his own blue line to cover the opposing points, and to break out when his team gets possession.

DEFENSEMEN ON THE DEFENSE

Successful defensemen must work well together. Each must know the moves of his partner in order to form an effective defense unit. On the Rangers, the defensemen divide the ice in half. Generally, Brad Park plays the right side, with say Dale Rolfe on the left side. "Now let's say the puck goes into my corner. We both can't chase it, even if we both think we can reach it. One of us has to stay in front of the net to protect our goalie. This is not to say that Dale can't come over to my side and get the puck, if he thinks he can reach it ahead of me. That's okay. But you've got to keep talking to each other ('I've got it. . . . Go get it!') to let each other know who's going for the puck and who's covering up in front."

Incidentally, and contrary to popular opinion, it is by no means essential to have a right shot play right defense and a left shot play left defense. It is not a question of which side one shoots from, but to which side one turns more easily. Being able to turn swiftly toward an opponent who is trying to skate outside you is one of the fundamentals of defensive play. A right defenseman must be able to turn quickly to his right, and a left defenseman to his left. The only real disadvantage of being a left-hand shot and playing right defense is at the offensive blue line, and with a lot of work, this can be overcome and turned into an advantage because you'll be more directly in front of the net for a shot. But, for now, let's get back to your part as a defenseman on defense.

Brad Park attempts a poke check while his defensive partner covers up for him if he misses.

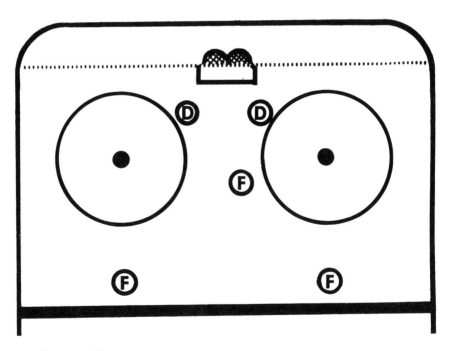

The zone defense.

As the Attacker Breaks Out. When the opposition launches an attack, here are the basic situations that most often occur and how you and your defense partner should normally react:

1. First of all, you both should know whether your forwards are going in to forecheck or are coming back out of your attacking zone to cover the opposing forwards.

2. If the attack is on your side of the ice and your forward on that side stays in to forecheck, you must make a snap judgment whether to move in to check, or to get back fast. If close enough, you may try to check the puck carrier, either with your stick or with your body.

3. If your defense partner goes in to check, then you should start back out of the attacking zone to cover a possible pass by the puck carrier.

4. When your forwards start to backcheck, or a clean breakout is evident, both defensemen should turn and race for the center line, and jump turn to face the attack. You both must see instantly whether one or both wings are covered, and whether it is a one-, two-, or three-man break.

5. If the wings are covered, both of you should try to stand at your own blue line, 10 to 20 feet from each other, so as to force the puck carrier to make his play before he crosses your blue line.

6. If the wings are uncovered, both of you should back in, forcing the play into a corner. Never allow the puck to be carried through the center.

In Their Own End. Once the opponents carry the puck into the attack zone, the defensemen must concentrate on their cardinal purpose: keep between the goalie and the puck carrier or another opponent. Here are some pointers that Brad would like to give to his brothers on the back line to accomplish this purpose as well as the important job of stopping a goal by the opposing team:

1. As we have stated several times, hockey is a game of moves and countermoves, and defensemen must be very careful not to commit themselves too soon because they give the attackers something to work on. You should remember that the less information you give your opponents the more difficult it is for them to make plays. Hold your ground and force the attacking players, especially the puck carrier, to make his move and then you'll have something positive

and definite to work on. By following this rule, you'll make fewer mistakes.

2. If a situation calls for a body check, do it correctly. Concentrate 100 percent on the attacker's body and make sure to hit him. A missed body check causes problems.

3. If you didn't or weren't able to body check or stick check the puck carrier, then your next duty is to turn quickly and skate alongside the puck carrier, keeping him between you and the boards and forcing him to a bad shooting angle. Remember always to force the play away from the center into the corners.

4. When covering a player with the puck along the boards, use your arm and leg closest to your opponent to ride him off and to pin him against the boards. That is, the arm in front and the leg behind. Use your skate or stick to gain control of the puck.

5. There should always be one defenseman stationed 5 to 15 feet in front of the net to protect your goalie. But don't move in too close to the crease because you'll be in goal range where a well-directed shot may score. In fact, if you back in too close you may help the opponents to score by unintentionally screening the shot from your goaltender or a shot may deflect off your skate or stick into the goal.

6. In the strategic position in front of the net you should be ready to clear rebounds to the corners, and intercept pass-outs in front of the net. Of course, when in front of the net, maintain contact with the man you're covering, keeping your stick as near his stick blade as possible. Don't lose sight of the puck. If it is passed back to an attacker at the points, drive your man out of the goalie's view. Also, if passed in front of the net be sure to hurry the attacker's shot as much as possible so that it will be less accurate.

7. Around the net, you should always body check the puck carrier. An error close to the net can be disastrous, especially if the misplay involves the puck carrier. Thus, the nearest defensive player should body check the puck carrier any time he comes within a 15-foot radius of the net. Remember that within this radius, always play the puck carrier rather than the puck.

8. Get the puck out of your defensive zone as quickly as possible. Whenever stopping an opposition attack, you should try to control the puck and make an immediate play to get the puck into the center zone, where it will be harmless for a few moments. But don't attempt

to control the puck or carry it out of your defensive zone if you're the last man back.

9. Never pass or carry a puck across the front of your net when an opponent is nearby. Always skate behind the net and start your offensive breakout play from there.

10. Don't try to block high shots from far out. In general, the defense gives the goalie a clear view to handle all long shots. If the shooter is close enough, however, the shot may be blocked by dropping in front of it.

11. The defenseman into whose corner the play has been forced covers his position. That is, when the puck is in the corner to the goaltender's left, then the left defenseman goes after it and the right defenseman stays in front of the net. Should the puck go into the right corner, the left defenseman remains in front of the goal. Keep in mind that a defenseman never allows a puck carrier to stickhandle his way out of the corner to the front of the net.

12. When your team has regained control of the puck and starts to move up ice, the defenseman, on the side the puck is being brought out, should trail the puck carrier out of the defensive zone. This trailer action will prevent any opposing player who checks the puck carrier from perhaps breaking quickly in on goal or setting up a play. The trailer should stay on his job until the puck is in the attacking zone, at which time both defensemen can take their position on the points.

POSITIONAL PLAY

Positional defensive play isn't as evident in hockey as it is in such sports as basketball and football, but nevertheless it's an important part of the game. While there are several systems of positional play employed in hockey, the one used is primarily the concern of the coach. However, the better conception each player has of the general fundamentals of defensive strategy, the better player he'll be. For this reason we've described the four most popular systems used in the NHL.

Zone Defense. In this system players are aligned so that the wingers cover the points and the center covers the slot. The defensemen are responsible for their respective corners and the area in front of the goal. As the puck is moved around, the winger on the puck side must check his opposing defenseman who comes up to cover the point most closely.

One of the defensive wingers should step into the slot to give assist-

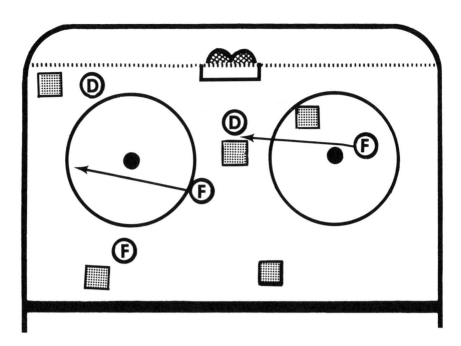

The sliding zone defense.

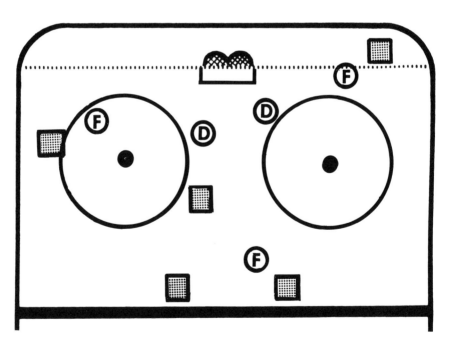

Man-on-man defense.

ance to the centerman. One defenseman must always play the puck in the corner, the other defenseman plays the man in front of the goal. Their positions reverse when the puck moves to the other side of the net. Sometimes your center is the last man back. If this is the case, the first winger back should cover the slot until the center returns. When using a zone defense, close coordination is most important since the important areas in front of the net must be covered.

The Sliding Zone. The sliding zone supplies added strength in front of the goal and in the corners. The alignment has the center covering the point man on the side where the puck is. The winger and defenseman on that side both go for the puck while the other winger moves in to cover the slot and the other defenseman covers the front of the net. With the puck in the left corner, the winger (left) in the slot moves to cover his winger and the right winger moves to cover the slot. The center covers the point on the puck side. If the puck enters the right defensive zone, the right winger moves back to cover his winger, the left winger moves back into the slot, and the centerman moves across to cover the puck side point. Occasionally, the winger in the slot will have to come out to cover a shot from the other point position.

Man on Man. Another method of defending in your own zone is to play man on man. In this system each winger checks his opposing wingman. However, the wingers may change men if the attacking wingers crisscross. The center checks the point on the puck side and the defenseman on the other side must be prepared to go out and block shots from the other point. This system provides good defense in your vulnerable area, the slot. However, there are two disadvantages: The point man on the side away from the puck is left uncovered and any quick breakout pattern by your team will be retarded because your wingers are deep, covering their respective wingers.

Double Teaming. Sometimes a superstar is given double coverage. That is, two forwards are assigned to cover this attacking star when he has the puck. The other remaining forward takes care of the next most dangerous attacker. The disadvantage of such a defense plan is that the third attacking player will be free to take a pass. But, with say a Bobby Hull, this is often a reasonable risk to take since there are still the two defensemen to take care of the free man.

Double teaming should be started as soon as the opponent's breakout occurs. The two checkers assigned to the superstar should keep on each side of him to reduce his maneuverability. Also by escorting him in this

Don't screen your goalie as Brad Park is doing here.

Even with the "help" of the defenseman, a goal was scored on Dale Rolfe's shot in the fifth game of the 1972 Stanley Cup finals.

manner, the checkers can guard against a pass to the free man. Once in their defensive zone, the checkers should force him into the defensemen. He'll have to be a real superstar if he can beat four men.

TYPICAL PLAY SITUATIONS

In specific play situations, the defensemen have definite assignments. Terms such as one on one and two on one refer to situations where there is one attacker against one defenseman, two attackers against one defenseman, and so on. All coaches have their own preferences in handling such rush situations, so we've detailed here the methods we teach our defensemen at Skateland Summer Hockey School.

One on One. Try to force the play early, not back in the goal area. Start when your opponent starts, stop when he stops. Keep your head up, look him in the eyes, stay in front of him at all times. Always try to make the attacker commit himself first. Ignore the puck—keep your eyes on the attacking player and take him out of the play. That is, when you get the chance tie him up; then and only then, go for the puck.

When an opponent is carrying the puck from behind his own net, try to force him between yourself and the net, tie him up, then go for the puck. If the puck carrier, coming from behind his net, goes to the outside, rush over to cut off the angle to the boards. Play the man, not the puck. Similarly, if he shoots the puck up the boards, play the man first, tie him up, then go for the puck. If the puck carrier tries to pass it close by, stay in front and briefly tie up the man, being careful not to receive an interference penalty. Go for the puck when the opponent is out of the play. The opposition should never score in a one on one situation.

One on Two. In a one-man rush, the two defensemen shift across the ice laterally in order to get into the path of the oncoming player and should the puck carrier come within checking range, he should be body checked. If the attacker attempts to split the defense (go between the two defensemen), he should be body checked simultaneously by both defensemen. If the attacker should try to go around one of the defending players, this defenseman should skate in the same direction as the puck carrier, keep him between himself and the boards, and skate him off to a bad shooting angle. The other defenseman should take up his position in front of the net.

Two on One or Three on One. Here the defenseman must protect the defensive alley (the area extending out from between the goal-posts). The defenseman orients himself while skating backward by watching the opponent's goal. Stay in this area and try to force all shots to come from outside the alley. If possible, delay the play until you get help from your teammates.

In a close position with a two-on-one situation, the decision to take the puck carrier or the other player is the choice of the goalkeeper. Most of them, including our two goalies, prefer to take the puck carrier and have the defenseman take his partner. Tony Esposito of the Chicago Blackhawks, on the other hand, wants his defenseman to take the puck carrier.

In the case of three on one the defenseman must remain in the middle of the ice, but must make sure not to back up into his goaltender or block his vision. The attackers will almost certainly get off a shot, so position yourself to clear the rebound, when there is one.

Two on Two. Mentally divide the ice into two zones. Keep fairly far apart, but never so far that the center is weak. This will force the offensive attackers wide. It is very important to talk to one another all the time. Try to make the offense declare themselves early and try to make any shots come from bad angles outside the defensive alley. If the forwards crisscross, switch men; the defense should never criss-cross.

Three on Two. When three attackers are moving down on two defensemen, the defensemen must keep well spread and stay between the attacking forward line and the net. Always try to force the puck carrier into the corner, thus giving your teammates time to come back and help.

A defenseman never feels worse than when he screens his goalie and it results in a goal. But sometimes this can't be helped. It's the nature of the game; so many players gang around the net that the goalie's vision simply is blocked. What Brad Park does then is try to reduce the percentage of screening. "For instance, I'll talk it over with him. I'll tell him that I can't get out of his way and if I see I can't block the shot, I'll hold my legs together. That way he'll at least know that the puck is coming at him from one side or the other."

FACE-OFFS IN THE DEFENSIVE ZONE

The face-off in the defensive zone must be played by the defensive team as though it will lose that face-off. This means that every offensive

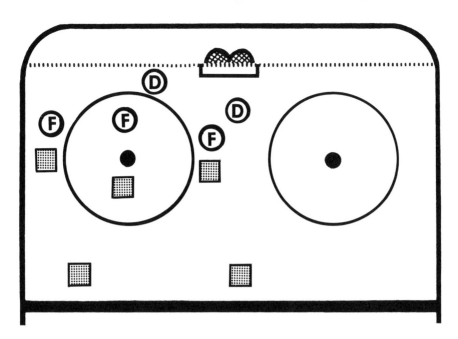

A typical face-off situation in the defensive zone.

man must be covered. Nonetheless, be positive about the face-off even though you are ready to cover every man if it is lost.

The positions taken by the offensive team will determine how you set up your defense. Assume the face-off is to the right of your goal. If the offensive team is positioned in the natural way (a winger on each side of the center) the lineup is as shown. The center should always try to draw the puck back into the corner where the defenseman can take it and move into a breakout pattern. In this diagram the left winger will break to cover the weak-side point and the center checks the opposing center but will move to the other point if he loses the draw.

To win a face-off, follow the tips given on face-offs in Chapter 6.

PENALTY KILLING

Every hockey team must be prepared to play one or two men short at some time in a game. When this occurs, teamwork becomes of vital importance. The shorthanded team, if it's one man short, uses a defensive unit of two defensemen and two forwards. These forwards, known as "penalty killers," usually are defense-minded players with exceptional skating ability, excellent stickhandling and passing skills, and

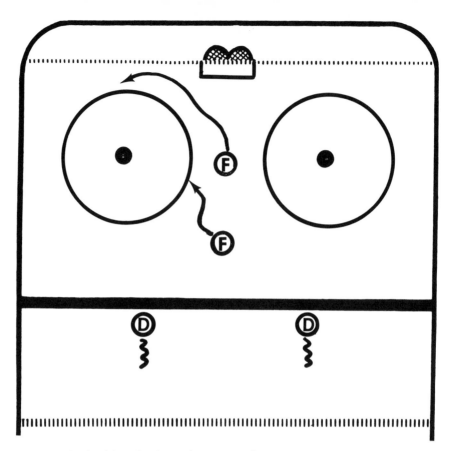

Two methods of forechecking when a man short.

nerves of steel. Most penalty killers play in tandem, and most teams use one penalty-killing duo predominantly. But, because penalty killers must skate hard for the period of time they are on the ice, few play the full 2 minutes of a penalty. Most teams in the NHL have two sets of regular penalty killers. On the Rangers, we have several of the finest penalty killers in the NHL—Bruce MacGregor, Ron Stewart, Glen Sather, Bill Fairbairn, and Walt Tkaczuk.

In a game a few years back against Los Angeles, Walt and Bill's defensive unit controlled the puck for 1:37 straight and 1:44 of the Kings' total 2:00-minute power play. In addition, the Rangers got off two shots on goal and the Kings didn't get any. But in Bill's view a "perfect" 2:00-minute penalty killing turn would be to control the puck for 1:58 and then score shorthanded at 1:59.

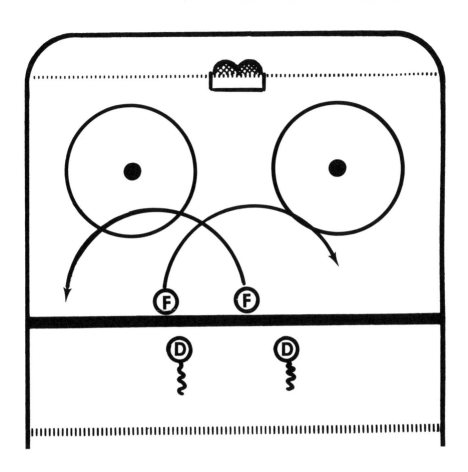

There are two distinct methods whereby a team may play a man short: by (1) forechecking, or (2) backchecking. All four men on the penalty-killing unit must know which method is being used, and all must play accordingly. In addition, it's vital that the penalty-killing unit know each other's playing styles and moves so that they are able to back up each other.

Forechecking. When a team uses a forechecking method of killing off a penalty, then press, rather than wait. The forwards or penalty killers, following an iced puck, should check the puck carrier before he can get help. Their play differs from normal forechecking in only one respect. The approach they take when swooping in on the puck is such that if they miss or a pass is made, they are already moving back fast to pick up checks. The defensemen on the points should not take

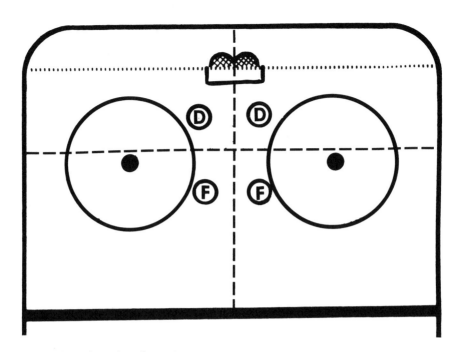

The four-player box formation.

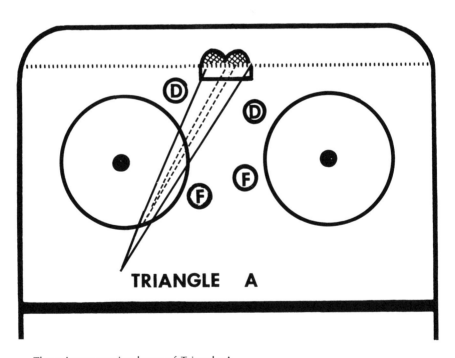

The primary scoring lanes of Triangle A.

chances at getting to the puck carrier coming out in order to back up the forwards' play. They are alert to cover up for one another, yet must capitalize on mistakes like blind passes caused by the pressure of their persistent forwards.

As we stated earlier, teams have their own methods of forechecking in the opposing team's end. This is true even when they're short-handed. For example, one of the most popular systems of forechecking and one our team most often employs is to have the penalty killers crisscross in front of the goal to pick up the wingers of the opposing team. The forecheckers move quickly down the ice into their opponents' zone; first one swings, then the other. The first forechecker pressures the puck carrier, then each man returns covering a winger. The two defensemen block off the center area. The defenders must coordinate their actions with those of the puck carrier and opposing wingers. Make it difficult for the attackers to carry or pass the puck. When the play crosses the red line, all four men should play up ahead of their blue line to put pressure on the attackers. That is, congest the on-side area at all times, forcing the attackers to shoot the puck into your end rather than carry it in. A disadvantage of this system is that the centerman isn't covered.

Another method we sometimes use is called the tandem system. As the play starts deep in the opposition's end, one penalty killer goes in to forecheck the man with the puck to steal the puck or to force him to make a bad pass. The second penalty killer falls back in the center area behind the first forechecker and watches for a loose puck or a bad pass. If his partner comes back, he may go in to forecheck, trying to keep the opposition bottled up in their end. If the power-play unit begins to break out, the two forecheckers then pick up the opposing wingers. The theory is to force the play away from the center area and make the weaker winger carry the puck. This is done, naturally, by covering the stronger players. The key to success with this system is to anticipate the attackers' moves. In addition, the two penalty killers must be strong and hard skaters.

Backchecking. A team using the backchecking method gains time to get into position, by shooting the puck into the other team's end at every opportunity. The penalty killers backcheck, picking up their men over the attacking blue line if possible, and under no circumstances go in after the puck carrier. The backchecker stays between his man and the puck all the way into the defensive end.

The defensemen move into position just over the center line as soon as the puck is shot down the ice. They play about 12 to 20 feet apart, as the puck carrier swings down center to shoot the puck in to start a power play. If he veers to one side, both defensemen move laterally to meet him. They must not let him split them. If unable to stop him, they should slow him up by forcing him wide. This delays the play enough to prevent an attacking winger from bursting over the blue line at top speed. Thus, when the puck carrier finally shoots, the backchecking wings have a chance to get to the puck first, and, turning, fire it back down the ice.

Whenever possible you should force your opponents to shoot the puck into your zone rather than have them carry it in. Because the opposing team usually attacks with four men abreast and because they can't pass over two lines, try to have your four defenders stand up against them at your blue line. If done properly, this technique will force the attackers to shoot the puck into your end. If you gain control in the center-ice area, control the puck as long as possible. Move the puck around quickly and waste as much time as possible before clearing into the opponents' end.

If you manage to shoot the puck into their end and you see they've got to hustle back to get it, it's a good idea to put on a little pressure yourself. One man goes in deep while the other hangs back. You try to keep them disorganized, especially when you see they're having trouble getting an attack formed. But—and this is the most important item of all—don't get trapped in their end of the ice. That's going to give them what amounts to a two-man advantage and could result in a goal. You have to think defensively more than anything else when you're killing a penalty.

Defending in Your Own End. What we do on the Rangers whenever the puck is in our own end of the ice and the opposition is pressing us is to go into a box formation. It works like a zone defense in basketball. That is, each man is responsible for a certain area of ice. To play the four-man box correctly when shorthanded, the primary scoring lanes must be blocked at all times. Triangle A is an example of a scoring lane. When the puck is at the top of the triangle, the player at the top of the box on that side moves out to cover, but always attacks from inside to outside, forcing the play toward the boards. This decreases the angle of the scoring lane. One defenseman stays in front of the net at all times, while the other moves to the side where the puck is located. He should also attempt to force the puck into the corner without actually going there himself.

The box should move in a coordinated fashion dictated by the position of the attackers and the puck. As the scoring triangle becomes more extreme, the box formation must not become too spread. Always force the attackers but don't gamble and get out of position. That is, you take a zone and stick to it. You cover anyone who comes into it. What you're looking for is for them to make a mistake (just as they are looking for you to make a mistake). You'll try to tip away a pass, or hurry a shot. The only time you'll charge the point man is when you're sure —absolutely sure—he's going to shoot. Then you try to block his shot.

When your team is shorthanded, it's usually most difficult to carry the puck out of your defensive zone so the best thing to do is to shoot it *carefully* down ice. (The shorthanded team has only one advantage in a penalty situation—it can clear the puck the length of the ice with no icing call, where the puck normally is brought back for a face-off.) We say shoot the puck because many players get excited when the pressure is on them and they clear the puck carelessly, and instead of getting it out of their zone they invariably feed it right back to the opponents. Always, in clearing the puck down ice, remember to look up for a clear opening to shoot the puck through safely, and get a good piece of the puck and drive it out with plenty on it.

Ragging the puck—the art of stickhandling in such a manner that the opponents can't get possession—is a most effective method of stalling when shorthanded. But we would like to stress another important point: Don't rag the puck in your half of the ice. Shoot it out. When you're inside your own blue line, the best way to do this is by banging it off the sideboards or, even better, shooting it down the middle of the ice. This area is usually unprotected.

Two Men Short. Two men in the penalty box places great pressure on the remaining three players. When possible the checking should begin in the opponents' zone. The centerman moves toward the goal, then swings tight to cover the center area. The defensemen move up quickly to guard the long pass. The three can't cover the whole blue line so they should not stand at each line as when they are one man short. You must give the attacking team room on the ice and wait for them to make a mistake when you are two men short.

In your own zone when you're two men short, a tight triangle is formed in front of the goal. One player plays at the top of the triangle and tries to force the opposing point man toward the boards. If possible, he should try to make the point man shoot from as far out as he can. The two defensemen must adjust their positions in respect to the position of the puck. One should always be in front of the net, while the other moves to the puck side.

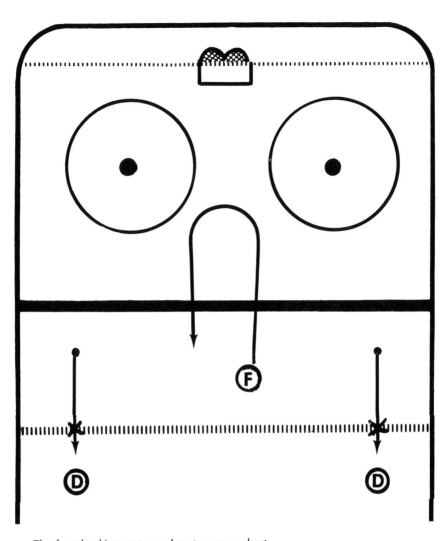

The forechecking system when two men short.

To play the triangle properly, the players must make sure they keep their positions. The triangle should be tight, each player responsible for a zone. Try to keep one defensive player between two offensive players. If possible, force all shots outside of the primary scoring lanes. Defensemen should try not to screen the goalkeeper on shots from the point. The man at the top of the triangle tries to make all shots come from the outside.

Here are some points to remember when you are two men short:

1. Keep pressure on the attackers when they are in their own zone, approaching center ice, and approaching your blue line, but don't get caught up ice.

2. Try to get them to shoot the puck into your own zone.

3. Protect the main scoring areas well. That is, cover the corners, and above all cover the points.

4. At every opportunity shoot the puck hard down the ice. The best clearing shot from the corner is diagonally hard and high across the ice, hitting the boards near the blue line.

5. Cover all loose pucks quickly.

6. Force the opponents to use their weakest shooter.

7. If you can't clear, force a face-off.

Face-Off Alignments. Face-off alignments are most important when you're playing shorthanded. You should try to (1) gain possession of the puck, or (2) at least put the other team at a disadvantage.

At center ice, one defenseman moves up to cover the winger who is free. The centerman attempts to shoot the puck into the attacking zone or draws it back to gain control and help to kill time. If the puck is faced off just inside the blue line, a defenseman again moves up to cover the free winger. The second defenseman moves into position behind his centerman.

During the face-off inside the opponents' blue line, it is extremely important that all the defensive players take up the proper positions so that the attacking players can be quickly covered. Every player must be assigned to cover a particular man.

In the defensive zone two defenders, a winger and a defenseman, are usually kept in front of the goal. After the draw the winger moves out to cover the point, the centerman moves out to cover the point on the other side. The defensive team quickly skates for any loose puck, and always keeps pressure on the puck carrier.

When you're two men short in the defensive zone, position one defenseman in front of and one defenseman to the side of the goal. The

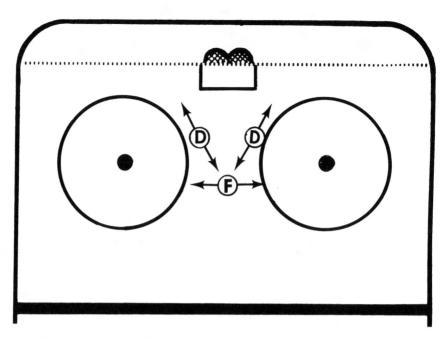

The three-player triangle formation.

center tries to clear toward the boards or draw to his teammate. Form the defensive triangle as quickly as possible. Also with a two-man disadvantage be prepared to attack from the face-off. At least get your stick on the puck.

A final word: When in a shorthanded situation, get off the ice if you're tired. Penalty killing can be a demanding job. If you're working at it, you usually can't go for more than a minute at top speed. And if you can't make the play because you're tired, you're not doing your team any good. In fact, any time you're tired you should take yourself off the ice as soon as possible.

PULLING THE GOALKEEPER

If the opposition's goalie is pulled in favor of an extra attacker, the defensive team must break through to cover the shooter. One defenseman must be kept in front of the goal at all times. The first duty of the defensive team is to play it safe and get the puck out of its own defensive zone—not to score into the open net.

8

Goaltending— the Toughest Job in Sports

BRAD Park's first position in an organized hockey game was goalie. "There was a little rink outside Toronto in Unionville where my father used to referee juvenile hockey games. My brother Ron, who was eight, had joined one of the hockey clubs in the league playing there, but I was only six, which was too young to play. One day while waiting for a goaltender on my brother's team to show up, I persuaded my dad to let me take his place. My pleading worked and soon I was installed as the goalie.

"Early in the game, one of the fellows carrying the puck for the other team came skating down along the boards, and I protected the goal on that side. But on the first shot, he put the puck in the net on the other side and I started crying. My mother, who was sitting behind the net, asked me what was wrong and I yelled, 'He wasn't supposed to do that.'

"Fortunately for me, my career as a netminder was very short-lived, and when I really entered organized hockey I was playing forward. While neither of us has ever played goalie professionally, Rod and I have played with some of the best—Ed Giacomin, Gilles Villemure, Gump Worsley, Jacques Plante, Terry Sawchuck—and we have attempted to shoot past the likes of Glenn Hall, Bruce Gamble, Johnny Bower, Tony Esposito, Roger Crozier, Ken Dryden, and many other good goalies."

Hockey players should study their own and opposing goalies carefully. As a forward, Rod tries to learn the moves of the opponent goalkeepers in hopes of finding ways to get the puck past them. You can be certain that there's a book on every big-league goalie kept by the majority of forwards, especially the seasoned ones. It doesn't take long for word to get around that Chicago's Tony Esposito is relatively

A goalie can expect things in his net other than the puck. For example, here Rod ends up in the cage after missing the net with the puck. No goal, of course, while he's in the cage, or in the goalie's crease. For this reason the goalkeeper tries to keep Rod caged in.

weak on long shots or that Buffalo's Roger Crozier is vulnerable on the high shots or that Philadelphia's Doug Favell doesn't handle low shots with the greatest of ease or that Boston's Gerry Cheevers has a good glove hand, but he'll give you those corners quite often.

Defensemen while on the bench should pay close attention to the play of both goalkeepers: the opponent's for the same reason forwards do, and their own for ways to improve their defense play. You can learn a great deal about goaltending as well as about the goalie himself by watching the play around the nets.

There is no question about it, the goalkeeper is the most important player on the ice. He is the last bastion of a team's defense. All winning teams have at least one aggressive, dependable goaltender who instills confidence in his teammates. Most good goalies are a breed apart from the rest of us. They must endure whizzing pucks, flailing sticks, flying skates, and occasionally a hurtling body. Of course, many of us on the Rangers accuse our coach of being partial to goalies. But if he is, it is understandable because Emile Francis was a goalie for over 15 years. And to show his loyalty to the goalies' Spartan code, there's a story that tells of a game he once played for New Haven in the American League. He had suffered a dislocated shoulder but refused to stay off the ice. In order to play he hooked a chain from one goalpost to his arm in such a way that it restrained his movement and prevented further shoulder damage.

What do we look for in selecting a goalie candidate from among our students at the school? One thing is a player who directs a team through leadership; the other players must have faith in him. He must also have the ability to come up with the big saves. Another important factor is concentration. The goalie must think of nothing but the puck. Lose sight of it and it can take his head off. Relax one second, and the red light indicates a goal and you lose the game.

Size is not too important. NHL goalies range from 6 foot 4 inch Gary Smith and Ken Dryden to our 5 foot 8 inch Gilles Villemure. But a goalkeeper must be mobile and quick as a cat. And he must have a tremendous amount of courage. Today's game of shoot, screen, and rebound necessitates a strong physical and mental makeup. "Hockey can get to a man," points out Emile Francis. "It moves at such high speed and the players must build themselves up emotionally like thoroughbreds, but it's not 14 games like in football. It's 78 games for the season and you're on skates, which are artificial legs, and you use sticks, which are artificial arms. Sometimes it gets to the point where

Goalie's special equipment (clockwise from left): body pad, catching glove, leg pad, stick glove. Equipment in use is shown below.

the goals and the crowd not only bother you but get the best of you."

Because the physical strain of the long NHL season is so great, all teams have at least two goaltenders on their squads. In fact, this policy is being employed in minor league, amateur, and college hockey too. Most goalies, despite their competitive desire to be No. 1 goaltender all the time, realize that platooning helps them remain sharp and can also prolong their careers.

Probably the biggest mistake young would-be goalies make is that they get the idea they don't have to be good skaters. It may be hard to believe, but it's just as important for a goalie to be a strong skater as it is for a forward or defenseman—maybe even more so, since the goalie is the only man who is on the full game. If you work on your skating, it'll strengthen your legs, and in any sport—hockey, baseball, football, or basketball—an athlete's legs are the most important part of his body. But beyond this, if you're a strong skater, it'll help you acquire all the moves that are needed to become a good goalie. So we can't emphasize enough: Skate with your teammates in practice. Take part in the sprints and the stop-and-go drills. Do it with your pads on, too. This will strengthen your legs even more.

EQUIPMENT

Due to the nature of his job—the toughest in sports—the goalie's "tools of ignorance" (the name given to his equipment by fellow teammates) are bulky in appearance. But we must remember that they are designed to help him keep the puck out of the net, as well as affording protection for himself. The goaltender's equipment appears to be cumbersome, but the major consideration in its selection is that it be the right size. Gear that is too heavy or that doesn't fit properly will hinder the goalkeeper's mobility in the net.

Skates. The goalie's skates are of unique construction. They have no radius; the entire blade on a goalie's skate meets the ice, providing the balance and stability so necessary in his job. The blade is also wider and is sharpened with a much flatter surface which makes it easier for him to stand motionless during stops in the action (the goalie never gets a bench respite during a game), and it increases his braking power when needed.

The skates used by the goaltender have sections which close the gap between the blade and the boot. This prevents the puck from going through them. The goalie's special skates also have extra protection around the ankles, Achilles tendons, toes, and the sides of the foot. Foot-bone injuries would take a long time to heal.

Goalies around the league differ on the sharpness of their blades. Many play an entire season without ever sharpening their skates. They claim that sharp blades have a tendency to grab the ice, hampering their sideward slide movements.

Sticks. The goalie's stick is also quite different from others, but it should be chosen with the same care for proper lie, flexibility, weight, and length. (According to regulations, a goalie's stick can't exceed 3½ inches except at the heel of the blade, where it may not be more than 4½ inches. The wide section of the stick can't extend more than 24 inches up the shaft.) Most goalies use from 11 to 15 lie. (On our team, Eddie uses a 12, while Gilles employs a 14 lie.) A higher-lie stick is generally used by a "stand-up" goalie. The weight and length should be such as to make the stick easy to handle. But don't make the mistake many young goaltenders make in cutting their sticks too short. Use as much of the stick as you can with comfortable control; however, remember that an extra inch or two may be all that is needed to make a save.

A goalie should put a good-sized knob of either black or white tape on the end of the handle. White tape is preferred because black tape leaves a smudge on the glove. The blade, however, is usually covered completely with black tape.

Gloves. A goalie wears two completely different types of gloves. On his catching hand he wears a "trapper" mitt, which is similar to a first baseman's mitt in baseball. It has big, flexible webbing and an extra-long sleeve top that reaches almost to the elbow, preventing pucks from breaking wrists and other lower arm bones. The palm is generally thinner and more flexible than the outside glove so that he can grab the puck easily and also release it quickly. This glove, like all hockey equipment, should feel comfortable on the hand.

The stick glove, sometimes called the backhand glove, has a fiber back which is very stiff and acts as an extra goalie pad. Not only does this protective padding protect the hand holding the stick, but by moving this hand up and down, the back of the glove can be used to deflect high as well as low shots. This stick-glove back should not exceed 8 inches in width at any point, nor should it extend more than 2 inches beyond the extended finger.

Chest Protectors. All netminders wear chest protectors to cover the area from below the chin to the top of the thigh guards in the pants.

They resemble baseball chest protectors, except they are not quite as bulky. The goaltender's chest protector is about 1½ inch thick, but it must not restrict the agility of the goalkeeper.

Shoulder Pads. The shoulder pads should cover the points of the shoulders, upper arms, forearms, elbows, shoulder blades, and clavicles. As a rule, these pads are heavier and more protective on the netminder's stick side, where there's no glove to catch shots. Many goalies wear elbow pads in addition to the protection afforded by the long shoulder pads.

Leg Pads. Shin or leg pads may be hinged at the bottom to cover the instep, and should allow flexibility at the knees. They should be just long enough to cover the thighs. The goalie today wears his pads much higher than his counterpart of even ten years ago. Common sense is prevailing. Today's pads are well reinforced at the sides to give added strength. But, even with special reinforcement, the edge at the inside of the leg will eventually weaken by wear so that when the goaltender presses his pads together, a hard shot might sneak through. By the way, most goalies prefer to keep the top straps loose and the lower ones snug.

Pants. Regular hockey pants are worn except that a thin layer of felt should be used as a substitute for the plastic thigh pads. This will help prevent rebounds. Also, there should be an added pad on the inside seam of the pants.

The Face Mask. Almost every goalie from peewees to the NHL wears a face mask. Actually, all should wear them since the puck travels too fast for any goaltender to trust his reflexes and instincts to the point where they're the only protection for his face. Jacques Plante introduced the mask in the 1960's and, although he was first kidded about being the masked marvel, his face mask paid off for him many times. But the best example occurred during the 1970 Stanley Cup playoffs when he stopped a terrific shot on his mask. On his way to the hospital he stated, "My mask saved my life."

The lightweight fiberglass and the wire-mesh baseball type are popular and are recommended for the best protection and confidence. When selecting a face mask make sure it fits properly without blocking vision or impeding head motion. Before purchasing it, check to be sure that you could see a puck at your feet and that it doesn't block your peripheral vision. Don't file the eye slits larger, however, since the puck may enter or it may weaken the structure. If a mask fits too tight, a severe bruise or bone damage may result. Some masks have a resilient pad on the inside to absorb shock. Of course, the time may soon come

When a goalie goes sprawling over the ice (top), he's totally at the mercy of the shooter. Shooters like Rod Gilbert show little mercy as he puts the puck past the prone netminder. On the other hand, a stand-up type goaltender (bottom), coming out of his cage to cut down the angle, doesn't give an opponent too much to shoot at.

when the goalie's whole head will be encased in a helmet such as a football player wears and have a built-in face mask.

THE STYLES OF PLAY

Every goaltender should develop his own style of play. In other words, don't try to pattern yourself identically after another netminder. True, there are goalies who stand up, those who sprawl, some who roam, others who stay in the cage moving only to cut down the shooting angle. On the Rangers our two goaltenders have two completely different methods of playing the net. Ed Giacomin prefers to roam about, scramble all over the ice, and challenge the shooters to skate in and beat him. Ed relies very heavily on his fabulous reflexes to stop the puck. Gilles Villemure always stands rather erect and plays the angles— trying, that is, to minimize the size of the net by skating toward the shooter and blocking out portions of the net with his body. One thing these two have in common, however, is that they keep the puck out of the net. In 1970–71, they won the Vezina Trophy, which is awarded to the goaltenders whose team allows the fewest goals. Thus, there isn't any "textbook" goaltender.

But there are some basic principles that will help a goalkeeper improve his style and action in the net:

1. Stay on your feet. This is one of the toughest things to master (especially for a young goalie). We know it looks great to make those diving, sprawling saves—after all, this is what really draws us to goaltending—but a goalie off his feet is all too often left in a helpless position. Unless you're lucky, it's almost impossible to stop a rebound when you're sprawled out on the ice. And you know how frustrating it can be to give up a goal on a rebound. Of course, you'll have to dive for some pucks. In fact, you'll have to be a circus acrobat to stop some shots. Our point here is that if you can make a save and stay on your feet, do so.

2. Don't touch shots going high or wide of the net. You may turn a harmless puck into a dangerous one.

3. Watch the puck, not the attacker's body. This is more important than watching the attacker's head for a tip-off when he is going to shoot. However, split vision will be developed with experience, with which the goalkeeper can check (from the corner of his eye) the position of the attacker's head as he approaches.

The best way to play the post when the puck is behind the net is to keep the leg hard against the inside of the post.

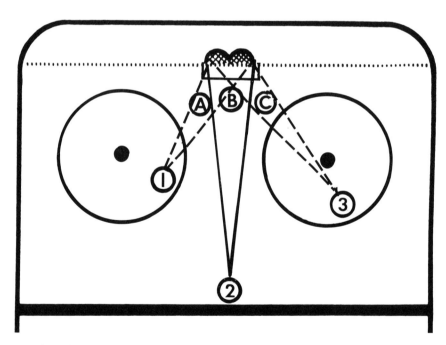

When playing the angles, the goaltender should use the crease as his guide. For example, he should move to locations A, B, or C to stop shots coming from 1, 2, or 3, respectively.

4. Don't turn the body around to look at a puck behind the net. Look over the shoulder, with the body facing the front of the net so that you will be in position if the puck is shot out quickly.

5. Familiarize yourself as much as possible with the shooting habits of each puck carrier—most have favorite or characteristic ways of getting off a shot. Most goalies keep a book on forwards as forwards keep one on them. When Rod first came up to the NHL, "I used to have the habit of winding up for the slap shot or setting myself before I shot. In other words, I was telegraphing my shot. The goalies knew it and had time to get set. I'm not doing that now. I'm using a wrist shot more, shooting faster, and getting the puck past the goalkeeper more often."

6. Always play the puck and the puck handler. That is, when a player has the puck on his stick, think first of him—not one of his teammates who might be getting into position for a pass.

7. Catch the puck whenever possible. This prevents rebounds and gives you a chance to play the puck in any direction. Always try to get some equipment blockage (pads, skates, or stick) behind all shots. Whenever possible, get squarely in front of the shot so that there is total glove and body blockage. Practice without a stick to improve your catch, equipment blockage, and footwork. Because some goalies feel more at home with something in their backhand glove hand, they use a cut-off butt end from an old stick when taking part in a stickless drill.

8. When the puck is behind your net or in the corner, hug the post nearer the play, with the heel of your skate tightly braced against it. Watch the play behind you by looking over your shoulder; if it appears to be coming out the opposite side, slide fast to jam your other foot against that post. Use your stick to stop pass-outs, or to check a puck carrier coming out from behind.

9. Keep the puck away from the goal mouth. On rebounds clear sharply into the corner with your stick if you have time; if not, drop to smother the puck with hand or body.

10. Never roam about the ice to stop pucks unless you know you'll get to the puck before an opposing player. While roaming, there's a danger that you may take your eyes off the puck in order to return to your net. This is something a good goalie never does. While there are several NHL goalies who successfully roam about their nets doing the work that defensemen normally do, we don't recommend this maneuver for young goaltenders.

11. Study the shooting angles to get the position in the net which gives the shooter minimum openings. Notice how moving out to your crease line, rather than remaining on the goal line, helps in this regard.

12. Good goaltenders are their teams' field generals on the ice. That is, the goalie directs his defensemen and forwards. Like a catcher in baseball, he is always talking and always directing. He knows where his opponents and his own teammates are at all times, and, by knowing, he can direct their movements in the defensive zone, alerting them to dangerous situations such as uncovered opponents.

GOALKEEPING MANEUVERS

The netminder's action in the crease is bounded by an arc instead of the rectangle or straight line of the crease. When moving around in the crease in relationship to the puck, you should always try to minimize the puck carrier's view of the open net. You should position yourself on a line extending from the puck to the center of the net. As the angle becomes sharper you must move to maintain your position on that magic line. To further cut down the target, you can move out of your net toward the attacker; however, you shouldn't move out too far.

You can make your job a great deal easier by playing your position in the goal mouth and crease with relation to the puck's position. For example, when a puck carrier is approaching with the puck on side—whether on his forehand or backhand shooting side—you know that the puck is in a basic shooting position. Therefore, you should move out to the front edge of the crease or a little further, directly toward the puck, thereby reducing the shooting angle. Remember that you want the puck to "see" the least possible amount of open net. As soon as the shot is made, you move with it.

Should the puck carrier approach you with the puck in front of him, he is primarily in a stickhandling position and would have difficulty making a shot. Therefore, you can move back a little toward your goal line, waiting for the puck carrier to make the next move. Frequently, under such circumstances, you throw a head fake toward him, thus making the puck carrier react.

It is a cardinal sin for a goalkeeper to be beaten on the so-called short side, that is, the side closest to the puck. To prevent this, you should employ the technique of telescoping. Use the posts as anchors but always move out from the goal arc and up the center of the shooting angle. Move into the goal as the attacker approaches. Telescoping cuts down the attacker's vision of the net. Practice moving around the goal arc following the puck. When a quick move from one goal post to the other is required, use a glide and drag movement. Turn the lead skate at a right angle to the other one, push with the rear skate and drag it behind. The move may also be done using the slide and drag. The skates are moved from their normal position in short slides. Learn to move quickly around the goal or from side to side when the play demands it.

As we have mentioned several times, the four corners of the goal are the most difficult areas to protect for goalies. Most goals are scored in the lower corners, particularly on the goalkeeper's weak side. To protect these lower corners use the stick, skate, pads, and gloves. On the upper corners use the gloves or preferably use the whole body. As mentioned earlier, always get as much equipment as possible in front of the shot.

Before each period of the game, most goalies rough up the ice in their crease. This is done to give their skates better purchase. Also make sure that there is no extra water in the goaltender's area. The onus is on the referee to have excess water removed, but the goalie must make the request.

The Stance. When the puck is at the opposite end of the ice, the goalie may relax. You may spend more than half the game under fire in your own end; therefore, learn to save yourself for the maximum efforts you'll then be called upon to make. Thus, while the other goalie is under fire, take a comfortable stance with your knees bent, legs slightly apart and your toes pointed outward. Hold the stick rather loosely so that when it slides on the ice, the entire blade is in contact with the ice. Position yourself in the front center of the crease.

When the puck reaches center ice, you must adopt the ready position. The feet are wide enough apart to keep the pads closed. The knees are bent just enough to allow you to move suddenly to either the right or left. Bend forward at the waist to bring your eyes closer to ice level, and to allow you to keep your stick flat on the ice in front of your skates. The stick is held in the upper hand, at the bottom of the narrow part of the shaft. Your head and eyes are up, intently following the puck. The free, or catching, hand is held beside the lower leg.

Move from this stance in a small arc from side to side of your net, keeping your body at all times centered on the puck. In this standard

The three most common goalie ready positions: the crouch (left), the stand-up position (above), and the butterfly or inverted "V" style (below).

The slide glide.

The full split.

ready position your stick and catching hand can readily cover one side of the net. (This side is your strong side; the other is known as your weak side.) The stick is used to prevent as many shots along the ice as it can reach. Remember to keep the blade perpendicular on the ice. Ice shots to the weak side are taken on the skate blade of that foot. Your pads take shots level with your knees or lower. Use your free hand to catch all pucks off the ice to the strong side, to trap high shots taken on the body, and to smother loose pucks on the ice when you have to go down. High shots to your weak side may be deflected by the back of your stick hand.

Goalies are individualists and they have variations of this so-called standard ready position. The three most common are as follows:

1. *The Crouch.* In the crouch the back is straight, the legs are in a deep knee bend, the hand grips the stick at the top of the wide shaft and the stick is placed directly in front of the feet. The catching glove hand is up and open. A crouching goalie generally uses a stick lie between 11 and 13.

2. *The Stand-up Position.* In the stand-up position the hand is higher on the handle of the stick and the knees are only slightly bent. The stick, usually a lie from 13 to 15, is placed in front of the skates, legs close together. The catching-glove hand is in the standard ready position. The back is straight and the body is bent slightly forward at the waist.

3. *The Butterfly Style.* In the butterfly style, the legs are wide apart and form an inverted V. The body is in the deep crouch position, back straight. The stick is between the legs and the grip is at the wide part of the shaft. The catching-glove hand is up and open.

As you play more and more shots at the goal, chances are that you'll develop a particular stance suited to your style of play. In fact, most fundamental goalie maneuvers mentioned in this chapter will be varied as you develop your own style of playing goal.

Slide Glide. This maneuver is frequently employed to get the goalie across the goal area quickly. When you wish to glide to the right, for example, you turn your right foot so the toes are heading in that direction. Push off hard with the other foot. To stop the glide, as you'll want to do when the puck has been stopped, you simply turn the leading foot sideways and dig the blade firmly into the ice. The action of the foot that leads the movement is governed by the hip on that side. For instance, when making the glide to the right, you turn your right hip outward in the direction of the glide. This automatically will turn

The half split.

your foot. Once the move across the crease is started, your front shoulder should follow your feet and should be kept as nearly as possible directly above your foot and knee. To help keep your balance, bend the knee slightly. While gliding across, carry your stick in the hand on the opposite side to which you're gliding, so that you are poised to sweep away the puck should it drop to the ice.

The bend of your forward knee determines the height of your glide across the cage. For instance, when moving across to stop or catch a high shot, the knee of your front leg should be bent just enough to maintain your proper balance. If the glide is for a medium-height shot —from the stomach to the hips—the forward knee needs more bending. On low shots, the forward knee must be even more bent. Actually by bending your knee you get your hand close to the level of the shot and thus if you misjudge it a little you can move it down or up as required. If you went across without bending your forward knee and the shot was lower than expected, you wouldn't be able to reach down far enough to stop it.

The Full Split. This move is employed to stop a low shot well to the side of the goalkeeper either on the ice or a few inches high. In making the maneuver, as its name implies, you do the split exactly as done by

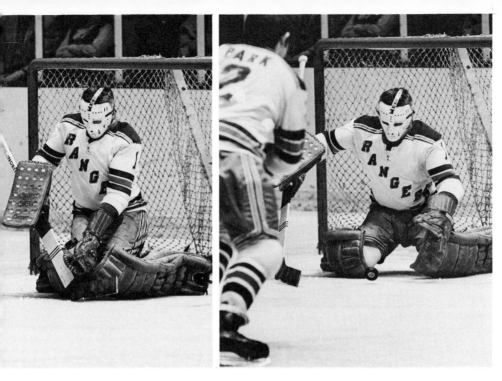

The butterfly drop.

a ballet dancer. The move is started in the same manner as the slide glide is started, with a push off the foot farthest away from the puck. At the same time the other foot is kicked out to the side toward the spot at which you expect to stop the shot. The toe of the skate should be facing directly upward and your leg should be straight at the knee. As your leg is kicked out, the push-off foot turns so that the toe of the skate is pointing in the same direction as your other foot. This foot is then moved as far back as possible so that your leg straightens. This brings your body down to the ice between the legs. As your forward foot is kicked out to the side to start the split action, the upper body is bent well forward over this leg and your head is kept forward with your eyes on the puck at all times.

While making a full split, the stick is moved at the same moment as the leg closest to the puck is kicked out. When the split has been completed, the stick blade should be out slightly past the foot with the outside edge flat on the ice and the toe of the blade facing up. Your free or catching hand should be ready to cover the vulnerable crotch area.

There are two basic methods of recovering from the split. You can bring the rear foot quickly underneath your body and then drive up-

Two ways of accomplishing the double-leg slide.

ward. Or you can pull your feet back in toward the center of your body, at the same time raising your body. It's vital that you should practice your recovery until you can do it rapidly and in good balance. The sooner you can regain your feet, the sooner you'll be back in the play.

The Half-Split. This move is excellent for shots low to one side and is also valuable because it leaves you in a good covering position. It is accomplished by dropping to one knee, with your other leg going out sideways as flat on the ice as possible. When your leg is moved out along the ice, the inside of your knee and the inside of the ankle should be facing down toward or right on the ice. It should be practiced to both sides. The stick should go out to the side with the blade in front of the foot. Actually, the stick is handled in the same way as when doing the split.

The Butterfly Drop. The butterfly drop is used against dekers and to cover shots along the ice. Drop on the inside seam of the pads, keeping your back straight, the glove hand up and the stick in front of the legs. The skate on the outside should be past the post. In performing this maneuver you get down to the ice rapidly in order to catch the puck carrier off guard. Surprise is of utmost importance in the butterfly drop. If done too slowly or if the move is telegraphed to the attacker, the puck carrier will have the opportunity to shoot underneath you as you go down, stop dead and fire over you as you hit the ice, or sidestep the move and leave you sprawling on the ice behind, looking and feeling very foolish.

The Double-Leg Slide. In the double-leg slide, throw the two feet out, one leg on top of the other, the stick hand or glove hand up, depending on the side. This move is excellent against the quick shot to the far corner.

The Pad or Side Kick. To make stops on quick low shots from the sides, most goalies like to use the pad or side kick. It's a simple movement that involves a quick, stiff-legged lift of the leg closest to the puck in a sideways action. During the kick, the pads should be kept facing square to the puck.

The Skate Save. The skate save is a quick move to stop low shots from the corners. When making this save you shouldn't go down the ice but rather aim the side of your skate blade at the puck. Your knee should be bent and the foot positioned with skate blade turned slightly outward, so that when the puck hits the blade it will be deflected outward and to the boards.

When doing the split to make a skate save, your rear leg should be

The side-kick save.

The goaltender makes a stick check.

dragged behind; the skate on this foot can be turned and used to stop the slide if it's too fast for the shot. Also be sure to place your stick between your legs for precautionary blocking and have your catching hand ready in the vulnerable crotch area. Practice skate-save proficiency with both feet and don't use the skate if you can use your stick and keep possession of the puck.

The Stick Check. The netminder who can use his stick quickly and efficiently will find this skill often pays off for him, especially during scrambled play around the net and when up against a deker. In stick checking, you must not use any sweeping motions or wild swings but should confine yourself to short, well-controlled jabs. The ability to use a good poke and hook check just as any other player does will often come in handy. A good example of this is when you're sprawled on the ice out of position. You can often make a stick-check movement and stop a goal.

STRATEGY OF GOALTENDING

Many suggestions that come under the category of strategy have already been dealt with. However, there are still a few to cover.

Playing Face-Offs. The netminder must have a clear line of sight to the face-off area, or else he's beaten to start with. When he sets up, he should locate himself at the corner of the crease so that the middle of the stick's blade rests on the point of his crease.

Blooper Shots. Every now and then a puck carrier may let go a high flip shot that becomes a bouncing puck. On such blooper shots, move out to the puck and get it before the first bounce whenever possible. Catch it if possible, smother all first bounces with the whole body. Great care must be taken with bouncing pucks since they are moving slowly down the ice twisting and turning in different directions and it is quite possible for them to change direction quickly in an unexpected, freak hop.

Screen Shots. The screen shot is, of course, the toughest shot a goalie has to handle because his vision is blocked by other players or just by the way the play is developing in front of the net, and he has lost sight of the puck. Many a goalkeeper has been scored upon without even seeing the puck. But if he's in the right position, he may be able to make the save by simply having the puck hit him. Also, by playing in a deep crouch, he may be able to peer through the maze of sticks, legs, and players. The goalie may also be able to detect the direction of

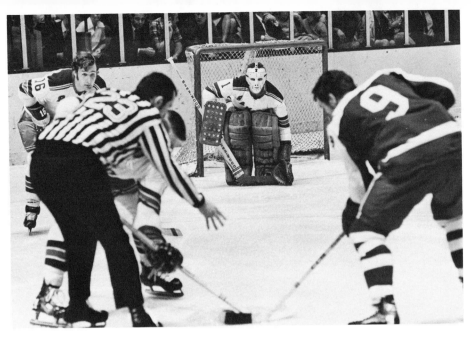

The proper position for a goaltender on the face-off.

impending shots by noting the body angle of the players who are screening him.

Long Shots. When the goalkeeper has the time on long shots, he should get his body behind the puck instead of just catching it with his glove hand. This will avoid a fluke goal which can result from a puck deflecting off his hand into the net. On long bouncing shots, move out on the puck and smother it. It is not uncommon to come way out of the net to do just this.

Faking. Just as a puck carrier can use faking to force the goaltender into making the first move and thus draw him out of position, so can the goalie entice the puck carrier into committing himself. Faking a stick check is an ideal way to force the puck carrier into making a move.

Holding the Puck. There are times when it's wise for you to hold on to the puck purposely until the referee blows his whistle to stop play. For example, if an attacker is very close to you, or there is a free attacker on the side to which you must clear, or if you're off balance after catching the puck, or if your team's defensive play is disorganized, or if your side needs a player change, it's wise for you to hold the puck. But remember that any unnecessary holding will only put your team at a disadvantage; it will mean a face-off close to the goal you are

Smothering a puck is sometimes a wise move by a goalie.

Carefully clear shots that are caught.

tending, and this may give the opposing team an opportunity to set up a scoring play.

Smothering the Puck. Dropping on the puck to smother it and stop further play is a good maneuver any time there is an attacking player dangerously close to a free puck. The best way to go down to the ice to smother the puck is first to drop your knees and then grab the puck or lie on top of it, curling your body around it. Don't try to dive or bellyflop on it since such maneuvers leave your body in the air too long.

If the puck is a short distance away and there is an attacking player attempting to get it, the best smothering technique is to take a couple of quick strides and then go down with your knees together, keeping your body between the puck and the goal. Once on your knees, you can throw your body toward the puck, reaching it with your hands to cover it. When making any smothering maneuvers be sure to keep your eyes on the puck until it is safely under your body or hands.

Clearing the Puck. Many goals are scored as a result of rebounds and poor clearing procedures. To control a rebound as much as possible, use the hands either to catch the puck or to trap it against the body or pads. Any time there seems any danger of a rebound being knocked in by an opposing player, you shouldn't attempt to clear, but should hold or smother the puck. If a stop is made with your body and the puck is trapped in your equipment, don't move until the whistle has been blown.

When clearing the puck, it is usually best to do so to the side and behind the goal if possible, because, even if it is recovered by an opposing player, he won't be in a position to make a scoring attempt before you're set again. If the puck is loose and you can beat the attacker to it, skate quickly out and clear it over the blue line. Snap judgment is the ultimate in this situation. Most clearing, however, should be to the side and behind the goal or to the corners, and let the defensemen do the rest. A clearing pass to a teammate should be attempted only when you're certain that the play can be completed. If there is even the faintest chance that it may be intercepted, a clearing pass shouldn't be made.

When making a clearing play, do so as quickly as possible after the shot has been stopped so that none of the attacking players can break in quickly for the puck. Holding the puck too long before clearing can get you in trouble or cause a face-off deep in your defending zone. It's a good policy when clearing to get rid of the puck as quickly as possible, especially if there is an attacking player anywhere near the goal.

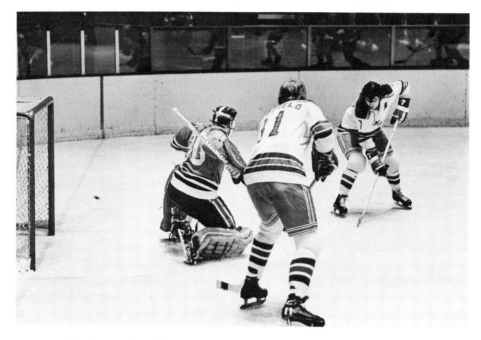

Situations such as this—two opponents against a goalie—make life miserable for goalies.

One-Man Breakaways. When a player breaks in on the net alone, remember that the puck carrier can't shoot effectively while in a stickhandling position. He must bring the puck to either his left or right, and you shouldn't commit yourself too soon. Wait for the stickhandler to make the move for you to work on. Watch his stick for a tip-off on his shot.

On a one-man breakaway, most goalies prefer to come out of their nets to cut down the shooter's angle. That is, skate out of your net a few feet, moving directly at the attacker, as described in Chapter 6. If the shooter comes within body length, you can make a surprise baseball-slide block at the puck to beat the attacker to the punch. In this slide, aim your leg pads at the puck and place one leg pad upon the other for increased blockage. If possible, slide when the puck carrier takes his eye off the net. Gump Worsley is one of the best goaltenders against a breakaway that we know of in the NHL. He rarely is the first to commit himself, but places himself in the middle of the goal and calmly waits for the opposing forward to make the first move in the one-on-one situation.

Two-Man Breakaway. This is a goalie's nightmare. When facing a two-on-one situation, you must concentrate on *not* making the first move. You must always play the puck, moving as best you can to stay in front of it at all times.

If the attacking player is not in a passing position (with the puck at his side), move out to the edge of the crease to reduce the shooting angle to both corners. If the puck carrier is in a position to pass (the puck in front of him), you must wait until he executes the pass or moves to shoot. If a pass is made, start shifting your position to the receiver side immediately, but stay on your feet, unless the pass is made within the body-length smothering distance. If the pass is one within your body length, hit the ice as the pass is made, slide with the pass, and take out the puck and the receiver. Since the receiver is in so close to the net, there is no danger of a return pass.

Penalty Shots. A penalty-shot play is simply a one-on-one situation, except that the player designated by the referee to take the shot must always move toward the goal once he has crossed the attacking blue line, and he receives only one shot. (No goal can be scored on a rebound of any kind.) The goalie must remain in his goal crease until the puck has crossed the adjacent blue line.

In a penalty-shot situation, the goalie must keep the shooting angle to a minimum (you can move much further away from the net since you don't have to worry about a rebound or other opposing players), and must force the attacker into the first commitment. There are several ways this can be accomplished. For instance, if the attacker is coming down the side, you can come out to meet him on that side. But when doing this, keep in mind how much net area you're giving the player to shoot at on the far, or unprotected, side of the cage. Frequently, by intentionally giving the attacking player a spot to aim at, you hope that he takes this "advantage" and you are ready to defend that area with stick or body. Also when coming out of the net to cut down the angle, shift from side to side, attempting to make the attacker guess where you're going to be in the next second or so. Another trick is to make the player shoot with his backhand because he usually has less power and control in this type of shot.

Getting Off Ice. The goalies should always watch the signals used by referees, especially when the puck is in the neutral or offensive zone. If the referee signals a delayed penalty, you must be certain which team is the offender. If it is your opponent, you should skate as fast as possible to your bench so your team can have another skater enter the offense. Remember that once the offending team touches the puck, play is stopped so there is no need for the goalie to be on the ice when a delayed penalty is called.

Pulling the Goalie. Most coaches will pull the goalkeeper near the end of the game in order to get another skater on the ice in an effort to get a tying goal. If this is your team policy, you should station yourself, according to the location of the puck, in a position on the ice where you can readily see your coach, who will give the signal when you are to leave the ice. Seconds count near the end of a game, and the move must be done efficiently. In fact, with a face-off at the opponent's end and seconds to go in any period, especially with a one-man advantage, our coach won't hesitate to pull the goalie.

Drills for the Goalie. Goaltending is a tough position and requires time and effort to develop the needed skills. Skating ability, as in every other position, is the most important skill that the goalkeeper must master. Therefore, it is important that he participate in all the skating drills at practice.

A goalie, as previously stated, practices without his stick. That is, he must block shots off the pads of the glove, arms, and body. In practice, his teammates should shoot so that the goalie also becomes adept at making skate saves.

There are, of course, many drills that can be used to keep a goalie sharp. One we use at the Skateland Summer Hockey School is to line seven or eight players up in front of the goal—about 15 feet away from the goaltender. At a given signal we have each player shoot at the net in turn. The puck handler must make certain not to shoot until the goalie has stopped the puck fired by the man ahead and the goalie is looking at him.

9

Conditioning and the Hockey Player

PLAYING better hockey requires top physical condition. Your heart, lungs, and body muscles must be strengthened to meet the demands of rugged competition. In fact, physical condition can often make the difference between a run-of-the-mill player and a good one. Being in good shape also can prevent many injuries.

Physical condition, however, is very much an individual matter. You must *want* to train; you must be convinced that you can produce your best efforts only when you are at the peak of condition. Take stock of yourself to determine where you are weakest. What muscles need the most strengthening? For instance, when Rod was a youngster, he never gave skating a second thought. "It was something I did naturally. Keeping my legs in shape was just part of an overall fitness program that I followed. Push-ups and sit-ups are the routine exercises any boy practices if he wants to develop a strong and healthy body. Then I'd go to the Montreal Forum and watch the Canadiens play. Guys like Boomer Geoffrion, Rocket Richard, and the others would smash pucks off the boards so hard sometimes you had to cover your ears. It made me realize what powerful wrists they must have. I decided to develop my grip and wrists, too.

"I went home and dreamed up an exercising device to help build the muscles in my arms and wrists. I got an old broomstick from my mother, cut it about fourteen inches long, and borrowed a drill from dad to cut a hole in the middle. Then I suspended a piece of iron from a rope through the stick. I'd roll the iron up, over and over again, to build my wrists. Slowly but surely I found my shot improving. I don't know how much that broomstick had to do with it, but pretty soon my shots were making a racket just like Geoffrion's."

Drills and exercises that we perform in training camp.

OFF-SEASON CONDITIONING

The best way to stay in condition is never to get out of condition. That is, a good hockey player is really never out of good physical condition. Thanks to the workouts we receive at our hockey school, we're both in condition pretty much the year around. Many of our teammates play golf as a form of relaxation and conditioning. In fact, Vic Hadfield, Jean Ratelle, and Bobby Rousseau are golf professionals during the off-season.

While a hockey player should keep his muscles in shape during the off-season and maintain close to his playing weight, a conditioning program must be undertaken three or four weeks before training camp opens. It should be pointed out that a hockey training camp isn't a health farm. Players shouldn't report to lose weight or develop muscles. They are at camp to prepare themselves mentally and physically for the hockey wars. Incidentally, the same holds true for all the boys going to any hockey school. Try to arrive in the best possible condition so that you can get right to work on hockey training.

Our Ranger preseason activity lasts but a month. After only one week, the squads are ready to play exhibition games, of which we're permitted to play a maximum of 12. During the off-season, a hockey player should always watch his weight and take care not to overeat. Brad can gain weight very easily—"If I report to training camp at more than a hundred ninety pounds (my normal playing weight) our coach really lowers the boom on me. I usually have to get rid of five to ten pounds before camp. Of course, the legs are of primary importance to a hockey player. Of all the exercises you can do to strengthen your legs and to keep them strong, nothing can replace walking or running."

Here's a program that Brad has found excellent for getting legs into shape:

    Slow jog—5 minutes
    Sprint 20 yards, walk 50 yards, repeat—4 minutes
    Slow running—4 minutes
    Backward running (full speed), turn, and run forward full speed, both 25 yards—1 minute
    Walk—4 minutes
    Hop on left foot 25 yards, then right foot 25 yards—1 minute
    Slow jog—5 minutes

Leg kick-up and groin-stretch exercises are good muscle - loosening drills.

The push-and-hold exercises are another good warm-up drill. One player pushes, the other holds, using the same stick.

This leg-strengthening program should be lengthened slowly from 25 to 50 minutes in duration. Running a slightly hilly terrain is better than on flat ground. Don't stand around after a workout but shower immediately.

There are many ways that you can develop your wrists, arms, and shoulders. Weight training (primarily with bar bells) is a good way to strengthen these muscles. Swimming, tennis, squash, and handball are also good. The latter is especially good for goalies since it toughens the palms of their hands, and the constant bending is good for the back muscles. Another trick for goalies is to put on a pair of regular hockey shin guards, not goalie pads, and play alone with a handball trying to keep the ball in play by kicking it back to the front wall, hitting it squarely in the center of the shin guard.

Before our students report to school, we send an instruction sheet containing five body-building exercises that have been developed especially for hockey players. As a result of a careful 25-year study of the functions and demands, plus types of injury, it has been determined that no other athletic functions are exactly like those of a hockey player. The feet, thighs, buttocks, and lower back are the parts of the body which make the difference. The following exercises are the best known for developing problem areas:

1. Lie on the floor with one foot against a dresser, or similar furniture piece, in such a position that your heel can be forced under it. The base of a dresser between the legs is a space well suited to this. Keep the back of your knees flat upon the floor and force your heel under the dresser as far as it will go. You will feel a pulling at your calf. Lie there a few moments, then switch to the other foot.

2. While lying or sitting, pull the feet up and curl the toes downward, holding as long as possible. Usually a cramping underneath the arch prevents holding this position too long. Repeat a few times.

3. Lie on your back upon the floor, bend one knee completely with your foot free of the floor, and swing your leg like a pendulum until eventually you can touch your buttock with your heel.

4. Lie flat upon the floor with your legs parted, and the inside of one foot against a heavy piece of furniture. The other leg, while still in contact with the floor, is pulled further away from the one which is held in place by the heavy piece of furniture. This you will notice gives the vague feeling of a slightly pulled groin. No matter how hard

you may work at this, you cannot injure yourself. Devote the same amount of effort to each leg.

5. This last exercise, with which many of you are already acquainted, is the most beneficial of all in so far as general freedom of movement is concerned. It incorporates foot, ankle, calf, knee, thigh, buttock, lower-back, and hip-joint exercises. To accomplish it, sit on the floor with both heels touching a wall. Extend your arms with fingers pointing toward the wall just above the toes. Lean backward just a little while breathing in deeply through the nose. Bend forward from the hips while breathing out through the open mouth, making sure that the back of the knees remain in contact with the floor. Eventually you should be able to punch the wall with your clenched fists.

You may find that any one or more of these exercises is quite easy to do, and the remainder so difficult that you feel you are made in such a way that they are impossible for you; we have heard it said so many times, but it has never been true. Any person who considers himself an athlete should be able to do them all with ease.

IN-SEASON CONDITIONING

If you're a member of an organized team, your conditioning program and practice are planned for you. But a hockey player must exercise constantly to keep in condition and to prevent muscular injuries. Players can suffer serious muscle pulls if they don't warm up properly. Muscles must be loose. If they're not, they will pull or rip and then you're out of action. Early in the hockey season, especially, groin injuries seem to be a common problem. While a groin pull isn't serious, it is painful. Only rest will heal it properly and that means no hockey playing. Illustrated are several muscle-loosening exercises that prevent such pulls from occurring.

Of course, before a game, the warm-up period is most important. Once on the ice, we both have about the same ritual: Skate around slowly, stretch and bend, and then skate a little faster. After taking a few shots and having passed the puck around a bit, we are ready both physically and emotionally for the game.

A practice session, during the season, is a good time to correct faults and develop better team play. A typical 2-hour Ranger practice session at Skateland is about as follows:

15 minutes: Muscle loosening exercises and skating drills, including crossovers, figure eights, and backward skating.

15 minutes: Shooting drills with goalies at both ends of the ice.

15 minutes: Passing and stickhandling drills as well as a checking
practice.

15 minutes: Special play—line rushes, breakouts, power plays,
and face-off drills.

45 minutes: Scrimmage under near-game conditions.

15 minutes: Stops and starts and similar drills. The session is
closed out by skating laps around the rink.

During the season it's important to eat properly. Eat well-balanced
meals with moderate amounts of liquid. Stay away from fatty foods and
don't eat a heavy meal later than 4 hours before a game. Don't smoke
during the hockey season—or at any time. Neither of us does. Also,
don't drink hard liquor— it doesn't mix well with hockey. Incidentally,
during a game, most team trainers have a liquid drink available to help
replace the loss of body fluids due to perspiration. Of course, several
of us still like the old custom of eating an orange between periods. But,
never fill up on water because it certainly can slow you down.

Proper sleep is most important to any athlete. Eight to 10 hours of
sleep is ideal every night, and be in bed at least by 11 P.M. This, of
course, is impossible on game nights, and here we are confronted with
a different problem. Many hockey players can't sleep after a grueling
contest, and 3 hours later they are still replaying the game. Of course,
most of us take a nap in the afternoon before a game. We have been
asked frequently how grown men can sleep for 3 hours before a game.
To be truthful, it's just a question of conditioning your body to it.
We're pros, and we know our entire livelihood depends on our being
in the best possible condition. So we do it.

10

Up the Road to the NHL

ALL young hockey players dream of the day when they'll be in the National Hockey League. Some fortunate boys, like us, have attained this goal. Others fall by the wayside, and many are forced to take the detours of life, but each ambition commences with a dream.

While about 99 percent of today's professional hockey players were born in Canada, it's only a matter of time until the United States has its own stars too. Junior hockey associations around major U.S. cities are developing some fine young people. Amateur hockey in high schools and colleges is also beginning to turn out good players. In fact, in 1972, Chris Ahrens, a young man who played his minor hockey at Skateland and attended our school, was the first New York metropolitan player drafted by a NHL team. The United States Olympic hockey team won a silver medal for its second-place finish in the 1972 games in Japan. Hockey is no longer just the national game of Canada, but it's *the sport of North America.*

We're frequently asked what's the best way to learn to play hockey correctly. The answer is to play on an organized team. Thanks to the facilities of today—there are skating rinks available in almost every major town or city in North America—almost every boy who has the desire can join an organized team. Coaching has greatly improved over the years, and with the formation of teams according to age and ability, each youngster has an equal opportunity. Playing under supervision eliminates the many bad habits of the self-taught individual. In recent years one of the fastest methods of learning the sport is to attend a summer hockey school. The last ten years have witnessed the growth of at least 75 such schools in the United States and Canada.

The idea of hockey schools is generally credited to our coach, Emile

239

Rod Gilbert gives his students at Skateland Summer Hockey School the "word."

Francis. In 1950 he joined a fellow named George Vogan in setting up the first hockey school ever. The place was Moose Jaw, Saskatchewan, Canada, and two years later they went to Grand Forks, North Dakota. The student body grew from 25 kids to 120, and the instructional staff included such hockey greats as Red Kelley, Glenn Hall, and Andy Bathgate. The idea for a hockey school came to Emile during a visit to the Vero Beach, Florida, training camp of the Brooklyn Dodgers. They had a baseball school there, and Emile thought, "If they do it in baseball, why not hockey?"

Of course, there are two types of hockey summer schools. One is a summer camp that includes hockey along with its various other programs. The second is a summer camp where hockey is exclusively taught. Our familiarity is with the latter type, and our remarks in this chapter are based on these schools.

When selecting a hockey school, attempt to learn its teaching philosophy. We operate under a "teach and have fun" premise. Skating, stickhandling, passing, shooting, checking, and play are emphasized, and there is a constant review of the basics in varying drills so that we "don't practice mistakes." True, each man has a different philosophy of teaching, but the experienced, mature, interested instructor will try to get to the individual. This is accomplished by working with smaller groups, say 20 to 25 per class, and by stressing individual play more than group play. Of course, team play, sportsmanship, the basic playing rules, and bench decorum are also emphasized. When the boys are ready for it, there are daily scrimmages.

In addition to normal concerns when selecting a summer camp—the food, the programs that are available, the supervisory staff, and accommodations—the hockey student has another consideration. What about the hockey teaching staff? We have seen a few schools that employ the big star, who rarely works with the pupils; he is there for window dressing, while younger assistants are actually doing the leg work and teaching. Both of us are at our school while it's in session.

Summer hockey schools are an excellent way to learn our game, but you must be a member of an organized team to put this knowledge to use. Most skating rinks are now sponsoring leagues like we have in Canada. Rod Gilbert joined an organized peewee-league team when he was eight. Canada's peewee and midget hockey leagues can be compared with the Little Leagues and Babe Ruth baseball leagues in the United States. Each league has a regular schedule and championship playoffs. Whereas the Little League has a championship series in Williamsport, Pennsylvania, the various kids' hockey leagues have their own different playoffs. The organization of the Little League and some of the peewee hockey groups is very involved and very much the same. In both cases they tend to put too much emphasis on the institutional aspects of the sport, detracting from the recreational value. To aid those who are interested in attending hockey schools, our associate, Allan Eisinger, along with other leading hockey school directors, formed an association to accumulate the necessary information on the various schools. To obtain a copy of this report, write to: Skateland, 3345 Hillside Avenue, New Hyde Park, New York 11040.

Once a boy reaches the age of fourteen he can join the junior amateur leagues. In Canada there are two basic sets of junior amateur leagues, Junior A and Junior B. The Junior A encompasses the ages of sixteen to twenty, while Junior B covers the ages of fourteen to twenty. The major difference between the two, apart from the age ranges, is that the quality of competition in Junior A is quite a bit better than in Junior B, although players have been known to graduate from Junior B to the professional ranks. Rogatien Vachon, the Los Angeles Kings goalie, is one such example, but for the most part players of high ability first play in the Junior A division and then make it to the pros.

Junior hockey, based to a degree on the Canadian system, is on the rise in the United States. There are over 150,000 registered Amateur Hockey Association players in the United States. The Metropolitan Junior Hockey Association, which comprises teams from the metropolitan New York area, for example, includes boys up to nineteen, and the brand of hockey played is steadily improving to where it could be considered about equivalent to Junior B or better hockey in Canada. In fact, several of our former students who played in the MJHA are now playing Junior A hockey in Canadian Amateur Hockey Association leagues.

In the CAHA, players in both Junior A and Junior B, while being regarded as amateurs, receive a weekly allowance to compensate for time taken away from school or job. In many cases the youngsters continue attending school while playing junior hockey. Junior A competition, by its very nature, is more intense than Junior B, because the Junior A stickhandlers are on the verge of professionalism and are constantly being scouted by major-league teams. Nowadays, many of the Juniors first play college hockey and then enter the pro ranks. Cliff Koroll, Ken Dryden, Keith Magnusson, and Tony Esposito are some of the college breed who have made it in the NHL.

UP THE ROAD TO THE NHL WITH ROD

"I guess you could say my hockey-playing days started when my parents enrolled me at Roussin Academy, a French-Canadian Catholic school that starts children in the first grade and has classes right up to what would be the equivalent of the fourth year of high school in the United States. Naturally, Roussin, like most Canadian schools, had hockey teams for every grade, and I began playing for them as soon as I entered.

"Besides playing hockey in school, I played in peewee leagues and at fourteen joined a semipro team called Mernier Refrigeration, sponsored by the company of that name. The latter presented a great challenge. For one thing, it meant I would be playing against skaters twice my age. For another, it meant traveling out of Montreal—something I'd never done.

"When I was fifteen I started to play Junior B hockey for a parish team called St. Eusebe in the Laurentian League, which embraces teams in and around Montreal. Once I realized I was doing well with St. Eusebe, visions of playing Junior A hockey began dancing in my head. At sixteen I qualified for Junior A, as far as age went. Several possibilities were before me. I could play for the Montreal-sponsored team in Hull-Ottawa, or I could play for a team sponsored by a different NHL club.

"You must realize that every French-Canadian kid dreams of the day that he'll play for the Montreal Canadiens. In Montreal hockey is a religion, and everybody, or at least it seems like everybody, worships at the altar of the beloved Canadiens. But I was about to become a heretic; I had made up my mind that I would try out for the Rangers. I made this decision because the Canadiens were a powerful team with a very, very big minor-league farm system. I considered the possibilities and soon realized that the odds were far greater against my getting a spot on the Canadiens because of this vast farm system, coupled with their already strong roster. There just didn't appear to be any room for me in the Montreal organization, plus the fact that my good friend and the man who shaped my entire hockey career, Yvon Prud'Homme, was a scout for the Rangers.

"It was Prud'Homme who arranged for me to try out with the Rangers' Guelph Biltmores in the Ontario Hockey Association. The

OHA was the strongest junior league in Canada. 'I don't think you're good enough to make it,' Prud'Homme told me. 'I expect to see you back in Montreal in a couple of weeks.'

"My parents were equally convinced I'd be back. To them the trip to Guelph was nothing more than my first excursion out of the province of Quebec, although they weren't too crazy about that, either, especially after a visit to our house by a member of the Canadiens' organization. 'What are you doing letting a French-Canadian boy try out for an English-speaking team owned by the New York Rangers?' he demanded.

"He intimidated my parents, who didn't realize that there already were several French-Canadian boys playing for English-speaking teams. Marcel Pronovost was a star for the Detroit Red Wings, Camille Henry with the Rangers, and Real Chevrefils with the Boston Bruins. 'He's right,' said Frère Eursise, who coached me at Roussin where I still was attending school. 'It would be improper to take him away from his education at the age of sixteen when he still hasn't graduated from the academy. I suggest that he stay in Montreal.'

"I felt cornered and guilty, since I myself was a Montreal fan and I worshiped the Boomer Geoffrion. Brother Eursise nearly had me convinced, until Prud'Homme pointed out that I was only going to Guelph for a tryout and he doubted very much that I could make the team. But the deadlock was finally resolved by my brother Jean-Marie. 'Let him try it,' he said. 'He can always come back—and he's already finished twelve years of schooling at Roussin.'

"That tilted it in my favor. Jean-Marie had played Junior B hockey. Several of his friends had moved on to Hull, where they found themselves in a *cul-de-sac* because the Canadiens had a surplus of good hockey players. 'There wouldn't be any room for you in the Montreal system,' he said, and I believed him. And the next day I went out and bought myself a round-trip ticket to Guelph.

"I climbed aboard the train to Guelph, a sixteen-year-old French-Canadian who couldn't speak a word of English. My destination was an Ontario city of some fifty thousand people, almost none of whom could speak French. The only common bond we had was a love of hockey. At least this was enough to make me feel comfortable, if not actually at home. As soon as I arrived, the team arranged for me to stay at a boarding house operated by Mr. and Mrs. Michael Woronka. Fortunately they were very special people. They not only took me in as a paying boarder, but they made me feel as if I were their son. They were friendly people, a happy family, and right off the bat we clicked. They wanted to help me enjoy Guelph and they were genuinely interested in teaching me to speak English. Were it not for their concern and sensitivity, I might very well have taken a train back to Montreal.

"This positive atmosphere reflected in my performance at training camp. I was motivated to work hard and surprised a lot of people. 'As soon as I saw you in the workouts,' said Prud'Homme, 'I knew you had the desire and the ability to make it that first year. You decided to give 120 percent, and that's what made the difference.'

"I knew that that extra effort would help put me on the team, and, after two weeks, the coach, Eddie Bush, told me I had made his club. Now this presented a problem. What was I going to tell my parents, who fully expected me to return home after training camp? How could I persuade them to let me stay? I knew I had one thing going for me —Prud'Homme, who was on my side now. I never knew how he did it, but my parents gave me permission to stay in Guelph.

"According to Junior A regulations, at that time, you were given your room, board, and tuition in school free, plus receiving $10 a week spending money. On Christmas and Easter you were given a paid vacation back to your home town. If you didn't choose to go to school, your $10 a week spending money was increased to $60, since the club didn't have to pay tuition. It was an incentive for many a young sixteen-year-old to quit school, for that amount of money in many cases was as much as the boy's father earned.

"I liked living and playing in Guelph, but it wasn't easy. School was especially difficult. Since I hadn't graduated from Roussin Academy, I had to continue my high school studies at the English school in Guelph. The first thing they did when I got there was drop me back a year because of my language deficiency. Fortunately, I learned fast both in and out of school. The boarding house was an especially big help. Mrs. Woronka, the landlady, was herself a teacher, and she had three children. I used to talk with them, and they, in turn, helped me learn. Wherever I went I carried a dictionary under my arm or in my pocket. When a word came up that was new to me, I'd flip the pages of my dictionary until I found it. We also had three English-speaking hockey players in the house, and they helped me, making things a lot more comfortable than they might have been.

"Eddie Bush, who was a former star NHL defenseman, coached me during that first year in Guelph, and then I played the next three seasons under Emile Francis, and each year I improved. In my third as a junior with Guelph, I had finished second in scoring to Chico Maki (now with the Chicago Blackhawks) who had been playing for St. Catherine's. I was good enough as a hockey player to get a tryout with Trois Rivières (Three Rivers), which was a Ranger pro farm team at the time. Trois Rivières had three games remaining on its regular schedule. In those three games I scored four goals and six assists for ten points.

"Although I was sent back to Guelph the next season, I knew that NHL teams would often invite their best junior players for two- or three-game trials near the end of the season, and I wondered whether the Rangers were considering me. I got my answer a few hours before Guelph's last regular 1960–61 season game. Emile Francis called me over in the dressing room. 'Rod,' Francis said, 'they want you in New York.' I felt a little dizzy. 'After our game, take the bus to Toronto and join the Rangers there.' I was so excited that I had difficulty understanding him. 'Mr. Francis,' I said, 'could you please repeat this for me? Really!'

"The next year, because of an operation to correct an old hockey injury, I didn't report to Kitchener, Ontario, where the New York club operated a team in the Eastern Professional Hockey League, until late December of 1961. As I stated earlier, it was from there that I joined the Rangers during the 1962 Stanley Cup playoffs and have remained with the New York club ever since."

UP THE ROAD TO THE NHL WITH BRAD

"After my dubious career as a goalie that I detailed earlier, my first team, at age seven, was the Eglington Aces. When I moved up to our local peewee-league team, I joined a team coached by my dad, and we were good enough one year to get an invitation to play at the International Peewee Hockey Championships held in Quebec City. We had no trouble reaching the finals, but what happened in the last game taught me an interesting thing about all coaches—even my dad.

"Prior to the final game our record was 29 goals scored and only one scored against us. By the middle of that championship game we were ahead 6–0 and really were making a shambles of the affair. After the second period, Dad came into our dressing room and said, 'Okay, fellas, we're by far the best team, but let's not make them look too bad. Ease up and pull back on your shots. When you have a good shot on net, miss it. No more goals . . . understand?'

"On the first shift of the final period, Syl Apps, Jr. (who was later my roommate on the Rangers and who now plays for the Pittsburgh Penguins) won the face-off and passed the puck back to me. I went to their end and passed it to Syl and then we just passed it back and forth, never letting them touch it. Finally we moved in on their goalie. Our other line mate, Bobby Griffin, had the puck right in front of the crease. The nearest opposing player was about 15 feet away, and all Bobby had to do was knock the puck into the net. But, remembering what his coach had said, he passed back to our man at the point. The second that occurred the crowd started booing and Dad benched my line for the rest of the game. This is when I learned that sometimes if you do as the coach says you're wrong and if you don't you're still wrong. However, in any case you must follow the coach's instructions. Needless to say, we won the championship.

"When I was fifteen, Dad was transferred to Montreal, so we moved there and my brother and I tried out for the same Junior B team. He was really hurt when I got a spot on the club, and he was rejected. For me, the experience was tremendous and for the first time I played defense. But before the season was over my father was transferred back to Toronto, and I moved back with the rest of the family. That following year, however, my dad coached the Neil MacNeil High School Junior B team, an affiliate of the Toronto Marlboros, who were linked directly to the Toronto Maple Leaf organization. I received a hockey scholarship from the school, with all expenses, tuition, books, uniform —everything paid. Besides that, they gave me $2.50 for each game. At 16, while I was technically still an amateur, I was actually being paid to play hockey. I couldn't believe it.

"The next season the Neil MacNeil team folded and I became a free agent. I then got an invitation to go to the Hamilton Red Wings Junior A camp. But the night before I was to leave for the Hamilton camp, I got a phone call telling me not to report 'because the Toronto Marlboros have put you on the priority draft list,' and I was to go to the Marlboros A camp instead.

"The camp was divided in half: the out-of-towners, who'd come to Toronto to try out with the Marlboros, and the in-towners, guys like me who lived in the city. I was real angry because Jim Greggory, now manager of the Maple Leafs, told my dad that I didn't have a chance of making the team, but I was determined to prove him wrong. On my first shift in the opening scrimmage, I lined up Brent Imlach for a body check. Brent was the son of Punch Imlach, the former Buffalo Sabers' and Maple Leafs' manager-coach, and a pretty good forward at that. As Brent skated toward me I waited, and then gave him the hip and sent him sprawling. A little later a forward named Terry Caffrey came in on me, and I sent him flying as well. That's all my confidence needed. From then on I knew I had a shot at one of the two defense openings. I opened the season as defenseman of the Marlboros A club.

"Our opening game was against the Oshawa Generals on Maple Leaf Gardens ice. There were 11,000 attending that afternoon because Oshawa was led by none other than Bobby Orr. I'd heard a lot about this guy, but I had no idea how to play against him. I found out on my very first shift. Orr got the puck and started on one of his patented rink-length dashes, coming directly at me. Bobby had been in the league three or four years and was a little older, so I watched him carefully as he cut toward center ice. I was getting ready to poke the puck away from him when suddenly I tripped and fell flat on my back. Orr went around me and passed to a teammate who scored. My first shift in my first Junior game was certainly a flop.

"Somehow I steadied down after that and kept my job as fourth defenseman throughout the season. We finished fifth out of nine teams that year and had a fairly good team. Our goalie was Al Smith, and up front were such players as Wayne Carleton, Terry Caffrey, and Gerry Meehan—all are now in the NHL. In the playoffs we reached the semifinals against Kitchener. We had a tie in the final game with 11 seconds remaining when Walt Tkaczuk, now my teammate on the Rangers, came down ice for Kitchener. Walt is a left-handed shot, but on this play he switched hands and beat Smith to win the series for Kitchener. The next year, however, we beat Kitchener and went on to win the Memorial Cup, Canada's Junior championship.

"I didn't start thinking seriously about an NHL career until my third Junior year. By then I'd become Rangers' property, a result of the Junior draft. In 1966 the structure of the CAHA and NHL was changed so that the sponsoring team didn't 'own' a player as in the case of Rod. The Junior hockey system of drafting is run similarly to drafts in other sports. For every player drafted, the team picking the player must reimburse the team that lost the player to the tune of $3,000. The NHL spends over $900,000 a year (almost $80,000 a club) helping the CAHA administer the far-reaching 'amateur' program. But drafting a player doesn't guarantee an NHL team a certain player. It must now negotiate with him on his professional contract. In 1967 I signed an agreement with Emile Francis and was invited to the Ranger camp in 1968.

"But after a very good training camp—I thought—I was sent down to the Rangers' farm club at Buffalo. On December 9, 1968, however, my dreams were fully realized; I was recalled by the Rangers and have been there ever since."

Hockey is a great sport. The ladder of success to the NHL is a hard one to climb. But dreaming didn't get us here. It is hard work to become a successful hockey player. Believe us, however, it's worth the necessary effort.

Appendix

Gilbert-Park Professional Record to Date

RODRIGUE GABRIEL (ROD) GILBERT

Right Wing . . . . 5 feet 9 inches . . . . 180 pounds . . . . Born Montreal, Quebec, Canada, July 1, 1941 . . . . Shoots right . . . . First Team NHL All-Stars, 1971–72 . . . . Single

			REGULAR SCHEDULE					PLAYOFFS				
Season	Club	League	GP	G	A	Pts.	Pen.	GP	G	A	Pts.	Pen.
1959–60	Three Rivers	EPHL	3	4	6	10	0	5	2	2	4	2
1960–61	Rangers	NHL	1	0	1	1	2	—	—	—	—	—
1961–62	Kitchener	EPHL	21	12	11	23	22	4	0	0	0	4
1961–62	Rangers	NHL	1	0	0	0	2	4	2	3	5	4
1962–63	Rangers	NHL	70	11	20	31	20	—	—	—	—	—
1963–64	Rangers	NHL	70	24	40	64	62	—	—	—	—	—
1964–65	Rangers	NHL	70	25	36	61	52	—	—	—	—	—
1965–66	Rangers	NHL	34	10	15	25	20	—	—	—	—	—
1966–67	Rangers	NHL	64	28	18	46	12	4	2	2	4	6
1967–68	Rangers	NHL	73	29	48	77	12	6	5	0	5	4
1968–69	Rangers	NHL	66	28	49	77	22	4	1	0	1	2
1969–70	Rangers	NHL	72	16	37	53	22	6	4	5	9	0
1970–71	Rangers	NHL	78	30	31	61	65	13	4	6	10	8
1971–72	Rangers	NHL	73	43	54	97	64	16	7	8	15	11
Rangers Totals			672	273	349	593	353	53	25	24	49	35

Product of Ranger organization.

Douglas Bradford (Brad) Park

Defense . . . . 6 feet . . . . 190 pounds . . . . Born Toronto, Ontario,
Canada, July 6, 1948 . . . . Shoots left . . . First Team NHL All-
Stars, 1969–70, 1971–72 . . . Second Team NHL All-Stars, 1970–71 . . . . Married

			REGULAR SCHEDULE					PLAYOFFS				
Season	Club	League	GP	G	A	Pts.	Pen.	GP	G	A	Pts.	Pen.
1968–69	Buffalo	AHL	17	2	12	14	49	—	—	—	—	—
1968–69	Rangers	NHL	54	3	23	26	70	4	0	2	2	7
1969–70	Rangers	NHL	60	11	26	37	98	5	1	2	3	11
1970–71	Rangers	NHL	68	7	37	44	114	13	0	4	4	42
1971–72	Rangers	NHL	75	24	49	73	130	16	4	7	11	21
Rangers Totals			257	45	135	180	412	38	5	15	20	81

Obtained in amateur draft, June, 1966.

Glossary

A. The letter worn on an assistant or alternate team captain's jersey. There are never more than three assistant captains on a team. (Both Rod Gilbert and Brad Park are at present assistant captains on the New York Rangers.)

ATTACKING ZONE. The area in which opponents' goal cage is located.

BACKCHECK. An attempt by forwards, on their way back to their defensive zone, to regain the puck from the opposition.

BACKHAND. A shot or pass taken on the left side of a right shot or the right side of a left shot.

BANANA BLADE. A hockey stick blade that has an exaggerated curve.

BEAT THE DEFENSE. To outwit and get by a defenseman.

BEAT THE GOALIE. To outwit and score on the goalie.

BENCH PENALTY. Involves the removal, for 2 minutes, of one player of a team against which the penalty is awarded. Any player of the team may be designated by the coach to serve the penalty.

BLIND PASS. Passing the puck without looking.

BLUE LINES. The lines on the ice to indicate the zone boundaries.

BOARDING. Violently checking an opponent into the boards.

BOARDING THE PUCK. To hit the puck against the side boards.

BOARDS. The wood surface that encloses the rink.

BODY CHECK. Slowing or stopping an opponent by using the body.

BREAK. Chance to start a rush when opposing forwards are caught out of position.

BREAKAWAY. The act of a fast rush generally with no opponent between the puck carrier and opponents' goal except the goaltender.

BREAKING PASS. Passing the puck to a teammate who is accelerating his skating speed for a breakaway.

BREAKOUT. When the attacking team comes out of its defending zone with the puck and starts up ice.

253

BUTT-ENDING. To jab an opponent with the butt end of a stick (the end farthest from the blade), while both hands are on the stick and no part of the stick is on the ice.

C. The letter worn on a team captain's jersey.

CAGE. See *goal cage.*

CAROM. A rebound of the puck off the sideboards or any other surface.

CENTER. The middle man of the three players who make up the offensive line.

CENTER FACE-OFF CIRCLE. A circle with a 30-foot diameter at the midpoint of the ice where the opening face-off of the game and every face-off after a goal is held.

CENTER ICE. The area between the two blue lines.

CENTER RED LINE. The line that divides the ice exactly in half. It is the center of the ice.

CHARGE. Charging across the ice to body check an opponent. Usually if more than two steps or strides are taken, it is considered to be illegal.

CHECK. Any means used to break up an attack.

CHECK BACK. Skating back toward one's own goal to help out defense and goalie.

CLEARING THE PUCK. Getting the puck away from in front of one's own goal cage area.

COVER. Stay close to an opponent on a play in his defensive zone to prevent the attacker from getting free to receive a pass. Same as *shadow.*

CREASE. A 4- by 8-foot box in front of each goal.

CRISSCROSS. An offensive play when the attacking wingmen change sides as the play moves up the ice.

CROSS CHECK. An illegal body check such as holding your stick across the body of an opponent to prevent him from passing.

CROSSOVER. A skating maneuver in which one foot is crossed over the other alternately.

CUPPING. The act of closing one's hand on the puck.

CUT-BACK ANGLE. Angle created when the puck carrier's cover overskates him, permitting him to cut back and get away from his cover.

CUTTING. Crossover skating stride when turning.

DECEPTION. Various actions with the body, stick, head, eyes, or anything else to force the other player to make the first move.

DEFENSEMEN. The two players whose job it is to assist the goalkeeper in preventing opponents from scoring.

DEFENSIVE ZONE. The area in which the goal cage of the defending team is located.

DEFLECTION. A shot or pass that hits some object such as stick, skate, etc., and goes into the net for a score.

DEKE. A fake by a puck carrier to stickhandle around an opponent.

DELAYED CALLING OF PENALTY. The referee signifies the calling of a penalty by pointing to the offending player, but does not blow his whistle and give the penalty until the completion of the play by the nonoffending side in possession of the puck.

DELAYING THE GAME. A penalty is called against any team that causes unnecessary delays in the game or has too many players on the ice at one time.

DIG. Fight for puck in corners.

DIGGER. A player who relentlessly hounds the puck until he comes up with it.

DIVING. Approaching puck carrier head on with very little chance of stealing the puck.

DOG A MAN. Cover an opponent very closely and persistently.

DRAG. Placing the skate at right angles to the forward motion so the skater can slow himself down.

DRAW. On face-offs, succeeding in getting puck to a teammate.

DRIBBLE. Keep control of puck on the end of the stick.

DROP PASS. An act in which the puck is left for a trailing player to pick up.

ELBOWING. Hitting an opponent with your elbow.

EMPTY NET. No one guarding the net, as when the goalie is pulled.

FACE. The front side of a hockey stick blade.

FACE-OFF. The dropping of the puck between the sticks of two opponents to start or resume play.

FAKING A SHOT. Pretending to shoot the puck but not doing so.

FEATHER. To handle the puck gently and lightly with the stick blade.

FEEDING. Passing the puck.

FEINT. A deceptive maneuver with the head and shoulders to fake an opponent into thinking that you are going to make a certain move.

FIGHTING. A major, double minor, or minor penalty may be handed out to a player who starts a fight. In turn, a minor penalty is awarded to the man who, having been struck, retaliates with a blow or attempted blow. However, the referee is provided very wide latitude in the penalties which he may impose under this rule.

FINISH-OFF PLAY. Scoring a goal.

FIVE ON FOUR. This describes play when a full team is attacking a team playing one man short. *Three on two* describes three forwards attacking two defensemen.

FLAT. The portion of a skate blade that touches the ice.

FLAT PASS. A pass in which the puck slides along the ice.

FLIP BACKHAND SHOT. A backhand shot in which the puck is flipped into the air to pass over an obstacle.

FLIP PASS. Lift or flip the puck over an opponent or his stick.

FLIP SHOT. A shot on the forehand in which the puck is flipped toward the net.

FLOATER. An offensive player who slips into the center zone behind the attacking defensemen. Same as *hanger* or *sleeper.*

FLOPPER. A goaltender who frequently flops to the ice to make saves.

FOLLOW IN. Normally this is what a player should do when he shoots, though there are exceptions. The shooter rushes in after his shot to play the rebound or intercept a clearing pass.

FOLLOW-THROUGH. The path the stick follows in the direction of the puck after a shot or pass has been made.

FORECHECK. To keep opponents in their end of the rink while trying to regain control of the puck. This is usually done by the forwards.

FOREHAND. A shot or pass taken on the right side of a right shot or the left side of a left shot.

FOUL. Any infraction of the rules that will draw a penalty.

FREEZING THE PUCK. Holding the puck against the boards with the stick or skates.

FULL STRENGTH. A full complement of players.

GET A SHOT OFF. Shoot the puck toward the goal.

GET THE JUMP. To move fast and thereby get a good start on the opponents.

GIVE AND GO. A maneuver in which the puck is passed to a teammate and the passer moves instantly in the direction of the goal to wait for a return pass.

GOAL. A point scored when the puck is put into the opponents' goal and has entirely passed over the red goal line.

GOAL CAGE. The cage, consisting of steel posts and netting, fixed to the ice.

GOALIE. The well-padded player who guards the open mouth of the goal cage. Also called *goaltender, goalkeeper, netminder.*

GOAL LINE. The 2-inch stripe between the two goalposts and extending in both directions to the sideboards.

GOAL MOUTH. A rather indefinite area in front of the goal.

HARD PASS. A pass made with considerable force and speed.

HAT TRICK. Three goals scored by a player in one game.

HEAD-MANNING. Passing the puck ahead to a leading teammate.

HIGH STICKING. Carrying the stick above shoulder level. It calls for stoppage of play and a face-off at the spot where the offense occurred, or a penalty if an opponent is hit with the stick.

HIP CHECK. Using your hip to knock an opponent off stride.

HOLDING. Using your hands or stick to hold an opponent.

HOLE. Area located halfway between blue line and goal, directly in line with the net.

HOOK CHECK. A side sweep of the stick close to the ice in an attempt to snare the puck from an opponent.

HOOKING. Using the stick's blade to impede an opponent from behind. When a player is checking another in such a way that there is only stick-to-stick contact, such action is *neither* holding nor hooking.

ICING THE PUCK. Intentionally shooting the puck from behind the center red line over the opponents' goal line.

INTERFERENCE. A penalty is imposed on a player who interferes with or impedes the progress of an opponent who is not in possession of the puck. In interpreting this rule, the referee must make sure which of the players is the one creating the interference. Often it is the action and movement of the attacking player which causes the interference since the defending players are entitled to stand their ground or shadow the attacking players. Players of the side in possession are not permitted to run deliberate interference for the puck carrier.

JUMP. A quick start in which a player is going full speed after one or two strides.

JUMP STOP. A jump into the air in which the skates are positioned so that when the player comes down, he can stop quickly.

KICKED GOAL. A goal kicked into the opponent's net intentionally. It is disallowed. The puck can be propelled on the ice by kicking the puck, but a goal cannot be scored this way.

KNEEING. A penalty charged to any player who uses his elbow or knee to check an opponent. A match misconduct is imposed on a player who kicks or attempts to kick another.

LEFT DEFENSEMAN. The defenseman who normally plays on the left side, looking toward the opposition's goal.

LEFT WING. The man on the offensive line who plays on the left side.

LIE. The angle made by the shaft of the hockey stick and the blade.

LIFT PASS. The puck is handled in such a way that it is made to leave the ice surface to pass over an obstruction.

LINE. The three forwards, or offensive players.

LOOSE PUCK. A puck not actually in play or in the possession of any player while the game is still in progress.

MAJOR PENALTY. A 5-minute penalty called for a major infraction.

MATCH MISCONDUCT. Any offense that causes a player to be put out of the game.

MINOR PENALTY. A 2-minute penalty.

MISCONDUCT PENALTY. Ten minutes or more against an individual player. His team may substitute for him during the 10 minutes.

NET. A synonym for the goal cage.

OFFENSIVE ZONE. The area in which the goal cage of the opponents is located.

OFFICIAL. One of the three on the ice—referee and two linesmen. Also the goal judges, timekeepers, and various others charged with the duty of keeping track of some aspect of the game.

OFF SIDE. When an attacking player precedes the puck into the attacking zone, play is halted and restarted with a face-off. Also when a puck is passed over more than one line and becomes a two-line pass.

OFF-THE-BOARD PASS. Directing the puck from one man to another by bouncing it off the sideboards.

ON THE FLY. Making player changes or substitutions while play is under way.

OPEN ICE. That part of the ice that is free of opponents.

PASS. The transfer of the puck to a teammate by sliding it along the ice or flipping it into the air to put it within his reach.

PASSING ALLEYS. Clear lanes of ice for passes to teammates.

PASS-OUT. A pass by an attacking player from behind an opponent's goal or the corner to a teammate in front of that goal.

PENALTY. A punishment for violation of the rules that involves suspension from the game for a specified period of time.

PENALTY BOX. An off-ice area where the penalized player sits while serving his penalty.

PENALTY KILLERS. The forward or two forwards who serve in a defensive role while their team is shorthanded because of penalties.

PENALTY KILLING. The defensive maneuvers employed while a team is shorthanded.

PENALTY MISCONDUCT. A 10-minute penalty for deliberate and serious misconduct involving officials or fans. A misconduct penalty can also be given for the balance of the match.

PENALTY SHOT. A free shot on goal with only the goalie attempting to block the puck.

PERIOD. A regular hockey game consists of three periods of 20 minutes each.

PLAYMAKER. The player, usually the center, who sets up the plays and gives any signals.

POINTS. The positions taken up by the defensemen on offense just inside the attacking blue line.

POKE CHECK. To dislodge the puck from the puck carrier by stabbing at it with the blade of the stick.

POWER PLAY. During a penalty, the team with the advantage sends five men with the puck into the penalized team's defending zone. Similar to a *ganging play*.

POWER SKATING. Skating techniques used in hockey which include starting, turning, stopping, and changing speeds and direction. Same as *agility skating*.

PUCK. A vulcanized rubber disc (1 inch thick, 3 inches in diameter, weighing between 5½ and 6 ounces) that is frozen for several hours before game time to prevent it from bouncing.

PUCK OUT OF SIGHT. Whenever the puck is lost by the referee, usually when the goalkeeper falls on it, the whistle is blown and play is stopped.

PULLING THE GOALIE. The removal of the goalkeeper from the ice and replacing him with a forward. Since this move leaves the goal unguarded, it is usually considered only as a last-minute resort used when a team is behind and the game is practically over.

PUSH PASS. Advancing the puck forward with a restrained shove rather than a full swing.

RAGGING. To retain possession of the puck by clever stickhandling.

REBOUND. A puck that bounces off the goalie's pads.

RIGHT-BACK PASS. To make a pass and expect to receive the puck right back.

RIGHT DEFENSEMAN. The defenseman who normally plays on the right side, looking toward the opposition's goal.

RIGHT WING. The man on the offensive line who plays on the right side.

RING THE POST. Hitting one of the iron upright posts on a shot for the goal but failing to make the goal by reason of the puck hitting the post and bouncing away from and not into the cage. Same as *hitting the post*.

RINK. The ice surface on which hockey is played, 200 feet by 85 feet wide.

ROCKER. The gentle curve in the blade edge of a skate produced by rounding the toe and heel of the blade.

ROUGHING. A small-scale punching or shoving bout.

RUSH. An individual or combined attack by a team in possession of the puck.

SAVE. The act of a goalie stopping a shot.

SCOOTING. A skating motion consisting of short thrusts designed to keep the skater moving in a confined area.

SCRAMBLE. When several players from both sides at close range battle for possession of the puck.

SCREEN SHOT. A shot on goal from behind a screen created by either one or more players (opponents or teammates).

SHIFT. A player's turn on the ice. Also a change of balance in which the man with the puck attempts to fool a checker.

SHINNY. The opposite of team and combination play. It actually denotes a poor form of hockey.

SHOOT. To direct the puck with the stick toward the opposing goal in an attempt to get it past the goalie into the net.

SHOOTING ANGLE. The shooter's position on the ice in relation to the goal.

SHORTHANDED. A team with one or more players in the penalty box is considered shorthanded.

SIN BIN. Another name for the penalty box.

SKATING BLIND. Skating with the head down.

SLAP SHOT. Bringing the stick back, then quickly forward, and slapping the puck ahead.

SLASHING. A player who impedes or seeks to impede the progress of an opponent by slashing with his stick is penalized. The referee can also call slashing on any player who swings his stick at any opponent (whether in or out of range) without actually striking him or where a player, on the pretext of playing the puck, makes a wild swing at the puck with the object of intimidating an opponent.

SLOT. The shooting area, about 20 to 40 feet in front of the cage.

SLOW ICE. A soft ice surface.

SLOW WHISTLE. This is used by the linesmen when an offside occurs, without doing actual damage to the defending team's procedure. If this is so, the whistle is withheld. If then damage does occur—an unfair advantage is gained in sequence resulting from the offside—then the whistle is blown. Also often a referee will call a penalty with gestures, but he does not actually stop play because the team committing the violation does not have the puck.

SMOTHERING. A maneuver by the goalie to stop the puck by falling on it.

SNAKE. To whip or lash the stick quickly at the puck.

SNAP PASS. A quick pass made with a snap of the wrists.

SOFT PASS. A pass made with moderate force.

SOLO. A rush by a player without assistance from his teammates.

SPEARING. Jabbing an opponent with the point of the stick blade.

SPLITTING THE DEFENSE. Puck carrier goes between the two opposing defensemen.

SPLIT VISION. The ability to look straight ahead and yet see players on either side and the puck on one's stick.

SPOT PASS. Passing to a spot rather than to a player.

STALLING. Delaying the game.

STICK CHECK. A maneuver with the hockey stick to sweep, poke, or hook the puck away from the opposing puck carrier.

STICKHANDLING. Carrying the puck along the ice with the stick.

STICK LIE. Angle between the blade and the handle constitutes the stick lie.

STOPS AND STARTS. A skating drill.

SUBSTITUTIONS. Players may be substituted at any time. When the puck is in play the subs enter the game on the fly by jumping from the bench to the ice as the other players approach the bench gate.

SUICIDE PASS. A pass that the receiver has to take by turning his head, thus becoming an easy target for a defenseman rushing him.

SWEEP CHECK. To use the entire length of the stick, flat on the ice, with a sweeping motion in order to dislodge the puck from the carrier.

TELEGRAPHING. Looking directly at a teammate before passing him the puck.

THREE ON ONE. Three men coming against one defensive player.

THREE ON TWO. Three men attacking on two defensive players.

TRAILER. A player who follows his teammate on the attack in position to receive a backward or drop pass.

TRIPPING. A penalty imposed on any player who places his stick, knee, foot, arm, hand or elbow in such a manner that it causes his opponent to trip or fall. When a player, in control of the puck in the attacking zone and having no other opponent to pass than the goaltender, is tripped, a penalty shot is awarded the nonoffending side.

TWO ON ONE. Two attacking players skating against one defensive player.

TWO ON TWO. Two attackers skating down on two defenders.

UNCOVERED. Player left unguarded in front of net.

UNDERLED PASS. A pass to a point behind or to one side of a teammate rather than to a spot where he can easily pick up the puck.

UNNATURAL SIDE. The right-hand side for a left shooter and vice versa.

WASHOUT. A signal by the linesman—same as a football official's motion meaning the point after touchdown was no good—meaning there was no icing or offside. Also used by the referee to mean that a goal is disallowed.

WINGS. The men in the forward line, the one playing on the right side of the ice being known as the right wing and the one on the left side being known as the left wing.

WRIST PASS. A pass of the puck in which the momentum is imparted with the wrist and forearm muscles.

WRIST SHOT. Propelling the puck off the blade of the stick with a flicking motion of the wrists.

ACKNOWLEDGEMENTS

The authors would like to thank the following for their help and cooperation in making this book possible: Allan S. Eisinger; Robert Scharff; Lawrence H. Rauch; Joseph R. Vergara; Emile Francis; John Halligan and Janet Halligan of the New York Rangers; Labatt's Breweries of Canada; Hawthorn Books, Inc.; Rawlings Sporting Goods Company; Dodd Mead & Company; and the staff of Skateland Summer Hockey School.

PHOTOGRAPHIC   CREDITS

Paul Bereswill: Pages 6, 10, 12 (top), 14, 16, 22, 24, 56, 64, 80, 85, 94, 96, 99, 101, 104, 112 (bottom), 120, 122, 126, 130, 132, 134, 136, 142, 148, 158, 178, 182, 204 (bottom), 210, 219, 220, 222, 224, 225, 228, 232, 240.
Dan Baliotti & Bob Rush: Pages 12, 26, 27, 28, 29, 32, 33, 38, 42, 43, 46, 47, 49, 58, 59, 69, 76, 77, 108, 110, 112 (top), 116, 118, 136, 159, 160, 188, 214, 215, 216, 218, 220, 226, 234.
All line drawings by Mary Puschak.

Index

74 75 10 9 8 7 6 5 4 3